D1287063

Advances in Office Automation

VOLUME 1

WILEY HEYDEN ADVANCES LIBRARY IN EDP MANAGEMENT

Edited by Thomas A. Rullo

Other Advances Series in the Library

Advances in Office Automation

VOLUME 1

Edited by
KAREN TAKLE QUINN

Industry Specialist
Engineering and Scientific Support Center
IBM Corporation
Palo Alto
California

A Wiley Heyden Publication

JOHN WILEY & SONS

Chichester · New York · Brisbane · Toronto · Singapore

Library of Congress Cataloging in Publication Data:

Advances in office automation.
    (Wiley Heyden advances library in EDP management)
    "A Wiley Heyden publication."
    Includes bibliographies and index.
    1. Office practice—Automation—Addresses, essays,
lectures.   I. Quinn, Karen Takle.   II. Series.
HF5547.5.A28 1985 v. 1   651.8'4   83-23256
ISBN 0 471 90398 1

British Library Cataloguing in Publication Data:

Advances in office automation.—(Wiley Heyden
    advances in EDP management)
    Vol. 1.
    1. Office practices—Automation—Periodicals
    651   HF5548.125

ISBN 0 471 90398 1

Typeset by Pintail Studios Ltd.
Duck Island Lane, Ringwood, Hampshire.
Printed by St. Edmundsbury Press, Bury St. Edmunds, Suffolk.

DEDICATION

To my parents, Carl and Gunvor Takle, who taught me 'I can' and to my husband, Frank, who gave the support so that 'I could'.

ACKNOWLEDGEMENTS

I would like to thank all my friends and associates who generously gave of their time and knowledge. I sincerely appreciate the opportunity Tom Rullo has given me to prepare this volume, and the editorial comments from Carol Christensen, friend and associate. And last, but not least I thank LaVerne Connie Forbes, friend, associate and indexer for this volume.

CONTENTS

LIST OF CONTRIBUTORS

JAMES H. BAIR, Hewlett-Packard Company, Cupertino, California 95014, U.S.A. (p. 3).

ED. R. BERRYMAN, Exxon Corp. B240/103, PO 153, 180 Park Ave, Florham Park, New Jersey 07932, U.S.A. (p. 231).

PAUL C. GARDNER, IBM Corporation, B85/Bldg 965, Poughkeepsie, New York, U.S.A. (p. 137).

NOEL J. GILSON, IBM Corporation V46/098, 5600 Cottle Road, San Jose, California, U.S.A. (p. 255).

AUDREY N. GROSCH, University of Minnesota, S98 Wilson, 309 19th Ave South, Minneapolis 55455, U.S.A. (p. 105).

ELIZABETH McGEE, McGee and Associates, 1270 Montclaire Way, Los Altos, California 94022, U.S.A. (p. 75).

LENA S. MENASHIAN, BNR, Inc., 685A East Middlefield Road, Mountain View, California 94043, U.S.A. (p. 161).

BEVERLY K. MILLER, University of Wisconsin, Eau Claire, Wisconsin 54701, U.S.A. (p. 53).

KATHRYN J. NELSON, Los Alamos National Laboratory, 120 Canyon Vista, Los Alamos, New Mexico 87544, U.S.A. (p. 3).

RAYMOND R. PANKO, College of Business Administration, University of Hawaii, 2404 Maile Way, Honolulu, Hawaii 96734, U.S.A. (p. 191).

JACK B. SIART, Pacific Telephone and Telegraph Co., AOS Planning, 575 Mission St. Room 200, San Francisco, California 94105, U.S.A. (p. 37).

DEBRA WIERENGA, Mary Street Studio, 346 Mary Street, Box 711, Saugatuck, 49453, U.S.A. (p. 21).

PREFACE TO THE WILEY–HEYDEN ADVANCES LIBRARY IN EDP MANAGEMENT

Information, to be of value, must be timely, accurate, and accessible. By addressing each of these criteria, the *Wiley–Heyden Advances Library in EDP Management* has proved to be a unique and valuable source of information for managers.

The timeliness of the material is maintained by issuing additional volumes within each series. These volumes build upon the base of previous ones to provide new insights and add topics of current interest. Because we continue to generate new ideas our readers receive the most up-to-date information.

The second attribute of useful information is accuracy. To create the *Wiley–Heyden Advances Library in EDP Management*, we assign a separate editor to each volume as an expert in the field, that editor being responsible for the overall content of the volume. Each chapter is in turn developed by an expert in a specific area and then submitted to the volume editor for review. Wherever necessary, additional technical review support is obtained. Because of this detailed editorial and review process, a high degree of accuracy can be assured.

The third attribute that makes information of value is accessibility. This feature is the least commonly discussed and the most difficult of the three to accomplish. In fact, the lack of easy accessibility to information was the main reason for developing the *Wiley–Heyden Advances Library in EDP Management*. Our primary role as developers and managers of this base of material is to provide our users with the information they want in a form in which they can readily use it. This task is accomplished through the selection of relevant topic areas, maintenance of a consistent level of content, and organization of material in line with its intended use. Although we have achieved our timeliness, accuracy, and accessibility objectives, we strive to improve the library through the added dimension of communication with our end users. Thus we welcome any suggestions for improvement of our current series or expansion into new areas.

Thomas A. Rullo
Executive Editor

PREFACE TO VOLUME 1

Office automation has sprung into prominence in the last five to ten years. The advantages of both stand-alone word processing systems and integrated computer systems have caused them to become integral parts of academic, municipal, small business, and corporate offices.

In this volume we deal with a full spectrum of office automation issues. The authors selected to present this material have developed their expertise through practical working experience. The chapters are intended as individual tutorials on a particular aspect of Office Automation. This series is not intended as a product comparison or product evaluation, as this information appears in other publications. Authors have been asked to be generic rather than specific in reference to products or corporations. However, they have been encouraged to express their own ideas and opinions.

This series is intended to provide a source of tutorial chapters for a wide range of readers, allowing them to examine and compare the strategies and approaches in different office settings. Since the needs, structure, and operating environment of the organization affects the choice of office automation tools, these volumes have been divided into the following five sections:

- Strategies
- Environments
- Essentials
- Productivity
- Appendices and Indices.

This is expected to be the general format of the continuing volumes in this series.

The appendices will be included in some volumes and, therefore, they are listed in Section V. To make the series useful as a reference tool, an extra effort will be made to keep the indexing terms consistent between chapters and between volumes. Future volumes are expected to include more references to the published information sources.

It is hoped that you, the reader, will find this a useful and illuminating series.

Karen Takle Quinn
Editor

Section I: Strategies

Advances in Office Automation, Vol 1
Edited by Karen Takle Quinn

Chapter 1

USER NEEDS AS THE BASIS OF STRATEGIC PLANNING

James H. Bair
Hewlett-Packard Company

Kathryn J. Nelson
Los Alamos National Laboratory

INTRODUCTION

Before computerized information services for the office environment can be developed for use within any organization, two crucial actions must be undertaken:

- User needs must be defined.
- An implementation strategy must be established.

Although these requirements seem nearly self-evident, in fact it is quite common for one—or usually both—to be ignored. In either case, the chance for failure of the system increases dramatically. In this chapter, we first identify the target groups of office workers to be supported. Next, we describe typical user needs and how to identify specific needs in a particular organization. We then discuss the factors that are critical for establishing an implementation strategy that has a reasonable chance of success.

Who Needs to be Supported?

The first task is to identify office workers for whom an increase in productivity would provide the organization with the largest return on investment.[25]

Historically, automation efforts have largely been directed at the clerical support staff. Their general function is to record, retrieve, and transmit information for data processing systems and for the professional staff.[10] More recently, secretaries have been provided with new tools, including word processing systems, copiers, data entry systems, and OCR (optical character recognition) devices. As a result, office automation systems are still viewed by some managers as another way of spending more money on secretarial and clerical functions; the popular trade literature continues to describe compatibility problems among word processing systems; and the ranks of 'office automation specialists' are peopled by former word processing and data processing staff.

The emphasis on secretarial and clerical workers has left a set of potential users known as 'knowledge workers' virtually unsupported.[8] These knowledge workers include managers and professional people whose function it is to interpret information and make decisions. There are pioneering systems that have addressed the needs of knowledge workers. The most famous of these is probably Augment, which was originally developed in the 1960s by Stanford Research Institute, where it was known as NLS; Augment is currently available from a major timesharing network.[9] In addition, the boom in microcomputers is on the verge of creating a new status symbol for managers, the personal computer. More generally, though, it has been thought that a telephone and a secretary were adequate to make knowledge workers productive and that outfitting secretaries is equivalent to investing in the knowledge worker. For knowledge workers who lack the status of a secretary to provide direct support, word processing centers have been considered adequate.

Now, the organization considering integrated office systems as a potential source of increased productivity must identify which of these sets of office workers are to be supported by the new technology. Although the traditional emphasis in office systems has been on the secretarial–clerical staff, managers are now becoming aware of the cost of the unproductive time of knowledge workers, since knowledge workers are more expensive and more numerous (see Figure 1-1).[1] They also are frequently in a position to make or contribute to very expensive mistakes when using inaccurate, out-of-date, or incomplete information.

Let us assume that the secretarial–clerical staff have already been supplied with the word processing gear that is *de rigueur* in any self-respecting organization,

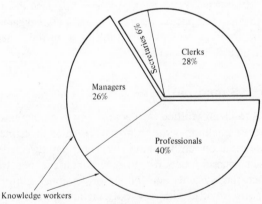

Figure 1-1.   Labor costs for white-collar workers in
the U.S.

and that the organization's attention is now to be focused on its knowledge workers. Whereas it was fairly straightforward to identify secretarial–clerical activities and—so it was thought—to find ways they could be made more productive, determining what knowledge workers need in order to be more productive is a larger challenge.

THE ACTIVITY MODEL

A series of studies undertaken by Bell Northern Research (BNR) between 1980 and 1982 addressed the problem of identifying ways to make knowledge workers more productive. At the heart of the studies is a view of organizational structure and professional productivity that can be described as the 'activity model'. The activity model accepts the premise that the actual products of knowledge workers are intangible and must be evaluated primarily by qualitative rather than quantitative measures. Ways to increase productivity must be identified by focusing attention not on their products, but on the activities they engage in while doing their job.

Using the activity model, we assume that improvements in an organization's performance can occur if the introduction of new, more flexible tools can either reduce the amount of time spent in nonproductive activities or increase the efficiency of work performed. Underlying this model is the pair of assumptions that (1) the work products of the organization are necessary and useful and (2) the specific jobs being performed in the organization are matched to its goals and objectives. If either of these assumptions is invalid, the organization has a management problem that computerized systems cannot solve.

THE ACTIVITY MODEL AND USER NEEDS

The studies based on the activity model were conducted in a variety of commercial, research and development, and government organizations. They demonstrated that the needs of knowledge workers could be grouped into three main categories: communications, information processing, and personal support. These results corroborate numerous other studies of organizations.[18]

Communications Needs

Communications needs turn out to be the most important.[14] They include, in order of the importance disclosed by the BNR case studies, a desire to:

- reduce interruptions, especially those caused by the telephone
- reduce delays in producing written communications
- reduce phone call nonclosures
- increase flexibility of contacts
- reduce unnecessary contacts

- reduce misunderstandings
- locate easily the people they need to contact
- reduce travel
- make more convenient the recording of meetings and telephone calls.

Typically, up to 75% of a knowledge worker's time is spent in communication activities, including face-to-face meetings, telephone conversations, and written communication (see Figure 1-2). Communication for the nonmanagerial knowledge worker is only slightly below this.[21] Clearly, any improvements in the mechanisms used for transmitting information carry a significant leverage in making the knowledge worker more productive.

There is some irony in the list of communications needs. For example, the telephone, which for many years has served as a cost-effective and time-efficient tool for nearly all knowledge workers, is now perceived as a hindrance to productivity. With 75% of the time spent in communications-related activities, those activities are crucial in the performance of a manager's function as a decision maker. But the results of these studies, as well as many others, indicate that communication is also the greatest problem for managers, as for all knowledge workers.[22] What is being asked for is not less communication, but communication at each manager's convenience. This clearly leads to a conflict of needs. Managers—indeed all knowledge workers—want to be able to talk to anyone they want to, but only when they themselves want to. It is difficult not to be sympathetic to this view of the world, but it does not hold much promise as a method of operation.

However, many exchanges of information do not require an interactive situation to be set up between the people involved.[13] Many are one-way—that is, one party needs only to give information to another party; no reply is necessary (and sometimes no reply is wanted). However, most traditional communications

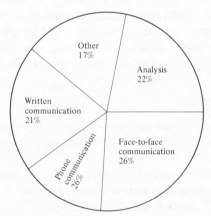

Figure 1-2.   Typical   knowledge
worker activities.

mechanisms (telephone calls and meetings) force people into an obligatory exchange of information, even when an exchange is not logically appropriate. Written mechanisms usually are too formalized or too slow to handle this kind of exchange, so they customarily use the telephone with its own limitations. The most important contribution of the office automation era is the focus on the need for more varied communications mechanisms and especially on the need for rapid, flexible (formal or informal, short or long) noninteractive communications media. The exact forms of the possible implementations—for example, enhanced telephone systems, digital voice messaging, and electronic mail systems—are perhaps less significant than the recognition of the need. It is possible, for example, that some improvement in communications requirements can be made by changes in management styles and in modifications to the communication channels.

Information Processing

The BNR studies identified several information processing needs: increased access to remotely stored information, reduced redundant information, and reduced irrelevant information. These needs historically have been satisfied (or not satisfied) by data processing departments.[17] Worldwide interest in office automation has focused attention on the need for the widespread availability of accurate, complete information, on demand. Computing and communications technologies have been developed sufficiently so that 'on demand' implies flexibility, rapidity of access, and even direct use of computerized information systems by managers or their staff.

Personal Support

For personal support, respondents identified the following needs: reduce uneven workloads, support composition (writing), provide support for routine calculations, and support personal calendar management. Most of these chores have historically been handled for managers by secretaries and for nonmanagerial knowledge workers by hook or by crook. These functions may still be handled by secretaries for many upper-level managers, but the secretaries and the nonmanagerial knowledge workers can have office systems to help them keep track of themselves.

METHODOLOGY FOR IDENTIFYING SPECIFIC NEEDS

The consistency of needs expressed by subjects in these and other studies of office systems makes the general areas for improvement clearly identifiable for a varied set of people.[7] However, within any given organization, it will be necessary to identify the particular ways in which these problems appear. This is the implementer's first task.

A common approach to need identification is to simply ask people what they want; the lists of wants then supply a master list that determines the services to be provided. The problem with this approach is the 'fallacy of perceived needs'. In marketing, where the measure of success is the volume of sales, perceived needs are simply another way of saying 'demand'. However, if the task is to make people more productive, they must be guided to what they really need, not necessarily what they report they want. If offices are automated on the basis of reported needs rather than real needs, productivity is much less likely to be improved.

Perceived needs can be misleading for several reasons. One problem comes from knowledge workers who are familiar with computers but may not be expert in their use. They may be aware of the functionality that can be provided by computers and are enamored of the equipment, either because it is faddish or because they are so accustomed to using it that they are not aware of other ways of doing things. These needs are technology-driven; that is, people perceive a service to be needed because hardware or software is able to offer it. Although this solution may have a very practical application in some places, it may provide more 'toys' than solutions to real problems. In short, care must be taken to avoid determining needs simply on the basis of the availability of tools. Sometimes better management policies can provide a much more productive atmosphere than a new spread sheet that has 87% more cells and also allows you to keep your grocery list.

On the other side are the people who know absolutely nothing about computers except that the local catalog-order house can never seem to keep orders straight. Like the computer-literate knowledge workers, these people will describe a set of perceived needs that are limited to their experience. Because their views of the possibilities can be so limited, and perhaps also very biased against computers, they may not be able to list actual needs accurately and completely. This assumes, of course, that a need is in part defined by the possibility of a solution. One hundred years ago people did not generally feel they needed telephones because they had no idea what could be accomplished once they were made available.

If people cannot be counted on to accurately and completely describe real needs, what can be done to discover them? Since the alternative is for the implementer to become a (perhaps) benign technocrat who tells people what they need and how they are going to be rescued from their narrow vision, it would seem desirable to find some way to accurately identify real needs and still involve the people who are to use the tools.

It is important to get the cooperation of prospective users in determining their needs because you not only want the tools to provide solutions to real problems, but you also want people to use them. That is, the system to be implemented must be both effective and accepted, because if it is not used, performance will not improve, however glorious its capabilities.[26] In fact, multimillion-dollar computing systems of various breeds have been thrown away because users would not accept them. So much for the benign technocrat.

The problem, then, is this:

> How can you predict what innovative technologies will meet *real* needs and be accepted by potential users, based on current attitudes and behaviors?

Although the perceptual problems just discussed may hinder people's ability to identify innovations that would improve their productivity, they usually are able to describe what they do (function) and how they do it (activities). The activity model implies that the implementer can use this information to identify target activities where productivity can be increased by the application of innovative tools. The required data can best be obtained by sampling the organization population using two complementary mechanisms, questionnaires and interviews.

Questionnaires

Questionnaires are used to collect well-structured data on the work conditions and habits of people in the organization. Although individual respondents will find it difficult to answer some of the questions accurately, the aggregate should provide a useful portrayal of the organization's activities. The following questions on oral communications needs and habits suggest the kinds of things that can be asked to acquire useful data:

- How many phone calls do you receive in a day?
- How many phone calls do you initiate in a day?
- How long do you talk on the phone in a day?
- How many meetings do you host in a week?
- How many meetings are you called to in a week?
- How long are the meetings you attend?
- Does someone answer your phone if you are not there?
- How many phone messages does someone take for you in a day?

To further illustrate what the questionnaire can be used to discover, the following questions are some of the ones that might be asked with regard to written communications:

- How many memos do you write?
- Are your written communications prepared on a word processor?
- Do you mind typing?
- What is your typing skill?
- Do you use word processing equipment yourself?

Because these data should be analyzed in quantitative ways, multiple-choice questions are most useful for the questionnaire. Questionnaires should be completed by approximately 5 to 10 per cent of the people in the organization.

Interviews

The questionnaire can be expected to generate adequate data to describe how people spend their time. This information will enable the implementer to judge where the leverage is; that is, it will be possible to identify one or two widespread needs for which innovative tools may provide a more productive alternative. However, such data can at best give only part of the needed information because they do not supply adequate information about people's attitudes.

Attitudes are best discovered during personal interviews. The sample size for interviews should be 10 to 20 per cent of the questionnaire sample size. The purpose of the interviews is to gather unstructured and unexpected information that cannot be obtained from a list of easy-to-answer and easy-to-analyze written questions. The interviews should reveal additional qualitative data to help interpret the structured data obtained from the questionnaires. They also provide the opportunity to find out how much people understand about computerized information systems and to begin to measure attitudes toward system implementation. In addition, it is possible to start the education process by describing new capabilities that may be feasible.

If care is exercised and adequate time is allowed for testing the questionnaires and interview guidelines, the implementer can collect much useful information about what people spend their time doing (both the functions and the activities undertaken to perform those functions), how much time they spend doing it, and how likely they are to respond favorably to the introduction of new tools. Ideally, the implementer would have the assistance of someone experienced in obtaining this data, since considerable care must be taken in preparing questionnaires, conducting interviews, and analyzing the results.

CRITICAL FACTORS FOR SUCCESS

However, a successful implementation not only requires a good understanding of user needs, but also must be coordinated by a carefully planned, fully supported strategy that takes into account a set of factors that are critical to a successful implementation. Although every implementation failure occurs in unique circumstances, the underlying cause of failure is usually user rejection. For example, knowledge workers typically are not forced by the nature of their jobs to use computers. Hence, any system that is to be used must lure people away from an existing set of activities and tools, ones that have long been accepted and long known to 'work'. An important part of the process of determining user needs must be a thorough understanding of these traditional activities and tools. The critical factors that must be addressed in order to encourage usage are described in this section.[23]

Physical Environment

Special attention must be given to the physical environment in which individuals will use the computer technology. Improper lighting (too much, too little, badly placed), badly designed workstations, inappropriate chair, a room vibrating because of heavy machinery and noise, will alienate all but the most enthusiastic users. Ideally, users would inhabit a physical environment specifically designed for modern computing and communications equipment, but in fact, most users will inhabit offices built for a more traditional set of tools. Consequently, any new system will probably be installed in existing facilities that may provide a less-than-ideal environment. Care should be taken to include the cost of office modifications in estimates of system cost.

Personality of Equipment and Systems

Not only must the environment be carefully managed, but the equipment selected—both hardware and software—also must be designed for comfortable use by human beings. Hardware factors, such as display resolution, keyboard touch, size of the screen and its reflective characteristics, and the range of adjustments (brilliance of displayed characters, tilt, swivel, position of keyboard) affect the overall utility of the system. Lack of concern for these ergonomic factors can result in user rejection, sabotage, or even lawsuits.[29]

Although the characteristics of the software are not likely to be the subject of a worker's compensation dispute, they do play a major role in user acceptance. Assuming, of course, that the functionality provided addresses needs that have been identified, the software must provide a friendly, preferably even convivial, atmosphere.[4] It must be responsive, reliable, and easy for a person unfamiliar with computers to use. To accomplish this goal, its user interface must have the following characteristics:

- Each user action must have a predictable effect. For example, the break key should not terminate a process in the mail system and destroy a file in the word processing system.
- Command structure must be consistent across all functions. For example, entries in a room scheduler should be made in the same way as entries are made in a personal calendar.
- Files must be able to be shared by all people working on a common task. For example, all members of a development project should have access to the proposal and all progress reports related to the project.
- The shared resources of a system must support existing equipment, including terminals and printers.
- Actions required of the user should be efficient—that is, few keystrokes (and little thought) should be required to perform a function.[5]

Usage Level

Realization of the full potential of integrated office systems requires that extensive on-line time be available to users.[2] Unlike traditional data processing applications, which have provided minimal on-line support, office information systems assume frequent interactive use by knowledge workers. Users are expected to do most of their information management tasks using a terminal, either directly or through an intermediary.

It is especially important during the early stages of implementation that people be encouraged to use the system regularly and at length so they can acquire and maintain an adequate level of skill. Unfortunately the procedures for using most currently available systems are rarely self-evident, except where the level of capability is minimal. Computer usage in a business environment requires an investment in skills development that can result only from direct, personal experience with the system. If people are deprived of on-line time, they tend to stop using the system altogether. The time people must spend familiarizing themselves with the system is a nontrivial part of the implementation cost and must not be overlooked.

The executive, however, may not have the necessary time to become dexterous with the new system, may believe typing to be a menial task, or may be afraid of seeming baffled by the system. Because people at this level can afford to have assistants, the executive's reluctance should not be discouraging. He or she can still benefit greatly by the system implementation through intermediaries. The selected assistant simply becomes the one to learn the system and deliver printed or oral versions of the computer-based information to the executive.

Since a high usage level is important for success, one thing to avoid during the initial implementation stages is charges that are based on the rate of usage, which essentially penalizes for increased use. This means that connect-time charges and processor usage charges should be avoided. Instead, charges can be based on a fixed, flat-rate subscription for participation in the system. This will encourage people to sign on more, stay signed on, and use more resources. Who can resist the opportunity to get more out of the system than what they think they are paying for?

Critical Mass of Users

The system should serve all knowledge workers in the organizational units being automated, regardless of their formal role, and should ultimately include all knowledge workers in the entire organization. Peer pressure is an important part of a successful implementation; it is difficult to resist using a system that is used by one's colleagues, or better yet, one's supervisors.[16]

This is especially true where an electronic mail system is involved. Electronic mail works effectively only if all people communicating with each other use the system daily. Reliability of the users is nearly as important as system reliability. Sporadic use of the system is destructive: users will stop sending messages to anyone who gets a reputation for not viewing mail frequently, and the effectiveness of the system can be seriously diminished.

Communications Opportunities

The user population should form a community defined by a communication network based on common needs or goals. Common goals, tasks, management, and interests generate communication traffic. The absence of an explicit need to communicate renders it meaningless to implement an integrated office system that facilitates communication. There must be a need for users to communicate with other members of the offices selected at each stage of implementation. In fact, the absence of a need to communicate can lead to the rejection of a new system, regardless of the other services available.[2]

Interestingly, one phenomenon associated with implementation of a new communications system is that it actually generates an increased need for communication among system users.[6] In part, this is due to the ease of communications that is introduced: the easier it is to exchange information, the more inclined people will be to do it. In addition, the new technology itself generates a need to communicate about the system itself. If the data network links users of other systems, communication potential is, of course, increased, and the range of people with a new shared experience to communicate is expanded. In this context, it may be reassuring to know that in our experience piles of electronic junk mail are not a necessary consequence of computer messaging systems.[12]

Access to Equipment

Although convenient access to equipment is sometimes viewed as an extravagance, it is in fact vital to success. It is consistent with the usage-level factor described above that each person have his or her own terminal and easy access to a high-quality, medium- or high-speed printer.[27]

Hardware and software must be capable of supporting large numbers of users, and in particular must support a high input/output workload. Because of the nature of the workload, individual microcomputer workstations linked by data communications to mainframes and to data networks are likely to provide the most successful architecture.

Within 5 to 10 years, traditional office furnishings will be replaced by the computer workstation as organizations evolve toward use of the 'multimedia office' (not the 'paperless office' that is frequently advertised).[28] The system implementer in the 1980s should have as a goal the provision of computer equipment as a basic tool for the knowledge worker, equivalent to the current attitude toward the telephone.

User Support

Many users of office systems will have had no previous experience with computers and therefore will require considerable handholding. Users will need training, documentation, and ongoing consultation in the use of the system.[19]

The fact that a system is, or purports to be, 'user friendly' should not be interpreted to mean that a casual user will be able to sit down at a terminal and do a sophisticated budget analysis with no assistance. 'User friendliness' is the ability to get novices doing simple tasks in a hurry, and the ability to use the system in an incremental way so that a large investment in training is not required for a small incremental increase in capability. However, no matter how easy a system is to get started on, and no matter how reasonable it is to learn more about it, sophisticated use of a system demands a thorough understanding, and a comprehensive training and consulting program is essential.

Assessment

Planned, ongoing assessment makes it possible to identify shortcomings in the system and take corrective action. At the organizational level, assessment provides data about changes in productivity, turnaround time, communication patterns, employee morale, responsiveness to customers, and the time consumed in adjusting to and operating the innovative technology.[3] Planned assessment also provides a mechanism for terminating a serious mistake gracefully, since it implies that an explicit decision for continuation is required.

STEPS TOWARD A SUCCESSFUL IMPLEMENTATION

The implementation plan must call for official administrative oversight and the establishment of policies and procedures for a gradual building of user expertise. At the beginning, emphasis should be on the development of understanding and the seasoning of representative groups within the organization rather than on providing service to the largest group as rapidly as possible. This emphasis is necessary so that the organization can integrate the system into its standard business operations using an evolutionary approach. The implementation takes place in three phases: the pilot phase, the assessment phase, and the expansion phase.

Pilot Phase

1. *Determine Organizational Commitment*

Because the implementation of an integrated office system will almost inevitably cross organizational boundaries, the opportunities for political intrigue are rife. The commitment of an organization to increasing its productivity by providing integrated office systems for its knowledge workers can be gauged by the attention it gives to administrative and political issues.

At least two kinds of power struggle can be anticipated. At one level will be the fight to take control of the implementation. The telecommunications, data processing, and office administration departments, for example, are each likely to feel most qualified to manage the system; they may concede the need for support by the other organizations, but they will each see leadership as most appropriate to themselves. On another level, departments on the receiving end of the implementation may have those who are very interested in change, but they may also (or instead) have people who are very resistant to change. The threat or opportunity to participate in the implementation may arouse a series of battles over small fiefdoms; these conflicts may be much harder to recognize than the major department-level battles, but they can be destructive nevertheless.

The organization that fails to recognize the early stages of implementation as primarily a political rather than a technical event will end up frustrated by the sometimes subtle and sometimes blatant social obstructions that will occur.

2. *Appoint a Facilitator*

A responsible person within the organization should be selected to manage the implementation and act as liaison between users and the vendor. The 'facilitator' (heretofore referred as the 'implementer') is the resident expert, planner, and 'pusher'. This person, who should report directly to upper management, has been found in case studies to be critical to the success of system implementation.[9]

One of the main functions of the facilitator is to control the flow of information and technology into the using organization. The facilitator may be technologically sophisticated, but most importantly he or she must be able to assess the applicability of innovations for the organization. By reporting to upper management, the facilitator will have sufficient status in the organization to influence decisions and comprehend the far-reaching implications of the innovation for the organization's future. A capable technical support team should be able to supply the facilitator with sufficient technical advice to prevent the facilitator from being baffled by the technical erudition of vendors.

The facilitator should participate in a user community of facilitators in other organizations undertaking the same sorts of implementations. Vendors must rely heavily upon facilitators for scheduling, support coordination, strategic planning, feedback, and input for continued development. Periodic meetings of facilitators and vendors can enable organizations to share learning experiences and thereby solve common problems.

3. *Identify the Pilot User Group*

Once a commitment to automation has been made and the facilitator selected, a pilot group is identified for the initial implementation phase. The facilitator must understand how the pilot group functions and what its role in the organization is. Experience has shown that groups of 25 or 30 people, including a wide variety of roles but with common tasks and goals, are most likely to be successful. The group should have a potential application that can be readily defined; it should be constituted such that the critical factors for success can be applied; and group members must be motivated to explore alternative ways of working. They should not find innovations personally threatening or a potential cause of a loss of position or status.

4. *Define the Initial Application*

Defining the initial automation application requires considerations not necessary with subsequent applications. A visible, immediate product that does not require complex procedures or extensive skill at using the system is crucial. Less tangible applications, such as communication support within the group, may not be as effective as the production of a document or the building of a small data base. Participation of the pilot group in the selection of the application generates involvement and motivation and also assists the facilitator in understanding the application environment.

5. *Select the System*

Once the users and the application are identified, the traditional system procurement process takes place. That process should include four steps:

- definition of system requirements based primarily upon study of communication flow in and adjustment to the user group
- development of a request for proposals from qualified vendors who are likely to meet the requirements
- evaluation of vendor responses
- selection of a vendor based upon the proposed system's interface design functions, user support, reliability, and the vendor's reputation and financial soundness. A review of the vendor's fiscal status is recommended to ensure that the company will survive to provide the needed service.

It is important to find a vendor who will work closely with the implementing organization to ensure delivery deadlines are met, provide rapid maintenance, and fully support the training, consulting, and documentation efforts.

6. *Begin Technology Implementation*

Implementation begins with hardware installation, work procedure design, consulting, training, and delivery of documentation, as required parts of the package. This necessitates a minimum scale of operation, adequate computer support, and a long enough commitment to warrant the investment on the part of both organizations (six months to as long as five years), during which time cost/benefits must be deferred. Enough timesharing computer power must be available to support the pilot group adequately.

The service provided should include a vendor consultant who will work closely with the facilitator. A trainer should also be assigned to an organization on a continuing basis. As one might expect, continuity is important in these relationships, particularly for the consultant. During this process, the consultant and his or her support staff learn about the organization, its structure and personality; this is of comparable importance to the participant organization's understanding of the system and its applications.

Assessment Phase

Unless the pilot project is evaluated, no one can be certain that improved performance is actually being attained. It is possible for an integrated office system to be designed and/or implemented that does not improve performance, or, even worse, that degrades performance.[4] A second major outcome of the evaluation can be a cost/benefit projection for an organization-wide system. Another outcome is the sharing of the experience of implementing and using such a system. An evaluation serves as the vehicle for disseminating this experience to the rest of the organization.

There are typically three steps of assessment in the overall evaluation process:

- *Baseline performance*   Measurements are made of the pilot group's performance as the basis of comparison after the system is fully operational.
- *System monitoring*   The system and its use are monitored to determine the level at which the different features are being utilized. User proficiency and system reliability are monitored to ensure that these factors do not interfere with using the system.
- *Post-test evaluation*   The methods used to measure baseline performance are repeated, and a comparison is made between the baseline and the post test. The difference represent changes in performance.

The changes that occur when new technology is introduced are extraordinarily complex and difficult to interpret. Because the changes can result from causes other than the newly introduced support system, expert analysis is required to determine the actual cause(s) of the measured changes. (For a complete description of evaluation methodology, see Reference 3.)

Expansion Phase

As successful use of the system is achieved, applications should expand to larger groups of users and additional applications. The user group size can reasonably be doubled at each incremental increase. The incremental increases can be expected to occur at gradually shorter intervals: the first increase at six to twelve months, the second at three to nine months afterward, the third at three to six months later, and so on. Automating an entire organization can require years, during which the addition of new technological developments has to be accommodated.

Applications may be added as fast as the users have mastered system usage for the initial applications. For example, the production and coordination of documents can be extended to larger groups, and a calendar facility can be put into operation. As the user population increases in size, computer-based mail can replace other modes of communication for users.[6] More advanced applications, such as the integration of data processing with the integrated office system, are incorporated in stages as growth proceeds toward complete use of the system for all information activities.

CONCLUSIONS

Implementing integrated office systems can increase or decrease productivity.[20] In other words, it can have the positive effect of allowing knowledge workers to produce better quality work faster, or it can have the negative effect of interfering with people who are trying to get their work done. We have discussed ways of identifying user needs, isolated several critical factors for success, and provided the steps of a strategic plan for implementation, all of which are based on more than 15 years of experience and research into what makes systems succeed or fail.

REFERENCES AND SUGGESTED READINGS

The literature in the following bibliography provides more information on the subjects discussed.

1. Bair, James H.: Communications in the Office of the Future: Where the Real Payoffs May Be. *Business Communications Review*, **9**, No. 1, January–February 1979.
2. Bair, James H.: Strategies for the Human Use of Computer Based Systems. In B. Shackel (Ed.), *Man–Computer Interaction: Human Factors Aspects of Computers and People*. Rockville, Maryland: Sijthoff & Noordhoff International Publishing Co., 1981 (NATO Advanced Studies Institute Series E: Applied Sciences).
3. Bair, James H.: Productivity Assessment of Office Information Systems Technology. In Robert Landan *et al.* (Eds), *Emerging Office Systems*. Norwood, N.J.: Ablex Pub. Co., 1982.
4. Bair, James H.: Designing the VDT Interface for Human–Computer Productivity. *Visual Display Terminals: Usability Issues and Health Concerns*. N.Y.: Prentice-Hall, 1983.
5. Card, Stuart, *et al.*: The Keystroke-Level Model For User Performance Time With Interactive Systems. *Communications of the ACM*, **July 1980**.
6. Conrath, David H., and Bair, James H.: The Computer as an Interpersonal Communication Device: A Study of Augmentation Technology and its Apparent Impact on Organizational Communication. *Proceedings of the Second International Conference on Computer Communication*, Stockholm, Sweden, 1974.

7. Culnan, Mary, and Bair, James H.: Human Communication Needs and Organizational Productivity: The Potential Impact of Office Automation. *J. Am. Soc. for Inf. Sci.*, **34**, No. 3, 215–221, May 1983.

8. Drucker, Peter: *Management: Tasks, Responsibilities, Practices.* N.Y.: Harper and Row, 1973.

9. Engelbart, D. C., Norton, J. C., and Watson, R. W.: The Augmented Knowledge Workshop. *AFIPS Conference Proceedings, National Computer Conference-21, June 1973*, **42**, 9–21.

10. Giuliano, Vincent E.: The Mechanization of Office Work. *Scientific American*, **September 1982**, 149–164.

11. Harkness, Richard C.: Office Information Systems: An Overview and Agenda for Public Policy Research. *Telecommunications Policy*, **June 1978**.

12. Hiltz, Starr Roxanne, and Turoff, Murray: *The Network Nation.* N.Y.: Addison-Wesley, 1980.

13. Johansen, Robert: *Electronic Meetings: Technical Alternatives and Social Choices.* Menlo Park, CA: Addison-Wesley, 1979.

14. Kerr, Elaine B., and Hiltz, Starr Roxanne: *Computer-Mediated Communication Systems.* N.Y.: Academic Press, 1983.

15. Landau, Robert, Bair, James H., and Siegman, Jean (Eds): *Emerging Office Systems.* Norwood, N.J.: Ablex Publishing Co., 1982.

16. Lederberg, Joshua: Digital Communications and the Conduct of Science: The New Literacy. *Proc. IEEE*, **66**, No. 11, November 1978.

17. Lucas, Henry C.: *Why Information Systems Fail.* N.Y.: Columbia University Press, 1975.

18. Mintzberg, Henry: *The Nature of Managerial Work.* N.Y.: Harper and Row, 1973.

19. Nickerson, Raymond S.: Why Interactive Computer Systems are Sometimes Not Used by People Who Might Benefit From Them. *INT. J. Man–Machine Studies*, **15**, 469–483, 1981.

20. Olson, Margrethe H., and Lucas, Henry C.: The Impact of Office Automation on the Organization: Some Implications for Research and Practice. *Communications of the ACM*, **25**, No. 11, 838–847, November 1982.

21. Panko, Raymond: Studying Management Work. Presented at the *Fifteenth Hawaii International Conference on System Sciences, University of Hawaii, 1982*.

22. Panko, Raymond, and Panko, Rosemarie: An Introduction to Computers for Human Communication. *University of Hawaii, National Telecommunications Conference, 1977*.

23. Picot, Arnold: Lessons Learned from German Studies On The Introduction of New Communication Technologies in Offices. *Proc. Office Automation Conference, San Francisco, California: April 5–7, 1982*. Washington, D.C.: AFIPS Press, 1982.

24. Strassmann, Paul: Managing the Costs of Information. *Harvard Business Review*, **October 1976**.

25. Strassmann, Paul: Organizational Productivity, the Role of Information Technology. In B. Gilchrist (Ed.), *Information Processing 1977—Proceedings of the IFIP World Congress.* Amsterdam: North-Holland, 1977.

26. Tapscott, Don: *Office Automation: A User Driven Design.* New York: Plenum Press, 1982.

27. Tucker, Jeffrey: Implementing Office Automation: Principles and Electronic Mail Example. *Proceedings of the Conference on Office Information Systems, Philadelphia, 1982*. Washington, D.C.: AFIPS Press, 1982.

28. Uhlig, Ronald P., Farber, David J., and Bair, James H.: *The Office of the Future: Communications and Computers.* N.Y.: North-Holland, 1979.

29. Vallee, Jacques: *The Network Revolution: Confessions of a Computer Scientist.* Berkeley, California: AND/OR Press, 1982.

Advances in Office Automation, Vol 1
Edited by Karen Takle Quinn
© 1985 Wiley Heyden Ltd.

Chapter 2

ERGONOMIC CONSIDERATIONS IN THE DESIGN OF THE AUTOMATED OFFICE

Debra Wierenga

Mary Street Studio

ERGONOMIC CONSIDERATIONS

Shortly after the publication of *The Soul of a New Machine*, author Tracy Kidder's documentation of the extraordinary efforts of a group of young engineers in the development of a new computer system, a *New York Times* reporter set out to interview the man who led that team, J. Thomas West. Hoping to gain some insight into the motivations and desires behind 'the computer industry's latest living legend', the reporter questioned the engineering manager closely regarding rewards and incentives: salary increases, promotions, stock options, dreams of starting his own high-technology company. Well, the 'legend' conceded after much probing, it really would be nice to have an office with a window.[14]

Microprocessor technology has initiated many changes in American society, not the least of which is that many highly educated professional/technical people such as Mr West are now working in corporate offices. In fact, as the demand for timely information grows exponentially, the demographics of the office worker become increasingly complex. The information society employs people with a wide range of skills and educational and professional backgrounds to generate, manipulate, and communicate the data that western society thrives on.

But in the concern over white-collar productivity and the excitement over the rapid developments in computer technology designed to improve it, the individual physical and psychological needs of the office worker have been largely overlooked: if Mr West is not likely to leave his well-paid position and stock options for want of a window, his desire for—and lack of—this seemingly small physical amenity is telling nevertheless.

Concern for human needs in the office workplace has only recently begun to evidence itself in the United States. Ergonomics, the study of workers' relationships to their physical environments, has been practiced more extensively in Western European countries—Sweden, The Netherlands, and West Germany in particular—where studies of the impact of the physical environment on worker satisfaction and productivity have in many instances led to national standards and laws governing the design of office buildings and equipment.

That the movement toward a more human-oriented view of the work environment and technology is beginning to take hold in the United States can be partially ascribed to falling productivity, which is bringing quality of work life issues to the fore. As U.S. corporations take on management styles which are more participatory in nature, environmental design issues are more likely to be raised and considered. Another source of the interest in the effects of the environment on the worker is the evolution of the human rights movement from minority and women's rights in the sixties and early seventies to individual rights in society and in the workplace in more recent years.

But probably the most significant stimulus to the raised ergonomic consciousnesses of U.S. corporations has been the recent influx of computer technology into all levels of office work.

In the early days of data processing, designers of equipment and office spaces could count on the fact that their designs would be used by technically-oriented, computer-knowledgeable people who would be more interested in the functionality of the equipment than in its ergonomic qualities. Today, the majority of the people required to interact with a corporate computer system are not computer specialists, but white-collar workers who find themselves for the first time part of a 'man–machine system' in which the machine appears to have the definite advantage.

The first wave of computer equipment to be used outside the heretofore sacrosanct confines of the DP department was designed with little attention to what ergonomists like to call 'man–machine interface'. Consequently, man had to meet machine considerably more than half-way, both physically and mentally. Corporate managements, hoping to improve office productivity, were anxious to implement the new computer systems. The general tendency was to accept the uncompromising qualities of computer hardware and software as given and to redesign jobs, work processes, and working relationships to suit the machine.

So, as the computer moved from the backrooms to the front desks of corporate America, it was not always viewed favorably by the people who sat at the desks. The first voices raised in protest were those of clerical workers whose jobs and working conditions underwent the most dramatic changes as a result of office automation. For clerical workers, computer systems generally meant more specialized, repetitive, and monotonous tasks, less control over how their work was performed, and less contact with other workers than they had with their pre-automation jobs. They also found themselves under new types of physical stress, suffering from eye fatigue and muscle strain due to the constant effort to accommodate their bodies to inflexible equipment and surroundings.

Working Women, a national organization of office workers, outlined the threats computerization posed to clerical workers' health, quality of working life, and future employment in a document called *Race Against Time: Automation of the*

Office. Exhorting office workers to organize to influence the application of microprocessor technology to clerical work, the study warns: 'Unless occupational safety and health findings are taken into account, office automation will integrate stress-causing factors directly and permanently into clerical jobs.'[24]

Since that time, interest in office automation as a social, managerial, and particularly as a health and safety issue has grown steadily. Scientists, psychologists, physicians, and other professionals representing a wide range of disciplines have undertaken and published studies documenting the impacts of various aspects of office automation on people's health, behavior, and mental outlook.

Although some of the recommendations for office and equipment design resulting from these studies have made their way into business publications, the majority are packaged for publication in scientific or academic journals, ultimately having little effect on the corporate decision makers who exercise control over the design, specification, and management of automated workplaces.

This is not to say that management is unaware of the problems that attend the introduction of a new computer system. As they watch their dearly-bought productivity gains undermined by high turnover rates or the subtle sabotage of unhappy employees—and as they begin to experience first-hand the frustrations and discomforts of the technology as it enters their own offices—corporate executives are demanding solutions from the designers and manufacturers of office equipment and furnishings as well as the architects, space planners, lighting, and HVAC specialists involved. Unfortunately, they often lack the background necessary to make informed decisions and to set realistic requirements for the design and management of the automated office facility.

It is the intent of this chapter to provide the reader with a brief overview of the findings and recommendations of ergonomics experts in areas impinging on the relationship between people and machines in the office. The references and suggested readings listed at the end of the chapter can serve as a starting point for more in-depth reading.

ERGONOMICS AND THE VDT

Ergonomics is an interdisciplinary field, drawing from physiology, anthropometry, psychology, engineering, medicine—and occasionally even sociology and anthropology. Ergonomic research analyzes the points of interaction between people and their work. The knowledge gained from ergonomic research is applied toward the fulfillment of two general objectives: the health, safety, comfort, and satisfaction of the worker, and the best use of the worker's time, skills, and abilities. In other words, ergonomics studies the effects of work conditions on the worker, and then redesigns the work conditions to better fit the worker's physical and psychological nature.

Although certain aspects of the office—the chair in particular—have been recognized as important subjects for ergonomic study and design in years past, the introduction of computers into the office has rendered ergonomic attention to the office worker's environment essential. The relationships between workers and their new electronic tools are more subtle, complex, and restrictive than interactions with pencil, paper, and telephone; the equipment dictates how workers perform their tasks and the physical postures they must assume while performing them.

Most ergonomic research of the automated office has, therefore, focused on the video display terminal (VDT). While the VDT is only one part of a computer system—which also includes the computer itself, software, printers, and other peripheral and interconnecting devices—it is the piece of equipment through which the worker interacts with every other part, and often with other people using the system. The design of the VDT and its placement relative to the user represent the most critical decisions in the design of the automated office.

Selection of the VDT should be based on two general criteria: the functions that the VDT will be used to perform and the specific needs of the individual user. If the user's job function requires only occasional use of the terminal to call up bits of information, for example, certain ergonomic features are less crucial than they would be for a user whose job requires continuous use of the VDT.

In the few years that VDTs have been in widespread use, manufacturers have improved their ergonomic design in several significant areas. Some of the basic features to look for are as follows.

The Keyboard

Along with the display screen, the keyboard represents a central point of interaction between the user and the VDT, and therefore a critical design feature. Positioning of the keyboard has a major impact on working method, and a keyboard which is detachable from the rest of the VDT offers great advantages in any job function. The keyboard can then be positioned on a different level from the screen or the worker's writing surface, and the user can position it for personal comfort, specific task, and level of typing skill (which is a factor in how often the user looks at the keyboard).

Thinness is another keyboard feature to look for. If the keyboard is too thick, it will be difficult for the user to position the surface supporting the keyboard (provided, of course, that the surface is adjustable) low enough to achieve the proper typing position while still leaving enough legroom under the work surface. Some ergonomists recommend that the thickness of the keyboard should not exceed 30 mm.[4]

A third important ergonomic consideration has to do with the color and finish of the keyboard surface and keys. To reduce glare and eye fatigue, keys and surface should be of a nonreflective color with a matt (as opposed to glossy) finish. Research has found that users' subjective ratings of eye discomfort are highest for keyboards with black keys, lowest for those with gray.[4]

The Display Screen

Legibility is obviously of central importance when considering the ergonomic qualities of a VDT display screen. Glare-reducing features such as the use of non-reflective glass and a tilt and swivel mechanism which allows the user to adjust the screen angle relative to light sources will help reduce reflected light, a primary threat to legibility. Other helpful options include controls which allow individual adjustment of screen brightness and contrast and a choice of colors for character display (most VDTs currently use white or green, but recent studies indicate that amber and orange characters may be more readable).[18]

VDT manufacturers are clearly taking steps toward making their products more adaptable to the user, and recent developments such as flat, plasma board screens and terminal and software designs which allow the user to communicate with the computer by pointing instead of keyboarding, promise that life with the computer will grow steadily more serene. In the meantime, however, the VDT is undeniably a more demanding and restrictive tool than those the office worker has been accustomed to, and sensitivity to both the worker's frustration and discomfort and to the ergonomics of the workplace can help ease the current incompatibilities between person and machine.

ERGONOMIC ISSUES IN THE ELECTRONIC OFFICE

One consequence of a poor match between worker and work environment is a less than optimum use of the worker's mental and physical capabilities, leading to a drop in work quality and productivity. Alternatively, the worker may expend more physical and mental energy to compensate for the inadequacies of the environment. This can result in higher stress levels for the worker and higher absenteeism and turnover rates for the corporation. Application of ergonomic principles to the design of the workplace obviously benefits both the individual and the organization.

Areas that require special attention in the electronic workplace can be discussed in four general categories: those that affect the visual interface between worker and machine; those that affect the posture of the worker in relation to the machine and other tools; environmental impacts, such as sound, temperature, and layout; and those that affect the psychological comfort and satisfaction of the worker with the changes office automation brings to working life.

Visual Considerations

Visual discomfort is a major source of irritation for workers in VDT environments. To begin with, the lighting levels required for work processes involving use of visual display screens are considerably different from those required for traditional office tasks, but the lighting of most VDT workplaces was originally designed for the latter.

In general, a VDT working environment requires a much lower level of illumination than an office designed for conventional office work typically provides. The American National Standards Institute recommendation for minimum illumination levels in a general office environment is nearly twice that recommended by some experts for offices using VDTs.[1,4]

The eyestrain associated with VDTs is most often the result of one type of glare or another. *Reflected glare* is the most common source of visual discomfort in the automated office. Light from windows or overhead fixtures reflected off the display screen severely reduces legibility by reducing the contrast between characters and background.

Based on their investigation into the health problems of VDT workers, the New York Committee for Occupational Health and Safety (NYCOSH) recommends installing indirect lighting designed expressly for VDT work, or, barring that, relocating work stations in relation to windows and existing overhead lights, and installing draperies and awnings. Dimmers on overhead fixtures will allow users to adjust lighting to the most comfortable brightness.[3]

Contrast glare is the result of a background which is too bright, such as a window or white wall, or any areas of excessive light contrast within the worker's visual field. Too much contrast leads to overloading of the eye's adaptation mechanism, and that leads to headaches and fatigue.

The position of VDTs in relation to light sources is an important consideration in minimizing contrast glare. Ergonomists recommend locating workstations at right angles to windows and fluorescent tubes, making sure that no light source appears in the visual field of the worker. Other treatments for contrast glare include repainting background walls in nonreflective, low-contrast colors and finishes and placing screens or partitions between workers and bright light sources. Such partitions, as well as work surfaces and other furniture, should also be finished in low-contrast colors. Designers of VDT office interiors should specify unsaturated colors in a matt finish for both walls and furnishings.[8]

The most troublesome incidences of contrast glare occur in the difference between the relatively bright lighting required for referencing hard copy documents, such as handwritten manuscripts or printed manuals, and the much lower lighting requirements for comfortable viewing of the VDT screen. Studies have shown that high luminance contrasts between source document and screen are associated with an increase in eye trouble among VDT workers.[10] The NYCOSH report advises allowing individual operators to solve this problem themselves by providing them with task lighting and display screens that are equipped with controls to adjust brightness. In this way, each individual can find the light balance between screen and source document that causes the least strain.[3]

There are other factors which favor individual control of lighting in VDT workplaces. For example, visual acuity decreases with age[4] and older workers therefore require higher levels of illumination than their younger colleagues. They are also more sensitive to glare.[11] Other conditions affecting visual sensitivity, such as the wearing of bifocals or contact lenses, are further instances of the wide range of specialized visual needs in today's office. Clearly, lighting designs which provide maximum flexibility in terms of individual control are the best solutions for VDT workplaces.

Postural Considerations

It is often difficult to distinguish between visual and postural problems in the automated office, as one very often is the result of the other. For example, in order to compensate for reflected glare from an improperly placed lighting fixture, the worker may unconsciously assume an unnatural sitting position, perhaps slouching in order to view the display screen at an angle that does not reflect the light of an overhead fixture. Researchers have found that many complaints of discomfort in working with VDTs come from workers who must maintain constricting postures in order to see what they are doing.

Viewing distance and angle are two important ergonomic considerations that affect both the visual and the postural comfort of the VDT worker. Proper viewing distance from eye to screen is somewhat dependent upon the size of the characters displayed on the screen, but most experts agree that a range of 450 to 500 mm is optimum. One study found that operators in workplaces with moveable terminals displayed a much wider range of viewing distances (from 450–800 mm) than the average range found in workplaces with built-in terminals. This indicates that workers do take advantage of the opportunity to move terminals in order to accommodate their individual preferences.[10]

Because viewing at these relatively short distances for long periods of time is especially fatiguing to the eye muscles, the National Institute for Occupational Health and Safety recommends regular breaks which allow workers to rest their eyes by viewing at greater distances.

The angle at which the operator views the display screen is also crucial, as too much tilting of the head either up or down will cause chronic neck aches. A natural and comfortable viewing position has the eyes looking slightly downward. The viewing angle most often prescribed for the VDT screen (at its center) is between 10 and 30 degrees below the horizontal formed by the user's eye level.[4,11] Grandjean[8] contends that the most comfortable head position of a seated worker is when the angle between line of sight and the horizontal is 32–44 degrees. Again, individual control seems to be the key to optimum conditions for the user. A tiltable screen or screen support which will allow operators to adjust the equipment to the most comfortable viewing angle is recommended by NYCOSH[3] and others.

The provision and placement of a document holder are also crucial to postural comfort. Minimizing the movement required when looking back and forth between source or reference document and VDT screen will reduce the stress placed on the inherently vulnerable neck muscles. Experts specify a document holder that is on the same plane and viewing angle as the display screen.[4] The document holder should be able to accommodate computer print-outs as well as standard sized papers and reference works.

When placing the VDT keyboard itself within the automated workstation, the most critical ergonomic measurement to consider is working height. If the work surface is too high, the user's shoulders and forearms must be raised to compensate, with painful results. If the surface is too low, a backache is often the consequence.

The correct keyboard height for any given worker follows from proper arm placement. The ideal work surface height is the one that allows the operator to use the keyboard while the arms form a 90-degree angle at the elbow, with forearms parallel to the floor. Since these heights will vary considerably depending upon the body proportions of the user and the thickness of the keyboard itself, use of a height-adjustable work table or dropped keyboard tray (which adjusts vertically *and* horizontally) is strongly recommended. As mentioned earlier, work surface height must also allow sufficient clearance for the legs under the table—a knee clearance of 170–200 mm is recommended.[4]

Placement of the keyboard on the work surface is largely a function of the specific tasks performed. A central position is the obvious requirement for job functions which entail continuous, two-handed keying. If the VDT is used only sporadically for calling up reference data, the keyboard may be placed to one side or the other for use with one hand. In any case, a keyboard which is separate from the display screen and can be positioned and repositioned by the user is distinctly preferable to any type of built-in arrangement.

When designing a VDT work station, it is important to consider any tasks the worker will perform in addition to those involving the use of a terminal. Even if the work is centered around the VDT, adequate space must be provided for laying out reference materials, taking phone messages, and other non-VDT functions. Another work surface may be required if the worker is required to do a significant amount of sorting, collating, writing, or other manual tasks, as the surface at proper height for keyboarding will be too low. Several experts recommend providing two work surfaces of *very* different heights—one for sitting and one for standing—whenever possible. Since the two positions use different sets of muscles, trading off between them allows for relaxation of those muscles not in use.[8,20]

The seated position, however, is the one in which most office workers—and especially VDT workers—spend most of their working days, and the chairs they sit in have a far greater impact on their health and comfort than they usually suspect. Orthopaedic research[13] and anatomical and physiological studies of posture and movement[6] have shown relationships between sitting postures and certain circulatory problems and lower back disorders. In electronic workplaces, where an increasing number of tasks are performed using a VDT, usually with the operator in a seated position, a properly designed chair is essential.

Height adjustability is a primary feature of an ergonomically designed chair. A good chair will allow any worker, regardless of height or body proportions, to comfortably assume the correct sitting posture for typing: thighs in a horizontal position when feet are firmly planted on the floor (or on a footrest); forearms parallel to the thighs. In too high a seat, the user's dangling feet are of little help in supporting the weight of the legs, resulting in excessive pressure on the thighs. If the seat is too low, the sitter is likely to compensate by rotating the pelvis forward, resulting in an unnatural outward curve of the lower spine.

An adjustable chair, together with an adjustable footrest are essential to attaining correct working height when work surface or keyboard height are fixed. In fact, this combination is probably the most economical solution to the problem of working height adjustability.[4] The footrest should be large enough to support both feet solidly and to accommodate some shifting of positions.

People performing non-VDT office work will frequently adopt a posture in which the trunk is partially supported by the arms placed on the work surface. Since this posture is an impossibility for the worker using a VDT keyboard in a two-handed typing position, a backrest which supports the lumbar (lower) region of the back is a necessity. The backrest should be adjustable vertically and at an angle to the seat to allow the individual user to best position it in support of the lower back's outward curve.

Both the backrest and the seat should be rounded and padded at their edges to avoid unnecessary pressure points on the back or thighs. For the same reason, most experts recommend a short seat surface—usually a seat depth of no more than 16 inches—to avoid excessive pressure on the undersides of the thighs.[13]

Light padding and textured upholstery are further features of an ergonomically correct chair seat. While some padding is required to avoid uncomfortable concentrations of pressure, too soft a seat leaves the sitter in a 'floating' position which requires extra muscular effort to maintain and which distributes too much weight to the thighs. A textured material surface (as opposed to vinyl or other smooth and 'slippery' fabrics) will provide a little extra friction to help the user maintain a stable posture.

There is some disagreement as to whether a flat or a contoured seat is more beneficial to the user, but all agree on the importance of a seat and an overall chair design which allow the sitter to shift positions freely and frequently. Even a good posture, if it must be maintained for a long period of time, becomes tiring and detrimental to the worker's health and productivity. Static positions held continuously contribute to muscle, joint, and circulation problems.

A working chair designed so that armrest supports and base or support legs do not restrict arm or leg movement will enable the user to assume a variety of positions. Armrests themselves may be a help or a hindrance, depending upon the task and the working style of the user. An adjustable-tension tilt mechanism which allows the sitter to periodically lean back to stretch the spine and strained back muscles (and consequently to stimulate circulation) is also helpful.

A less obvious but nevertheless central influence on the physical well-being of the worker is the design or organization of the work itself. Repetitive tasks and static positions which overload certain muscles lead rapidly to fatigue and chronic soreness.[2] Job organization which reduces the repetitive nature common to many

VDT-related jobs and promotes greater diversity of movement—such as from a seated to a standing posture—will also reduce musculoskeletal strain and the chances of work-related health problems.

Environmental Considerations

Beyond the design and furnishing of individual workstations, there are general conditions of the office environment that should be reconsidered when a new computer system is introduced. Especially in the large, open-plan offices which are increasingly common, quality of illumination, climate, sound, and space planning are largely outside the control of the individual office worker and must be designed to accommodate, as far as possible, a wide variety of needs and preferences.

The special lighting problems and requirements of the VDT user have already been discussed. As the NYCOSH study points out, however, solutions to the problems of glare and contrast may produce problems of their own.[3]

With lights dimmed, walls darkened, and windows draped or eliminated altogether, the automated office may seem a rather gloomy place to be. Researchers have found that a windowless workplace can notably exacerbate workers' already negative feelings about monotonous tasks and restricted movement, while the presence of a window under otherwise identical circumstances seems to alleviate some of the tension and feelings of unpleasantness.[5]

Besides whatever emotional boost a window may afford, there is evidence that the quality of the light it admits has important physical benefits as well. Unlike the fluorescent or incandescent lighting typical of most offices, natural daylight is 'full-spectrum'—that is it contains the full range of colors plus ultraviolet light. Studies have shown that people remaining indoors over a period of months, under typical indoor lighting—which provides little ultraviolet light—experienced impaired calcium absorption: a process stimulated by exposure to ultraviolet light.[25]

Natural daylight has several other important biological effects, and experts speculate that there are many more as yet unknown to science. At this point, the best course of action for those responsible for the specification of environmental lighting is to, as endocrinologist and medical doctor Richard Wurtman writes: 'not deviate markedly from the lighting environment under which people evolved in nature.'[25]

The office climate is something which has been given very little attention, but about which workers feel very strongly.[9] When considering the indoor climate, four areas should be taken into account: air temperature, humidity, the temperature of surrounding surfaces—such as windows and walls—and the movement of air throughout the space.

A visual display terminal gives off more than three times as much heat as a standard electric typewriter, and many VDTs in continual use can significantly raise the temperature of a workspace. When designing a space specifically for

VDT related work, this additional output of heat should be compensated for by the air conditioning system. When equipping existing offices for new computer systems, careful space planning can help to control the temperature problem. VDTs should be dispersed as evenly as possible throughout the space and should never be positioned so that their cooling systems vent warm air directly onto operators.

Some experts recommend treating the problem at its source by purchasing equipment with low thermal emission whenever possible. Treating the problem by increasing the air conditioning often leads to further worker discomfort caused by drafts around the legs and neck.[4]

Grandjean[8] advocates maintaining an indoor office temperature of 21 degrees centigrade in the winter and between 20 and 24 degrees in the summer, with the temperature of window and wall surfaces near the worker never differing more than two or three degrees up or down.

The humidity of the workplace may be indirectly affected by the use of VDTs in the respect that the additional air conditioning required to maintain comfortable temperatures may lead to an uncomfortable drying of the air. A relative humidity range between 30 and 70 per cent is recommended; relative humidity below 30 per cent has an adverse affect on the mucous membranes of the nose and throat.[8] Further research has shown that most people consider relative humidity between 30 and 40 per cent to be too dry, and some ergonomists therefore recommend that the relative humidity be kept at or above 50 per cent.[4]

The VDT is a quiet piece of equipment—so quiet in fact that in a VDT workplace distracting sounds from other sources may seem more disturbing in contrast. Office noise is typically defined in the literature as 'unwanted sound'. As such, it cannot be simply measured in decibels, but must be assessed in relation to the level of background noise, as well as the level of concentration required for the task to be performed. Researchers prescribe background sound levels of less than 55 decibels in task areas requiring a high degree of concentration, and less than 65 decibels in routine task areas. Equipment sound levels should not be more than five decibels over the general background level.[4]

The high-speed printers often used in conjunction with computer terminals are, on the other hand, fairly noisy pieces of equipment and should be located as far as possible from workers performing intellectual tasks.

Once the printer problem is dealt with, however, the background sound level may actually be *too* low, rendering normal conversational tones a distraction to workers who must concentrate. Studies have found that, especially in open-plan offices, overheard conversation is the noise-related disturbance most frequently mentioned by office workers. Interestingly, it is not so much the loundness of the conversation which is distracting but its information content.[19] To minimize this source of distracting sound—and maximize conversational privacy—ceiling, walls, and windows should be treated with sound-absorbent materials. Acoustical screens or panels surrounding individual workstations, or placed strategically between them, will also help to absorb and deflect speech sound.

If, after the above precautions have been taken, problems of overheard conversations persist, an electronic sound-masking system may be in order. Contrary to some popular assumptions, neither music nor the steady whoosh of the heating/air-conditioning system adequately cover speech; they only add new levels of sound. An expertly designed electronic system will produce unobtrusive sound that can be tuned to the specific wavelengths required to mask unwanted office sounds.

In addition to acoustical privacy there is a need for visual privacy: that is, protection from the visual distractions of nonrelated office activity. In a large-space office this is usually achieved through the use of screens or a panel system.

The layout of a workspace, as defined by the placement of screens, panels, and other furnishings, should always be designed around careful consideration of the amount and type of concentration, communication, and interaction required by the tasks performed there, as well as the traffic patterns of people and paper. The introduction of a new computer system is likely to have an effect—whether direct or indirect—on each of these variables. Communication which formerly took place face-to-face may now be accomplished via a computer terminal. Tasks which once required walking to some other corner of the office to access resources may now be performed without the worker ever moving from the VDT screen.

As office automation changes job roles and communication patterns, office layout should be re-evaluated and redesigned to support the new processes and relationships. Such changes may be necessitated by situations in which computer equipment—often a printer, less often a VDT—is shared between two or more people. Depending on how much the shared piece of equipment is used, it may be best placed at some distance from the workers (certainly if it is a noisy printer), perhaps on a stand-up height work surface to build some movement and a change of posture into the workers' tasks. A VDT which is referenced regularly by two or more workers, however, is best placed centrally where all can reach it easily, such as on a turntable located between users. However, the NYCOSH study reports that many workers find this 'cluster' arrangement, in which they are forced to sit facing other workers continually, to be stressful.[3] Because of the worker frustration and productivity loss that often cancels any benefits of shared terminals, these arrangements are becoming less and less common.

It is important to keep in mind that the line between privacy and isolation is a fine one and is dependent both on individual personalities and type of tasks performed. Working Women's report on office automation contends that modular work stations '... break down interpersonal communications between employees.'[24] And, indeed, there are indications that the automated office is perceived as a lonely and alienating place. A report prepared for the National Office Products Association predicts that the automated office, in which more and more communication is conducted through a computer terminal, 'may quite possibly become a more impersonal place in which to work ... a potentially far more lonely existence for the individual office worker.' Alienation of the office worker, the report goes on to say, is expected to be a growing problem.[22]

Psychological Considerations

There is evidence, however, that the perception of VDT work and modular work stations as isolating comes mainly from workers whose tasks are monotonous and repetitious and who feel they have little control over either the structure of their work or the structure of their environments.

A Canadian study of worker attitudes toward landscape offices found that *perceived control over the environment* had a direct relationship with how workers reacted to their office layout. The results of the study led researchers to hypothesize that workers who perceived themselves to have inadequate control over input to and from the environment also perceived a loss of privacy resulting from the open office design. Workers who perceived themselves in control over transactions with their work environment tended to cite the benefits of office landscaping: more effective communications, greater job satisfaction, increased productivity. Two workers, then, might have radically different attitudes about the same environment, depending on whether they felt they controlled it or it controlled them. A further consequence of this perceived degree of control was workers' perceptions of increased or decreased job performance; researchers conjectured that this might relate to actual job performance.[17]

A more recent study of workers in VDT environments indicates that this same principle may apply to worker attitudes toward office automation. This study compared the health and stress complaints of clerical VDT users to professionals using VDTs and to a non-VDT control group. Results showed that clerical workers, whose jobs were characterized by, among other things, 'involving rigid work procedures' and 'very little operator control over job tasks', had a much greater incidence of physical and emotional health complaints, as well as higher levels of stress, attributed to VDT use than did professionals using VDTs whose jobs 'allowed for flexibility, control over job tasks, utilization of their education, and a great deal of satisfaction and pride in their end product.' The researchers concluded that factors such as job content and task requirements interacted with environmental factors such as lighting and work station design to contribute to stress and health complaints. Because of this, they advise that solutions to VDT-related health problems include job redesign as well as workplace redesign if they are to 'deal with all the root causes of the problems.'[21]

Another study found that much traditional office work which was formerly accomplished through physical movement and human interaction is now limited to operating a terminal, and that VDT work in general was associated with repetition and monotony. Consequently, the researchers recommend that work be organized to reduce repetition and increase diversity of movement.[10]

Office Automation is often discussed as if it were a concrete phenomenon with definable limits, capable of transforming offices and work styles in set and predictable ways. In fact, the definition of the automated office rests largely with the management people who direct its design and introduction. The technology itself does not dictate the way in which it is applied. A computer system can be used to centralize or decentralize information structures; it can specialize or broaden job content; it can add to or detract from workers' comfort, sense of worth and well-being, and productivity. If the introduction of office automation takes into account human needs and abilities—that is, if it applies the principles of ergonomics—both corporations and individuals are likely to benefit.

REFERENCES AND SUGGESTED READINGS

1. American National Standards Institute: *American National Standard Practice for Office Lighting.* ANSI A132.1, 1973. Reprinted in *The Journal of IES*, October, 1973.
2. Ayoub, M. M.: Workplace Design and Posture. *Human Factors*, **15**, 3, 265–268, 1973.
3. Bergman, T.: *Health Protection for Operators of VDTs/CRTs*, New York Committee for Occupational Safety and Health, Inc, 1980.
4. Cakir, A., Hart, D. J., and Stewart, T. F. M.: *Visual Display Terminals*, Wiley, New York, 1980.
5. Collins, B. L.: Review of Psychological Reaction to Windows. *Lighting Research and Technology*, **8**, 80–88, 1976.
6. Floyd, W. F., and Roberts, D. F.: Anatomical and Physiological Principles in Chair and Table Design. *Ergonomics*, **2**, 1–14, 1950.
7. Fucigna, J. T.: The Ergonomics of Offices. *Ergonomics*, **10**, 5, 589–604, 1967.
8. Grandjean, E.: *Fitting the Task to the Man*, International Publications Service, New York, 1981.
9. Harris, Louis and Associates: *Comfort and Productivity in the Office of the 80s*, The Steelcase National Survey of Office Environments, No. II, 1980.
10. Hunting, W., Laubli, Th., and Grandjean, E.: Postural and Visual Loads at VDT Workplaces. *Ergonomics*, **24**, 12, 917–944, 1981.
11. International Business Machines Corp.: *Human Factors of Workstations with Display Terminals*, IBM, White Plains, New York, 1979.
12. Jones, H.: Designing Work Stations for the Information Age. *The Office*, **62**, 65–66, June, 1982.
13. Keegen, J.: Alterations of the Lumbar Curve Related to Posture and Seating. *The Journal of Bone and Joint Surgery*, **35**-A, 3, 589–603, 1953.
14. Klein, S.: The Man Behind the Soul of a New Machine. *New York Times*, September 20, 1981.
15. Koffler, R., and Dainoff, M.: Ergonomics. *Computerworld OA*, **16**, 55–61, 1982.
16. Makower, J.: *Office Hazards: How Your Job Can Make You Sick*, Tilden Press, Washington, D.C., 1981.
17. McCarrey, M. W., Peterson, L., Edwards, S., and Von Kulmiz, P.: Landscape Office Attitudes: Reflections of Perceived Degree of Control Over Transactions with the Environment. *Journal of Applied Psychology*, **59**, 401–403, 1974.
18. McCusker, T.: Ergonomics: The Human Factor. *Output*, March 1981, 24–27.
19. Nemecek, J., and Grandjean, E.: Results of an Ergonomics Investigation of Large-Space Offices. *Human Factors*, **15**, 2, 111–124, 1973.
20. Propst, R.: *The Office: A Facility Based on Change*, Herman Miller, Zeeland, Michigan, 1968.
21. Smith, M. J., Cohen, B. G. F., Stammerjohn, L. W., and Happ, A.: An Investigation of Health Complaints and Job Stress in Video Display Operations. *Human Factors*, **23**, 387–400, 1981.

22. SRI International: *The Future of the Office Products Industry*, National Office Products Association, 1979. Cited in *Office Hazards* by Joel Makower, Tilden Press, 1981.
23. Stammerjohn, Lambert, Jr., Smith, M. J., and Cohen, B. G. F.: Evaluation of Work Station Design Factors in VDT Operations. *Human Factors*, **23**, 401–412, 1981.
24. Working Women: *Race Against Time: Automation of the Office*, Working Women, Cleveland, Ohio, 1980.
25. Wurtman, R. J.: Biological Considerations in Lighting Environment. *Progressive Architecture*, **9**, 79–81, 1973.

Advances in Office Automation, Vol 1
Edited by Karen Takle Quinn
© 1985 Wiley Heyden Ltd.

Chapter 3

COMPLEXITIES OF INTERCONNECTING TECHNOLOGIES

Jack B. Siart

Pacific Telephone and Telegraph Co.

INTRODUCTION

Office Automation users, consultants, and vendors agree on at least one thing: The potential of office automation is realized only when the diverse OA technologies are interconnected to enable the users to create, send, and retrieve information with ease. They differ, however, on their ideas of the specific methods for interconnecting these technologies.

To say that interconnecting the various technologies involved in office automation is complicated is to state the obvious. Each of the technologies has a level of complexity on its own. This complexity is increased by a number of mutually exclusive standards for each of the technologies. Therefore, attempting to interconnect, or integrate, these technologies only adds more complexity. This is not to say that we should be paralyzed into inactivity, however. We need to simplify the technologies by understanding on a very general basis what each of them is from a user's perspective. Then we can evaluate the various strategic alternatives for integrating the technologies in order to realize their potential for simplifying our offices.

Each of the technologies currently considered applicable to office automation evolved separately. They were, and in the most part still are, discrete. Therefore, the systems and applications based on these technologies tend to be discrete from each other. Data processing and word processing are but two examples of this situation.

It is useful to explore the specific medium that comes in contact with the primary information user in data and word processing. In the United States the standard information form within offices has been 8.5″ × 11″ paper for quite some time, though, of course, we have exceptions for legal-size documents and engineering drawings. In word processing, this standard size (8.5″ × 11″) paper is largely followed. Word processing operators may use various size Video Display Tubes; however, they are not the primary users of the information. In data processing, a great many of the primary users of information utilize Video

Display Tubes. Data processing reports to managers, however, have been in the form of 11″ × 14″ printouts since the early days of data processing. These 11″ × 14″ reports are gradually being converted to 8.5″ × 11″ to conform with managers' standard-size office documents.

The following list of office automation technologies begins with a discussion of the various media that represent information from a user–interface perspective (i.e. we are not concerned here with machine readable media such as magnetic tape or diskettes).

INFORMATION MEDIA

Sound   The oldest medium that is used to convey information is the spoken word. It is used on a person-to-person basis via telephone, recorded via analog magnetic devices (and more recently by digital recording). Recent developments have enabled computers to 'speak' via voice synthesis and 'listen' via speech or audio recognition. Most commercial speech recognition systems are limited in their vocabularies and are speaker dependent.

Paper   The next oldest form of information representation that is used in offices is writing or drawing (graphics) on paper. Paper comes in various sizes, colors, and weights. However, as stated earlier, the office standard in the U.S.A. is 8.5″ × 11″, white paper with black print.

Micrographics   The 19th century gave us microphotography which used paper as the source or input document. Computer Output Micrographics (COM) appeared on the scene in the 1960s. All micrographic media require an enlarging device (called a viewer or reader) for the information to be used; therefore, the user–interface device would be the microfiche or roll film reader or viewer.

Television Monitor   Television has been with us for some time now in our homes. Video technology has recently been used in the form of videotape for training or one-way information distribution, and video teleconferencing, which is basically a closed-circuit TV broadcast between meeting rooms. Recent developments in the area of random access interactive videodiscs promise to expand on the usability of the television monitor in offices, especially for training applications.

Video Display Tube (VDT)   Closely related to the television monitor is the VDT. The resolution of a VDT must be greater than a television monitor in order to provide for readability of numbers and letters. VDTs can manipulate these numbers and letters on the screen under computer control whereas television monitors cannot. VDTs, which represent graphics (either black and white or color), often have even greater resolution than television monitors. Recent developments in VDT design include the 'flat panel display' where the screen upon which the information is displayed is flat and relatively thin.

WORKSTATIONS

Typewriters, computer terminals, word processors, personal (or micro-) computers, microfiche viewers, dictation machines, and the ordinary telephone can be defined as workstations. These devices serve as tools for conveying information, as described in the following detailed applications of the technology. The problem of differentiating some of these devices will be addressed later.

Word Processing

Word processing devices use many of the same electronic components as computers. Word processors range from the memory typewriters that formed the technology, to partial and full-page display devices with removable media (e.g. magnetic floppy disks) or shared hard disk systems. Many of the word processors in use today use VDTs, although electronic typewriters utilize paper printing systems. The primary difference between word processors and computers is that the former are designed to 'process' words and numbers in an unstructured manner, and the latter are designed to process computer files which have specific fields in which specific information must be present. Word processors also have special keyboards which have been optimized to facilitate the insertion and deletion of words, lines, paragraphs, and pages.

Word processors can be subdivided into stand-alone and shared, or distributed, systems. The stand-alone devices, as the name implies, are completely self-contained and are designed to be used by one person at a time. Shared or distributed systems are designed with two or more 'terminals' connected to a unit that facilitates sharing or distribution of the 'logic' of the system (central processing unit), magnetic storage devices, printers and/or communications.

The primary input method to word processors is via direct keyboarding of information by a word processing operator. The creator either dictates or writes the information. Systems can be configured with optical character recognition (OCR) devices for input of typewritten draft pages of information for later editing and revision on the word processor. This type of application takes advantage of the fact that the typewriters are already in place and the users are already trained.

Communication devices enable word processors to send or receive information in digital format from other word processors or computer systems.

The primary output method of word processors is the printed page. Printers can be high-speed draft printers, letter quality printers, or very high-speed page printers. Word processors equipped with communications can also output information to other word processors or computers for electronic mail applications, electronic filing, and/or conversion to Computer Output Microfilm.

The primary strength of word processors currently lies in their ability to correct errors and make revisions. In integrated office automation systems, word processors or systems with word processing capabilities stand a good chance of being the primary information capture device. Once information is captured digitally, we have the capability of sending the information to other devices in the same building, or to remote devices via some form of communications.

The cost of word processors ranges from as little as $1000 to over $15 000 per workstation. The price is based on the amount and size of internal memory, storage, printers, communications, VDT size and resolution, software, etc.

Word processing software can be added to microcomputers, minicomputers or mainframe computers. Conversely, data processing software can be added to word processors (many word processing vendors recently began offering the CP/M® (Registered Trade Mark of Digital Research) microcomputer operating system). Therefore, the differences between word processors and computers are becoming increasingly blurred.

In the area of standards, word processors sold in the U.S. have the capability of using the standard English alphabetic characters and numbers. However, there are no universal standards for such common control characters as centering, boldface, or underlining. This lack of standards becomes acute when information on one word processor is sent via communications to another word processor. This issue will be covered further under Communications.

Dictation Systems

Voice dictation systems capture the analog voice of the information creator for later transcription to paper or electronic form. Most voice dictation systems have separate components that are designed for the dictator and the transcriber. The dictator's device records the voice, and the transcription device (with foot controls) is used by the secretary or support personnel while at a typewriter or other keyboard device such as a word processor.

Dictation systems range from the simple microcassette recorder to endless loop telephone dial dictation systems. The microcassette recorders can be used as portable models for dictation while travelling. The recorded information is then given to the transcribing station physically in the form of the microcassette. There are dictation systems that are designed with the microphone in the principal's office and the magnetic storage and transcription device in the secretary or support personnel's work area. The endless loop telephone dial dictation systems are found primarily in word processing centers where any of a number of operators can access the dictation. The cost of dictation systems ranges from a few hundred dollars to $4000 to $5000 per telephone channel for a system with automated workload tracking and automated workload balancing.

The advantages of dictation over handwriting the information are: (1) output speed, (2) remote transcription, and (3) nonsimultaneous interaction with the transcriber. In general, we speak about seven times faster than we write. Keyboarding from dictation is also faster than from handwritten documents. Remote dictation via telephone allows us to dictate without regard for our physical whereabouts or time zone differences for travelers. Dictation systems allow the principal and the support person to interact nonsimultaneously, or independently.

This independence and freedom from interruption is viewed as one of the keys to increasing productivity. The only interface to other technologies is currently the telephone. The voice typewriter or voice word processor still appears to be in the distant future.

Recent trends in dictation equipment are toward multifunction, such as telephone answering with the dictation machine, and integration of dictation with Voice Store and Forward systems. Vendors are also making dictation systems more attractive to managers by adding workload recording and balancing features.

Optical Character Recognition (OCR)

Optical Character Recognition (OCR) technology is designed to convert information on paper to magnetic digital form. In that sense OCRs are the opposite of printers, which convert digital information to paper. OCRs are either uni-font (currently obsolete as they read only one typefont such as OCR-B), multifont, or omnifont. The multifont OCRs can read most typefonts (one typefont per page). Omnifont OCRs can read multiple typefonts per page and some handprinting. The accuracy of OCRs has improved greatly over the last few years; however, some users indicate that there are still many problems. Some of these problems can be overcome by additional training of typists.

OCRs range from the size of a desk-top copier to the size of a couple of desks. The prices range from $8000 to $200 000 depending on the number of typefonts read per page, disk storage, number of terminals, etc. There is usually an error factor associated with OCRs. Errors can be corrected at the OCR (which can slow it down) or at the word processor.

Some companies are mating an OCR to their word processor, which allows all of their existing typewriters to become input devices for the word processor. OCRs are also used to solve the interconnection problem between incompatible devices.

OCR speeds range from 20 seconds per page to two minutes per page. This speed sounds impressive when compared with keyboarding, though it should be remembered that the information on the scanned pages had to be keyed initially. The most efficient system appears to be to capture keystrokes electronically in the initial keying, depending, of course, upon the number of people keyboarding and the amount of information being keyed. Recent trends in OCR are toward smaller, cheaper systems.

ELECTRONIC MAIL

Many systems can fit into the definition of electronic mail. In fact, the telegraph systems that preceded the telephone were the first electronic mail systems. Later electronic mail systems included: (1) Teletype and Telex, (2) Facsimile systems, (3) Computer-Based Message Systems (CBMS), (4) Document-Based Electronic

Mail, and (5) Voice Store and Forward Systems (VSF). Electronic mail systems are frequently defined as the electronic transmission of a segment of the mail process.

Electronic mail systems can be passive, active, or have both capabilities. Passive systems require the recipient to check in to the mail system to see if he or she has mail. Active systems attempt to deliver the information to the recipient's location. Some systems allow the recipients to specify whether they want passive or active delivery.

Electronic mail can address the problems of slow mail services and telephone tag. One form of Document-Based Electronic Mail involves sending documents from one communicating word processor to another (point to point transmission). This can be a good alternative to overnight package or mail services and, in fact, can be faster and cheaper. In addition, the document can be easily modified at the receiving location.

Telephone tag (where a call-back slip is created a number of times before the parties connect) is quite a different problem. CBMSs have been in use for quite some time (at least 10 years) among computer professionals. A CBMS user can deposit a message in another user's 'mailbox' by using a computer terminal. The receiving user retrieves the message in similar manner. Both telephone tag and telephone interruptions are reduced for communications that are one way.

A Voice Store and Forward (VSF) system, frequently called voice mail, is similar in function to a CBMS except that the telephone is used instead of a computer terminal. Commands are entered via the 12 key pad, and messages are spoken into the telephone. VSF disadvantages relative to a CBMS include the lack of an audit trail on most systems, the lack of hard copy capability, and the lack of filing and retrieval capabilities. Since VSF technology is just a few years old, many users are just beginning to make system adjustments, such as the creation of a transcription voice mailbox for conversion of voice messages to hard copy for filing, etc. One VSF vendor has used the system to store and forward documents via facsimile devices.

The costs of electronic mail systems start as low as $7.00 per month per user for a VSF and can go up to several hundred dollars per month per user for a CBMS (including terminal rental).

At the present time, there are few standards for sending messages between systems. However, the National Bureau of Standards in the USA recently announced a CBMS message exchange standard for message content. Standards are not yet finalized in four other areas of message exchange, including addressing (i.e. the message envelope).

Computing

Computers of various sizes are covered in more detail in Chapter 6. The last few years have seen incredible advances in the power and performance of computer systems coupled with a reduction in price. This has presented us with the opportunity to install more computers in our companies, which can compound the incompatibility problem. In very general terms, the advantages of large mainframe computers over personal computers or Office Automation systems are:

1. *Large data bases*   Mainframe computers have a greater capacity for disk storage, therefore large data bases must be placed on mainframe computers. Also, sharing data bases is best done on mainframe computers.
2. *Large memory*   Mainframe computers have many times the memory of personal computers or minicomputers. Very large complex programs require a great deal of memory.
3. *Expensive peripherals*   Mainframe computers allow the sharing of expensive peripherals, such as high-speed page printers, Computer Output Microfilmers, OCR scanners, and high-density tape drives.

In the area of Office Automation, large computers can be used to share information. In this context, electronic mail and electronic filing of information are best done on large computers.

TELEPHONE SYSTEMS/COMMUNICATIONS

Voice and data communications systems and equipment have been with us for some time. Some recent trends are apparent: (1) voice telephones are being incorporated into VDTs, (2) local switching equipment (Private Branch Exchange (PBX) or Computerized Branch Exchange (CBX)) is gaining the capability of switching digital calls, (3) Voice Store and Forward capabilities are being considered for the PBX and CBX, and (4) Local Area Networks are being announced by virtually every major and minor telecommunications vendor.

In many ways the Local Area Network or LAN duplicates the functions of the telephone switching office, in that a LAN allows each device to connect to another device within a building or short geographical area. These LANs have what is called a communications processor to allow for connection to the telephone or other external network. In some LANs the communications processor is the PBX/CBX.

Many industry observers feel the LAN is the key to Office Automation. The advantages of a LAN include easy communications between any device in the building or close geographical area and the ability to easily share expensive peripherals, such as laser printers and Optical Character Recognition (OCR) Readers.

The field of data communications may have more 'standards' than any of the others. We have standards of speed (baud), half or full duplex, asynchronous or bisynchronous, even or odd parity, and then we get to the alphabet and numeric soup of communication protocols. Agreement is required on each of seven different levels of protocol to really effect communication between any two devices. This subject will be explored later in this chapter.

An unprecedented level of change is taking place in the communications marketplace. The industry is being shaped by a greater degree of computerization in switching, by new satellite communications networks, by the entry of competing and value-added communications carriers, etc. In addition, the regulatory agencies in the United States are in the process of making far-reaching decisions regarding the industry. One of the new services that has been announced in this fast-changing industry is the ability for the communications network to perform some of the protocol conversion that is the subject of this chapter. As of this writing, these services are only in the beta test stage. (Beta test is a stage of development testing before a product is announced. Selected customers agree to test the prereleased product to help test for faults.) Information on which protocols will be converted, and when and where the services will be available, is not yet public knowledge.

Computer Graphics

Computer graphics can be divided into: (1) Presentation Graphics for business presentations, (2) Decision Graphics to aid management decisions, (3) Computer Aided Drafting (CAD), and (4) Computer Aided Manufacturing (CAM). The last two are in the early stages of being combined into CAD/CAM. Computer Graphics systems allow editing and revision to graphic information in the same manner as word processors deal with words and numbers. The advantage, then, is to reduce the amount of effort necessary to create a revised 'drawing'. This allows the creation of more versions of a drawing before the final selection is made.

Computer graphics systems use VDTs to display the information that is being modified. This modification is done via digitizing pads, keyboards, and light pens. The output is reproduced via multipen plotters, color or black and white laser printers, color slide devices and/or computer imaging devices that produce output on micrographic or printing plate masters. The primary output for presentation graphics is the transparency for overhead projectors which can be created directly by plotters or laser printers.

The systems range from the simple personal computer to sophisticated image manipulation devices costing hundreds of thousands of dollars. Again, standards are few among vendors.

Recent trends show computer graphics capabilities being incorporated into smaller and cheaper devices. In addition, the high-end devices are duplicating the functions of entire printing shops, creating and merging text and graphics for creation of publishing masters. The CAD/CAM devices have application in engineering offices.

Image Systems

Image systems can be divided into: (1) Reprographics (i.e. printing, duplicating, photocopying), (2) Facsimile, (3) Videotape, (4) Videodisc, and (5) Micrographics (both source document and computer output). Image systems deal with text, graphics, numbers, etc. as images or whole pictures and therefore cannot manipulate letters, numbers, or parts of graphics displays.

Reprographics and facsimile have been around offices for quite some time. The latest trends in reprographics are towards intelligent copiers and even communicating copiers. This last trend in fact duplicates the function of a remote printer. The Japanese have created a machine which combines facsimile and OCR scanning.

Micrographics can provide rapid and economical access to static information archived from computers or received from external sources on paper.

Computer Output Microfilm (COM) is created by transferring information directly from a computer or from a $\frac{1}{2}''$ magnetic tape to either 16 mm or 105 mm microfilm rolls. The 105 mm microfilm rolls are cut into microfiche. Eye readable titling information and frame indexing is usually added while the film is being created.

Source Document Micrographics are created by taking 'pictures' of documents, usually paper.

Micrographic technology therefore utilizes the standards of both paper and computer for representing information. In addition, the microforms themselves have standards in terms of size and reduction ratio. Roll microfilm is generally either 16 mm or 35 mm (primarily 16 mm in office applications) at reduction ratios of $24\times$ (24 to 1), $32\times$, or $48\times$. Microfiche (French for 'small card') is a card of film that is approximately 4'' by 6'' at reduction ratios of $24\times$ for source document or $48\times$ for COM. Microfiche is much more prevalent in offices than is roll film.

Recent developments in micrographics include updateable microfiche where an image of a page (frame) can be added to the microfiche after it is developed.

Videotape is being used in offices for 'receive only' training and information distribution. Some companies have a 'video magazine' on videotape to augment other internal employee information.

Videodisc itself is a recent development. Media coverage of videodisc has concentrated primarily on the emulation of videotape for playing movies and the fact that current videodisc systems cannot record. Laboratory work is still being done on videodisc systems that can record as well as play (optical disc). A primary difference between videodisc and tape is the random access ability of some disc systems. A random access videodisc under microprocessor control gives us interactive video, which is excellent for training. Many companies and universities are working on integrating microcomputers with interactive videodisc players to form powerful Computer Aided Instruction (CAI) systems.

In each of the imaging technologies we again see a number of 'standards'. Facsimile systems employ 3 different transmission groups. Micrographics systems have multiple standards for film width, format, and reduction ratio. Three different videotape standards exist for two different tape widths. At least three different types of videodisc recording and playback systems are currently being marketed.

CURRENT INTERCONNECTION SITUATION

Most of the talk about fully integrated office automation systems is just that, talk. The lack of uniform standards in each of these technologies coupled with the lack of agreement on each of the following seven levels of data communication protocol has created the current interconnection dilemma for users.

The seven levels of data communication protocol break down as follows:

Protocol level 1/Physical control This involves specifications for plugs, voltages, etc.

Protocol level 2/Link control This involves message start and stop format, error procedures, sending and receiving 'addresses', etc.

Protocol level 3/Network control This level details how messages are grouped in the network.

Protocol level 4/Transport end-to-end control This level covers communication between different networks which could be in different buildings in various parts of the country.

Protocol level 5/Session control This level specifies the disposition of the message at the receiving destination.

Protocol level 6/Presentation control This level covers conversion of the binary bits of information to human readable language and formatting (such as spacing, indents, underlines, etc.)

Protocol level 7/Application control This level specifies formatting for the unique application. An electronic message will look different from a quarterly report, for example.

Closely related to the lack of communications standards is the lack of media standards. Information can be recorded on magnetic 'floppy' disks of 3.5'', 5.25'', or 8'' diameter, single or dual sides, and at varying densities (tracks per inch). In general, a floppy disk recorded on one system cannot be read on any other vendor's system. Information is also recorded on fixed and removable hard disks, $\frac{1}{2}''$ magnetic tape, cassette and microcassette tapes, and cartridge tapes.

The largest vendors are still in the process of creating fully integrated office information systems using their own previously discrete systems. They are able to do this by establishing their own standards. A recent trend was established when a vendor established a local area network and published the interconnection specifications in the hopes of having their LAN become the standard, which would maximize the probability of their furnishing the OA equipment. However, as can be seen from the seven-level data communications protocol, a LAN does not address all seven layers.

Vendor standards are designed to give the individual vendor the advantage of being a single-source vendor for the lucrative office automation market with his current customers. It is significant to point out that today not a single OA vendor has products in all of the technologies previously listed.

We may have a case of too many specialists both in the vendor community and in the user community in each of these areas of technology, with far too few information generalists. To use a medical analogy, imagine the problem of deciding which type of doctor to go to when you are ill when there are only specialists and no general practitioners. Many of the specialists in these technologies do not know enough about the other technologies to refer a user to another specialist in a different technology. The fact is that each technology specialist sees problems from his or her own perspective. A memorable statement was heard by the author at a recent conference: 'If the only tool you have is a hammer, all of your problems look like nails.' The fact that there are many different ways to accomplish the same end result with different technologies (and at very different costs) only compounds this problem. Word processing on micro-, mini-, and mainframe computers is but one example.

ALTERNATIVE INTERCONNECTION STRATEGIES

Users have the following general strategies available to them for interconnecting office automation technologies: (1) Single Vendor, (2) User Integration, and (3) Contractor or Systems House Integration. Of course, users can also press for integration standards, either individually or through user groups.

Single Vendor Strategy

The Single Vendor integration strategy necessitates selecting a single vendor to provide office automation hardware. Like all of the other integration strategies, it has benefits and weaknesses.

On the plus side, it leaves the integration problem squarely with the chosen vendor for today's systems as well as future developments, it simplifies problem isolation when the systems malfunction (and provides a measure of leverage with the vendor to solve the problem), it provides for maximum discount for volume purchases, and it simplifies the training process throughout the company. This training issue should be given a great deal of weight because the behavioral changes required of office automation users are painful at best (see Chapter 8 for a detailed discussion on training). Changing the system, and therefore reinitiating the learning curve, a few years down the road may be intolerable to the users. Besides, there will always be users who liked the old system better. In addition, with a single vendor the medium on which the information is recorded, such as floppy disks, can be interchanged physically within a building or even mailed. This physical media interchangeability may temporarily sidestep the local area network communications issue.

On the minus side, the user has to choose the vendor very carefully to assure that the vendor will remain one of the viable office automation vendors in the future. In the office automation field, as in other growth industries, a vendor shakeout is in our future. No user wants to be stuck with equipment that will become obsolete and will be difficult to service. The Single Vendor strategy is of course playing into the vendors' strategy of establishing their own standards. In many ways this is like taking a marriage partner. It is much easier to get married than to get divorced. Another drawback is the lack of features the chosen vendor may have relative to other vendors. Of course, if the feature is desirable to many users, the vendor will be motivated to incorporate it into his system. However, as the Office Automation market matures, vendors can be expected to seek niches that other vendors are not servicing. Therefore, the Single Vendor interconnection strategy may be short term at best.

User Integration Strategy

The most difficult strategy in the short term is for the users to perform the integration themselves. There are, of course, many different ways to accomplish this integration. The user may purchase 'black box' protocol converters that are designed to change the protocol from one or a number of vendors to that of the device that will be receiving the information. The user may designate a mainframe computer to serve as the network information buffer and protocol converter in a similar manner to the 'black boxes'. The user can program, or request the vendor to program, the sending device to create the protocol for the receiving device. The complexity of the User Integration strategy increases with the number of technologies and vendors involved. Future selections of vendors then may be restricted by the cost of adding another protocol to the conversion process.

The 'black box' protocol converter alternative can be a very expensive one depending on the number of devices the user currently has, as well as the number of different vendors that he would like to interconnect. A 'black box' would potentially be required on each device. A number of 'black box' vendors have designed their devices to convert protocols between the most popular brands of word processors. However, if the user finds that the vendor does not cover one of his devices he may have to purchase another 'black box' to satisfy the interconnection. You can easily imagine a stack of expensive boxes for interconnection. Obviously this is not a desirable goal for long-term office automation planning. However, small businesses or departments may see the short-term benefits as desirable.

The user network alternative may be attractive to those users who already have some sort of in-house timeshare computing capability. In that case, the user may write the protocol conversion program himself or contract with a software house to write it. An added advantage may be the ability to create an official company version of information on the timeshare computer for storage or archival purposes. This version can also be transferred to computer output microfilm for long-term archival storage so as not to tie up the timeshare computer's disk space with information that is no longer being actively changed or modified. A disadvantage of this alternative is the difficulty in obtaining the complete protocol from each vendor. Remember, most of the vendors would like users to adopt the single-vendor strategy. Another problem may be encountered when the user management tries to train users in the complex process of logging on to a timeshare computer, establishing a file, running a program to change the protocol to that of the receiving station(s), and/or retrieving a file left for them by another location. Training users of office systems is complicated enough today without expecting them to learn how to change protocols in this manner for remote recipients of their information. We must also consider the possibility that one document may have to be modified for many different protocols depending on the number of vendors' equipment it must be sent to within a large organization.

Requesting the vendors to program their devices to emulate the protocol of a competing vendor is at least theoretically possible. Gaining the cooperation of the vendors in this matter may be quite a challenge, however. The larger the potential order, the greater amount of attention a user can expect from the vendor. The key word in the preceding sentence is 'potential'. Vendors cannot be expected to be highly motivated towards converting equipment that has already been purchased.

An advantage of the User Integration strategy is that the user may choose each vendor based on the unique strengths of his features, geographical location, price, and support. Another plus is the fact, as stated earlier, that no one vendor is represented in all of the information handling technologies. Therefore, a degree of User Integration may be inevitable. The User Integration strategy also keeps all potential vendors in a competitive position to the users' advantage.

A disadvantage of the User Integration strategy is the knowledge that the user's Office Automation department must acquire in order to implement it. Specialists will be needed in each of the technologies. These specialists may need to be managed by the rare information generalist. Training for the users of different brands of equipment is complicated and reduces the economies of scale required for computer-aided instruction. Intradepartmental transfers of personnel may be inhibited due to the retraining problem. Problem isolation can become a major concern in multivendor environments. For some horror stories, consult with your data processing department. User-level problem isolation difficulties will require a greater level of expertise from the information users as well as from their systems people, who may be remotely located. A problem may be in the workstation, communications modem, local area network, computer hardware, or software. Or there may be an operator error, which requires a training solution.

Contractor/Systems House Integration

The selection of one of the two strategies listed above or this Contractor/Systems House Integration strategy may be very similar to the classic 'Make or Buy' decision process in other areas of business. This strategy frees the user from learning the technologies previously listed, establishing his own standards for the technologies, and also establishing the corporate interconnection strategy. To many user managements this presents a very tempting alternative. However, the existing managers in charge of the technologies, such as Data

Processing, Word Processing, and Telecommunications do not usually view the hiring of contractors or consultants in their areas of responsibility as attractive.

One advantage of the Contractor/Systems House Integration Strategy is the potential to get up to speed quickly and begin reaping the benefits of Office Automation. Also, a single source can be accountable for the overall plan and its execution. This strategy can also provide an opportunity for the users to learn how to set up interconnecting systems from the experts. It also provides an opportunity for selecting the best vendors for the user's particular office automation needs. Qualified Contractors or Systems Houses should have experience with many different user environments to draw from.

The primary disadvantage of the Contractor/Systems House Integration strategy is that there are very few experienced companies in this field. Unfortunately we do not yet have certified Office Automation professionals. In the interim, we can only be very careful to include performance warranties in our contracts with consultants or systems houses. This will not of itself guarantee a successful relationship, but it does force both parties to address the quality of the consulting and/or systems work.

USER INTERCONNECTION STATUS

Without consciously making the decision, many users have currently chosen the strategy of buying now and leaving the integration problems for the future. In part this is a response to the complexities of integrating today in a time of rapidly changing technologies and integration philosophy.

It should be obvious that the buy-now-integrate-later strategy has very short-term advantages with long-term problems. Some companies, of course, have standardized on a single vendor, or a few vendors for each of the technologies, such as computing and word processing. This will reduce the later integration problems. This strategy may be advantageous by minimizing the anguish of making a decision on an integration strategy while the user, in fact, waits for the Office Automation dust to settle.

A disadvantage of a wait-and-see integration strategy may be that the user's company is put at a comparative disadvantage relative to others in his industry. Other companies in the industry who automate may be able to respond more quickly and more cheaply to the marketplace. If the user chooses many different vendors for office automation devices he will have to integrate these devices at some time in the future. Another disadvantage is the possibility that one of the vendors will be a casualty in the very competitive office automation marketplace and the user will have obsolete, hard-to-service equipment.

COMPANY SIZE CONSIDERATIONS

The size of a company may be a factor in determining which of the aforementioned strategies is adopted. For example, a very large company probably already has a large data processing department with expertise in computers and data communications.

Additionally, the large company probably already has an existing inventory of minicomputers and mainframe computers along with the software to run on them as well as a number of word processors. The existing level of expertise in these large companies may make it more attractive to adopt the user-integration strategy. However, an existing inventory of a single vendor's computers and word processors may make the single-vendor strategy attractive.

Smaller companies, including small businesses, may find that developing the expertise required to adopt the user-integration strategy is too expensive to amortize over the limited number of office automation applications. Therefore, small companies may see the single-vendor strategy as attractive to them even though it will limit the features they will enjoy. Small companies do not have the purchasing power of larger ones and therefore cannot command the attention of vendors for feature additions to a selected line of office automation equipment. User groups may gain consensus on features that are desired of a particular vendor and communicate them to the vendor with the impact of large numbers. User groups can be either vendor-specific or application-general, such as Office Automation User Groups.

User Groups and Associations

Office Automation User Groups and Associations are emerging throughout the United States now. The primary function of these groups is to provide a forum for formal and informal discussions of office automation on a peer level. These discussions center on internal company strategies, justification to upper management, and problems with office automation systems or vendors. These groups could also be used to exert pressure on the vendors and standards-making groups (such as the International Electrical and Electronics Engineers, the American National Standards Institute, and the National Bureau of Standards in the United States) to simplify the complexities of interconnecting the diverse technologies of office automation. At the present time only a limited number of users sit on these standards-making boards. As stated earlier, standardization primarily benefits the users, not the vendors.

There are a few differences in how Office Automation User Groups (frequently called Office Automation Roundtables) and associations accomplish their goals of increased communication on topics of mutual interest. Office Automation Roundtables typically meet very frequently, perhaps monthly, and the groups are usually small—ten to twenty companies. Office Automation Associations (such as the International Information/Word Processing Association), on the other hand, have very large memberships (over 10 000) and meet only once or twice per year. Association meetings are usually combined with office automation equipment exhibitions.

Using office automation technologies, such as computer-based message systems or computer conferencing, is a relatively new phenomenon in the United States. One such group was established after the Office Automation Conference (sponsored by the American Federation of Information Processing Societies (AFIPS) in Arlington, Virginia) in 1982. Computer conferencing to discuss diverse issues of office automation between people located throughout the United States, and indeed, the world, may greatly simplify the process of communication and could potentially lead to consensus on office automation issues, including standards.

FUTURE OUTLOOK

It may be many years before we have universal standards that would eliminate the complexity of interconnecting the diverse office automation technologies. Many industry observers wonder if we will ever get to this point. In the interim, we can choose from the previously identified strategic alternatives for interconnection and press for standards individually and through user groups and associations. In this manner, we can realize today some of the benefits of improved productivity and communications that are the promise of office automation.

REFERENCES AND SUGGESTED READINGS

1. Stockett, Larry A., President, Micronet Inc., Washington, D.C. Private Communication.
2. Wakin, Edward: User Groups: Working Smarter Not Harder. *Today's Office*, 27–32, June 1982.
3. Mokhoff, Nicolas: Local Data Nets: Untying the Office Knot, *IEEE Spectrum*, **18**, No. 4, 57–59, April 1981.
4. Romei, Lura: Communication Software Powers the Multifunction Office. *Modern Office Procedures*, **26**, 63–74, April 1981.
5. Martin, Josh: Successful Office Automation, Part II. *Computer Decisions*, **13**, 108–124, 161–162, July 1981.
6. Walshe, Willoughby Ann: Solving the Standards Dilemma—Part II: Seeking the Solution. *Office Administration and Automation*, **44**, No. 2, 66–68, February 1983.

Advances in Office Automation, Vol 1
Edited by Karen Takle Quinn
© 1985 Wiley Heyden Ltd.

Chapter 4

CENTRALIZED WORD PROCESSING

Beverly K. Miller
University of Wisconsin-Eau Claire

CENTRALIZED WORD PROCESSING SOFTWARE

With recent advances in technology, computer systems are no longer being restricted to performing only data processing or 'number crunching' functions. Software suppliers have made tremendous strides in developing text editing or word processing systems that can be run on large mainframe computers. Therefore, excess capacity found on existing computer systems should not be overlooked when considering alternatives for implementing electronic word processing systems. The decision of whether to acquire an independent system solely dedicated to word processing (referred to in this discussion as a dedicated word processing system) or to utilize existing computer facilities coupled with a word processing software package (referred to as word processing software or text editing systems) should be based on the following factors: (A) the specific word processing needs that have been identified for the organization; and (B) the suitability of currently available computer resources for supporting the word processing capabilities necessary to meet those needs.

Identifying Word Processing Requirements

Word processing systems have repeatedly been shown to be successful in saving time and money while improving the quality of office correspondence. However, the types and volume of office correspondence produced, the time constraints under which the correspondence is produced, and the personnel structure of an office all significantly influence the types of equipment required. Offices in which a central secretarial pool produces large quantities of short, single-occurrence memoranda have different needs from offices in which distributed secretaries produce lengthy manuscripts which undergo constant revision.

While this chapter will not attempt to focus on the identification of these requirements, it is emphasized that they should be clearly defined before any type of word processing equipment is considered.

Determining the Suitability of Computer Facilities

All word processing systems are composed of two basic elements—hardware (including the keyboard, screen, processing unit, storage devices, and printer), and software (the machine-understandable instructions for storing and editing text). When evaluating whether a particular word processing system will adequately serve an office, one must look at both of these elements. When considering the use of an existing computer system, an evaluation must be made as to whether the present equipment can be adapted, or whether new equipment can be added to support the necessary elements of an office system. Secondly, the software must be evaluated to see that it will result in the gains in productivity necessary to justify implementation of a system.

The focus of this chapter will be on evaluating the alternative of utilizing computer-based word processing software rather than purchasing a dedicated word processing system to handle an office's automation needs. An attempt will be made to describe the various factors which must be evaluated relating to both hardware and word processing software features. After examining the various factors, their implications will be discussed. Finally, suggestions will be given for evaluating the feasibility of utilizing an existing computer system and choosing appropriate word processing software for that system.

EQUIPMENT CONSIDERATIONS

Terminal Networks

One of the biggest advantages of utilizing word processing software is that the existing network of computer terminals may act as word processors. These terminals are already in place—the communications cables and equipment investment has been made. Since the terminals can be used for both data entry and word processing, the proliferation of computer equipment can be somewhat controlled. Computer terminals which were being underutilized can be used more fully by combining their functions.

Attempts to implement centralized word processing or data entry systems often have problems because the people requiring these services are so far removed physically from the people performing the services. Office planners currently are recommending placing these services in as close proximity as possible. Many offices may not have had enough work to justify the cost of having video display terminal equipment within their immediate areas in the past. However, an office that could not previously justify the expenditure necessary to obtain a terminal for either of these uses could possibly afford it if both data and word processing functions could be performed on the same piece of hardware.

At the same time, attempting to utilize a terminal for more than a single function can have its drawbacks. Various types of computer terminals are available, and generally a type is selected that is specially designed for the intended usage. If the terminal was selected for use in a data processing function, it may not have features or a keyboard design that would make it convenient to use for word processing. While multifunctional terminals are available, the mere fact that they are designed for multiple uses suggests that they are not optimally designed for either function. While any terminal featuring a full keyboard can be used for word processing, lack of efficiency and frustration may result if the terminal is not well suited for its intended use.

Sharing a terminal between multiple functions is a fine idea if those functions must be performed at different times. However, the fact that the terminal is designed for various functions also means that the terminal will be tied up more often. Thus, when an operator wants to use it for word processing, another operator may be already using it for a data processing function. In addition, if two or more people are using the terminal (perhaps a word processing specialist and a data entry clerk), the terminal may be inconveniently located for one or more of them. Many times correspondence must be produced in a hurry, and the inconvenient location or unavailability can be a problem.

Central Processing Resources

Perhaps more important than an existing terminal network is the central processing unit of the computer. This, combined with main memory and disk storage, represents the major cost of either a data processing or word processing system. Since this investment has already been made, huge cost savings can be realized on the overall word processing system if some of the resident computing power can be utilized.

The capabilities of a mainframe's central processing unit can provide much more flexible advanced editing and file manipulation functions than could smaller units. Sorting or spelling verification functions may be available which would be limited on small dedicated word processing systems due to lack of memory and overall processing power. The speed of this processing may be highly improved by utilizing the capabilities of the large mainframe computer.

Central Storage Resources

Access to mainframe computer storage can be a big advantage for a word processing system. Instead of storing documents on diskettes or small disks, documents can be stored on the larger computer disk. This storage can be particularly helpful when dealing with extremely long documents, which might otherwise have to be broken up to fit onto the small diskettes now utilized on many dedicated word processing machines. Computer systems are usually set up to handle file manipulation, including long term storage and backup procedures.

The large amount of computer storage can present problems, however. Procedures must be developed for dealing with the numerous small files created as word processing documents. The seemingly 'unlimited' storage can cause people to become lax in removing unneeded documents, and directory records must be maintained to provide information regarding exactly what is located in storage. While computer storage may initially seem unlimited, the fact that a large number of keyboarders are creating word processing documents may mean that the on-line storage will fill up quickly. Typically, data processing files are packed tightly together, so only data is stored. Word processing documents, however, contain a great deal of 'white space' along with the text. Therefore, they become large files quite easily. If the increasing demand for storage space is not anticipated by the computer management, problems can result.

Printers

Typically, computer centers utilize a centralized high-speed printer for producing computer-generated reports. While rough drafts could certainly be produced here, word processing applications generally require the use of some type of letter-quality printer for final drafts. Since these printers tend to be quite expensive, procedures can be developed to have documents centrally printed and delivered to offices. However, the scheduling and distribution time involved make this alternative undesirable for most firms. While two or more departments may share a printer, this gain will require a great deal of coordination. If numerous small documents are created, printers should be located relatively close to the people using them.

SOFTWARE CONSIDERATIONS

Because dedicated word processing systems have software and hardware specifically designed to work together, they generally offer some helpful features that may be unavailable on central computer-based software systems. The following features, common to most dedicated word processing systems, may be totally lacking or cumbersome to use on computer-based word processing or text editing systems:

1. Design of both the hardware and software can be described as 'user friendly'.
2. Conversational user prompts indicate types of commands required.
3. Systems offer direct access into the word processing software, as opposed to wading through layers of software overhead when logging onto the system.
4. Status information is displayed at all times.
5. Fast and easy methods are available for correcting mistakes.
6. Advanced editing capabilities are available which are easy to learn and easy to use.
7. Text is highlighted on the screen when referenced in editing commands.
8. Equipment is constructed with document-oriented rather than line- and file-oriented architecture.

9. Text appears on the screen in the same format that it will be printed on the final document.
10. Document reformatting occurs immediately after a formatting command is entered.
11. Word processing operators need not be concerned with 'backing up' their files to some type of permanent storage media.

User Friendly Systems

Perhaps the biggest criticism of central computer-based word processing software is that it lacks the humanization and operator orientation that dedicated word processing system vendors seem to realize is essential. 'User friendly' is the phrase used most often to describe systems that are designed with the user in mind. These systems try to be as 'human' as possible. The software tries to duplicate previous manual procedures as closely as possible so the operators using the systems will be forced to make only minimal adjustments in their established routines. For example, some word processors offer a full-page display of black letters on a white background designed to resemble the way in which text would look on paper.

In addition, manufacturers of the word processing systems hardware components attempt to design their keyboards with operator convenience in mind. They will typically utilize a normal typewriter keyboard and place functional keys where they are within easy reach of the typist. Functional keys are offered for a number of common text manipulation features, usually including move, copy, delete, merge, and underline, along with cursor movement keys to allow positioning of the cursor anywhere on the screen.

Word processing software requires a considerable amount of computer resources, and general-purpose computers have many types of software programs running on them at one time. Therefore, the word processing software designed for these systems is often designed to run as efficiently as possible. This may mean that the extra 'human' touches may be missing on the word processing system.

As stated earlier, word processing or multifunctional data and word processing terminals are now available for use with a computer-based system, but keyboard designs vary in efficiency. Multifunctional terminals may have function keys that can be programmed to handle commands such as move, copy, and underline. These keys may eliminate the need for typing strings of commands; however, the keys may not be conveniently located for word processing functions, and they must be manually labeled for the designated function. Furthermore, if the word processing software was not designed to utilize the special function keys available on these terminals, or if a terminal is used which was designed for data processing functions and lacks programmable keys, the formatting commands must be keyed into the text.

The differences in location and availability of function keys can mean a great deal in terms of time and complexity of text entry. For example, on the word processing system terminal the keyboarder need only touch the 'TAB' key to indent a line. On one computer-oriented system evaluated the operator must key in the command '. in 5' on a new line within the document, type the line to be indented, and then type '. in 0' on the next line to stop the indentation. Needless to say, the second system requires a great deal more effort, both in keystrokes to command the function and in remembering the correct command.

User Prompts

Dedicated word processing systems typically provide a great deal of guidance for the keyboarder. They may offer a menu approach, whereby the keyboarder chooses from a list of operations to be performed or may simply provide various prompts when actions must be taken. These prompts are generally provided in a conversational format, such as 'please enter the document name' when starting an editing session, or 'move what?' when issuing a command to move text. The prompts take the operator through functions on a step by step basis.

The computer-based text editing system, in contrast, may require the keyboarder to key in specific commands whenever an operation is to be performed. The only prompt given may be a '*' to let the operator know that the system is ready to accept a command. Sometimes no prompts at all are provided. The operator must be familiar enough with the commands to enter the required parameters, such as entering the document name when issuing a command to start an editing session. Areas of text that are to be moved must be delineated before the 'move' command is issued.

Menu approaches and conversational prompts can make a system much more 'friendly' to an operator, and much easier to learn. This may give employees a more favorable attitude towards the automated equipment, and will almost certainly reduce the training time needed to make employees productive on the system. However, once employees gain experience on the system, these prompts and menus may become tedious. Pausing to answer several layers of questions can prevent productivity increases that would otherwise result.

Employees familiar with a system can generally issue commands without the benefit of detailed software prompts. In these cases it is nice to have the option of removing or overriding the menus. For example, when printing two copies of a document on a specified printer, some systems will force the operator to answer a series of questions, such as 'which document?', 'how many copies?', and 'which printer?' If the override capabilities are available, an experienced operator could rather simply issue a print command, the document name, the number two, and the description of the desired printer in a single string of commands.

Menu and prompt-override features such as those described are available on selected computer-based software systems and dedicated word processing systems. If they are not available on a specific system the ease of use of that system must be weighed against the less efficient operation of the system in the hands of an experienced operator.

Direct Access to the Software

When sitting down to work at a dedicated word processing system the keyboarder usually must do little more than turn the system on and begin entering new text or access an existing document for editing purposes. On the computer-based text editor the keyboarder must first log into the overall system, enter a password, ask to log into the word processing system, then start an editing session by either creating a new document or accessing an existing document. Ending a session generally follows the same pattern. With some software systems the operator must enter various modes, such as creating new documents, adding to existing documents, or editing documents. With these systems, a mode must be properly exited before entering a new mode.

The procedures will vary depending on the type of system, but generally the text editing start-up, edit, and shut-down procedures are more lengthy and possibly more confusing than the dedicated word processing system. The reason for the lengthy procedures is simple. When working on a centralized computer system there are many more options available regarding the type of work that can be performed through the on-line terminal. The word processing software is only one of several systems that may be accessed.

Status Information

In addition to issuing prompts for special operations, most dedicated word processing systems continually give the keyboarder information about the operating mode and position of the cursor, both in the line of text and position within that line. Page number, margin and tab settings, remaining storage, and special editing conditions may also be communicated to the operator. This is usually done through the use of a status line which is displayed at all times.

Most text editing systems provide little of this kind of information. At best, the systems may provide the data in response to special requests keyed in by the operator. This data may have different meanings from those one would expect. For example, line numbers may be meaningless for estimating the length and placement of text on a typewritten page if the text is not completely formatted on the screen. (This will be discussed later.) Rather, the line numbers may be used to access specific lines for display, duplication, or modification purposes.

Corrections

Correcting misspellings or replacing words is easily handled on a dedicated word processing system. The keyboarder simply positions the cursor below the letter or word to be changed and types the correct text, causing it to overlay the existing letters.

On a line-oriented text editor, however, the entire line may have to be re-keyed or a command must be made to replace a given string of characters. When this is the case, the command must be handled with care, for if the character string is not unique, the correction may be made at an unexpected place elsewhere in the text. Although this situation generally occurs only when data is transmitted to the computer immediately upon keying, it usually results in additional commands being given to check that the text was changed correctly.

Advanced Editing Capabilities

Most word processing systems on the market today, whether dedicated systems or computer-based software, offer capabilities for performing advanced editing commands, such as copying, moving, or merging text. While these capabilities are usually available, there can be a wide variation in how easily the commands can be invoked.

The keyboarder can usually see exactly what is happening when specialized operations are performed on the dedicated word processor. A labeled function key may be depressed, then step-by-step processes are followed and the keyboarder is prompted for the necessary input parameters.

For example, when moving text within a document, the operator may depress the 'move' key. The system responds with the question 'move what?' The operator then highlights the text to be moved by using the available cursor keys and depresses a key to indicate when the correct text has been highlighted. At this point the system asks the question 'to where?', and the keyboarder finds the desired location in the document, again depressing a command key when the proper location is reached. Once this command key is depressed the text is moved to the new location. The operator has the option to cancel the command at any time up until the final command is given, so there is no penalty for striking incorrect keys or reconsidering a decision.

Editing capabilities, while available, may be much more cumbersome to use with word processing software. With some systems, the keyboarder must describe the parameters of the command before issuing it. For example, when moving text, the keyboarder must place pointers, called 'start codes' and 'stop codes', at the beginning and end of the text to be moved. Once the command is issued (usually by keying in a control character and an 'm'), the text is moved. If an incorrect key is depressed or the area of text was not defined properly, the operation must be reversed by resetting the 'start' and 'stop' codes and using another 'move' command to return the text to its original position.

Highlighted Text

As mentioned in the previous section, when performing editing functions on an advanced word processing system the text being defined to be moved, copied, deleted, etc. is highlighted on the video display screen. This highlighting enables the keyboarder to know exactly which portions of the document will be affected by the command.

Systems which do not provide highlighting capabilities rely on small coded marks to designate boundaries. These marks may be easy to miss, and stray or unrecognized marks may interfere with the editing function. On these systems the keyboarder must check the text afterwards by a separate operation to confirm that the command was issued correctly.

Document vs. Line Orientation

A dedicated word processing system is generally screen or document oriented. This means that one can see large portions of the page and move a cursor or portions of text around to modify text on that page.

The computer supporting a text editing system, on the other hand, may be line oriented. If so, each line on the screen is sent to the computer as it is completed (actually, each character is sent immediately after being keyed). When asking to see portions of text, one line at a time is returned by the computer system.

While this method is very effective in providing fast transmission time for entering text, it creates special problems when attempting to correct mistakes. If a keyboarder realizes an incorrect key has been struck, he or she cannot simply backspace and overstrike the mistake with the correct keystroke. Rather, a series of control characters must be entered to inform the computer that a correction is to be made to some characters that were previously transmitted, or the entire line can be deleted and re-entered.

These restrictions can make a keyboarder extremely cautious when entering text, thereby reducing speed and productivity levels. In addition, this may create the necessity for separating sentences to allow for possible future additions or deletions of text. On this type of system only one line at a time may be changed.

Screen Formatting

Dedicated word processing systems generally format text directly on the screen so the keyboarder can see exactly how the document will look when printed.

A text editing system, in contrast, may rely on embedded codes to cause formatting to take place at the time a document is printed. The system may have two parts: the text editor and the formatter. Text is entered and changed using the editor. However, this text is completely unformatted. Formatting commands must be keyed into the text during the edit phase, and when the document is ready for printing it is run through the formatting program which arranges the text as commanded.

At this point, some systems will allow the operator to view the document through the video display tube before the actual printing takes place. Since most computer terminals can display only one character per position, however, some functions, such as underlining, still do not appear. Therefore, the keyboarder does not know exactly how the document will look until it is printed. At this point the operator may have to re-enter the editing mode and later, append, or delete some formatting commands to achieve the desired format. Then the entire formatting cycle must be repeated.

Figure 4-1 shows how a selected document might appear on a word processing system. Figure 4-2 shows how that same document might appear on the terminal screen prior to formatting it on a text editing system. While many text editors offer much better formatting than shown in Figure 4-2, it is a sample of documents actually prepared on one computer-based text editor, and it shows the range of differences that may be found between the types of software available.

Bev Miller

Nixon, J. R. "Zen and the art of implementing office automation", <u>Words,</u> Dec–Jan, 1981.

This article describes an imaginary company implementing an integrated word processing/data processing system. The article includes descriptions of the problems that were experienced as the company planned and implemented the system.

The first problem brought up dealing with people concerned the involvement of the data processing staff. Management could not understand the terminology being used by the staff, and they were afraid that the data processing department was jealous of the new system and wanted to take it over. These points demonstrate the problems of integrating areas that do not, as yet, understand the purpose and procedures of each other.

Figure 4-1. Sample document on word processing system.

```
.nj
.hy 1
.sp
.in 50
Bev Miller
.ll 60
.in 5
.sp 3
Nixon, J. R. "Zen and the art of implementing office
automation",
.ul 1
Words,
Dec–Jan, 1981.
.sp 2
This article describes an imaginary company implementing
an integrated word processing/data processing system.
The article includes descriptions of the problems that
were experienced as the company planned and implemented
the system.
.sp 1
The first problem brought up dealing with people
concerned the involvement of the data processing staff.
Management could not understand the terminology being
used by the staff, and they were afraid that the
data processing department was jealous of the new system
and wanted to take it over.
These points demonstrate the problems of integrating
areas that do not, as yet, understand the purpose
and procedures of each other.
```

Figure 4-2. Sample document on terminal screen prior to formatting.

As can be seen, the keyboarder operating a text editing system such as the one shown must have the capability of visualizing the final format of the documents prepared on the system. This requires a great deal of concentration and practice, and typically results in lower levels of productivity.

Re-Formatting Text

Word processing systems which format text immediately (as opposed to relying on embedded commands) differ in their characteristics. For example, some systems will change line endings and perform word wrap-arounds directly following the insertion or deletion of a word. Other systems will re-format the text only after the individual enters a command or depresses a format key, indicating that the editing is completed for that paragraph.

Proponents of the second type of system will claim that the constant re-formatting is a needless waste of processing power and can be distracting to the keyboarder, since even the slightest change can cause a delay while the formatting takes place. Further, it is said that having the text re-formatted can create problems when making changes from a printed rough draft, since the errors may not be in the same place once corrections have been made earlier and the text has been re-formatted (e.g., the words previously occurring at the end of a line may now be moved to the middle of the next line and are difficult to find).

Finally, proponents will argue that systems which format only upon the request of the keyboarder give the keyboarder control over how much of the text is re-formatted. An example of this advantage can be observed when the margins of a document are changed. Most systems rely on some sort of format line which sets the margins and tab stops. The systems usually permit changes to these format lines when the operator desires to alter the format of the text. Systems which require separate formatting commands often give the option of formatting one paragraph at a time. Therefore, if one wanted to leave a certain portion of text unchanged, the keyboarder could simply not issue the command to format those paragraphs.

In contrast, systems offering immediate re-formatting allow the keyboarder to immediately see the effects of any corrections, additions, or deletions made to the text. This immediate feedback simplifies decisions relating to hyphenation and general document formatting. These systems require fewer keystrokes, since a separate formatting command need not be entered. In dealing with varying margins for separate areas of text, the systems generally allow the operator to define new format lines wherever needed. Text following these format lines will be re-formatted, until a new format line is encountered.

File Back-ups

Another difference that can be found between various types of word processing systems (both computer-based software and dedicated systems) relates to methods of handling files. Many word processors handle files entirely without human involvement. In other words, the keyboarder is not concerned whether the file is being stored within the main memory or on attached storage devices, such as diskettes. Other systems make a distinction between text stored on the system (usually treated as temporary work files) and text stored permanently on off-line storage.

On systems maintaining a distinction, the keyboarder must periodically 'save' the page or document being edited, so that it will ultimately become a permanent file. This arrangement offers both advantages and disadvantages. By working with a temporary file, the keyboarder can experiment with changes to a document while maintaining the integrity of the original. If the decision is made to leave the original document unchanged, the edited document is destroyed merely by not 'saving' it and the original is left intact. No text is saved until the keyboarder requests that it be saved. The drawback to this is that until the new document is saved, the updates can be lost. If this happens, as it could in the case of a power failure or an operator forgetting to back up the file, any changes to that document would have to be re-done.

OTHER CONSIDERATIONS

Comparison of individual hardware and software features is a necessary, though not sufficient, basis for evaluating word processing systems. In addition to looking at isolated features, it is important to look at the effects which the combination of these features will have on the organization as a whole.

The following areas should be investigated when considering the implementation of a particular word processing or office automation system:

1. Training resources that will be required with the new system, and the increase in personnel productivity that can be anticipated.
2. Security and integrity of the information stored, regardless of whether it is stored in a central location or within distributed offices.
3. Detrimental effects that may result from overloading the existing computer system.
4. Ease of future expansion in office automation, possibly in the areas of electronic mail, personal productivity aids, and integration of data processing and word processing.

Training and Personnel Productivity

Word processing software on a centralized computer can make word processing capabilities available to anyone with a suitably logged-in computer terminal. However, as shown by the description of features found on some word processing and text editing software, little can be done on these systems without extensive training on the part of the personnel utilizing the software. Since the software is quite complicated and involves a network of interacting offices, the training must be quite extensive (see Chapter 8 for additional thoughts, ideas and strategies for training).

Training in utilizing the word processing software would involve two distinct areas: technical use of the software itself and procedures to be followed when dealing with the computer system.

Because the word processing software is quite complex, it is unrealistic to assume that an inexperienced operator could 'pick it up' merely by reading a manual. Some type of training program is needed, whether developed and conducted by in-house personnel or by the software supplier. Although this type of training would be needed no matter what type of word processing system was utilized, more complicated systems require a great deal more training time than simplified menu-driven word processing systems.

The second type of training required for computer-based word processing software deals with procedures. Individuals must be taught how to interact with the computer system itself, including how to 'log on' to the system, how to request that files be loaded or backed up, and even how to access the word processing software. As seen in the discussion of user interaction with the computer system, these procedures may be complicated, and new users will require time to adjust to the system.

The training required for complex systems can become very costly, particularly if an office experiences high staff turnover. Additionally, even after a person is trained on the software, a long period of time is required before that individual reaches a productive speed in using it. The learning curve involved will be much longer if the software is difficult to use.

There are noticeable advantages, however, once individuals are trained and experienced in the use of the centralized system. Employees who transfer to another office utilizing the centralized system need little or no training on the equipment, other than learning the procedures of that particular office. This provides increased back-up capabilities, since word processing operators need little or no training to substitute for individuals absent from other areas.

Peaks and valleys in workloads could be smoothed by transferring underworked personnel into offices experiencing the peak workloads. Or, if the physical movement of personnel is inconvenient, the excess workloads themselves may be shifted to other offices. Since all documents are stored in the central computer, they may be accessed at any CRT as long as the operator enters the correct passwords. The workstations used to enter or edit the text may vary.

Increased productivity may be realized when an individual is performing both data and word processing functions on a single piece of equipment. An individual must take time to adjust to a different keyboard, function keys, etc. when changing from one type of equipment to another. If a single terminal can be used for all functions, this adjustment time may not be necessary. However, if the terminal has programmable function keys which serve different functions depending on the task, some adjustment time would still be needed.

Security and Integrity of Information

Whenever documents are stored in a central location, security and integrity become important issues. Offices accessing their word processing files via the computer terminal must be certain their files will be kept private and safe from accidental loss or destruction.

Most computer systems have developed security systems to monitor the use of the computerized information. Typically a system of confidential user identification and passwords is utilized. These same systems will usually be appropriate for word processing files. Many systems have various levels of security, and may allow the individual creating a document to designate it as available only to the author, available to selected other users for viewing but not modification, or possibly available for unlimited public viewing and modification.

Computer personnel are also quite familiar with requirements and procedures for creating back-ups (copies) of files and storing them safely. They probably also have recovery plans for emergency situations which might otherwise result in the loss of some important documents.

Individuals using the computer system for word processing applications are often insecure when their documents are stored outside their own office. They may feel they are losing control of their information. Usually a thorough review of the security and back-up procedures being used to protect the office's files will aid in reducing this insecurity. In fact, in the majority of cases, the information will be safer stored on the centralized computer system than if merely stored on a small diskette in a desk drawer.

Effects on Computer Resources

Word processing software systems are designed to be highly interactive. Thus, they tend to require a considerable amount of computer resources in the form of central processing time and data communications line activity. In addition, the size of the word processing software and the volume of word processing files stored on-line require large amounts of memory.

As stated earlier, most computer systems have a certain amount of excess capacity to allow for expansion. However, as the use of the word processing system grows and the demand for the limited computer resources becomes heavier, users may experience increasingly longer response times due to an overloaded computer. Most computer systems can be expanded by adding main memory, disk storage capacity, or additional peripheral devices. These features, however, add to the total cost of the system. The cost of the features must be taken into account when calculating the total added cost of the word processing facilities.

The type of terminals utilized by the computer system can have a terrific impact on the amount of central processing time required at the mainframe. If the word processing system utilizes a series of 'dumb' terminals hooked to the mainframe, all of the processing must be done in the main central processing unit.

The system could experience wide fluctuations in response time depending on the amount of activity on the system. However, if 'intelligent' terminals (having some limited amount of processing power and memory of their own) are used, the word processing software may be 'down loaded' to the local terminal to perform word processing applications. This will alleviate the strain on the central processing unit and will not affect response time as heavily.

Advanced Office Automation Functions

Having a word processing system supported by a mainframe computer may offer particular advantages when an office is investigating the feasibility of developing some other office automation systems. Electronic mail, for example, can be facilitated easily on a centralized computer system. The word processing software will provide a method of creating and accessing the documents or messages and the computer storage will provide ample file areas for holding messages. Software is currently available on most large computer systems for distributing the messages to selected or multiple recipients.

Integration of word processing and data processing applications may also be facilitated by a centralized word processing software system. Since the word and data processing files are both stored on the same computer system, communications problems need not be resolved before utilizing the information in either application. While the two types of files may be formatted differently (codes in one may be unrecognized by another), the files can usually be easily converted to a usable format. Many systems make no differentiation between 'DP' and 'WP' files.

If the computer system has some type of ad hoc query and reporting software, an individual could use that data processing software through the video display terminal to select a population and build a file of information based on various input parameters. That file may then be manipulated by the word processing software for correspondence. Merging form letters with computer generated lists would be an example of this type of usage.

Larger computer systems offer the storage and processing power needed to provide some of the 'work savers' popular now, such as creating an automatic table of contents, indexes, numbered pages or sections, stored functions, and sorting facilities. Many of these functions are being offered on some dedicated shared logic and even stand-alone word processing systems; however, the memory size of these units often imposes limits on the size and complexity of these features.

EVALUATING THE EXISTING COMPUTER SYSTEM

After the specific automation requirements of the office have been identified, the following steps should be taken in evaluating the feasibility of utilizing the existing computer system as a base for implementing a word processing system.

First, check the present condition of the mainframe computer's central processing unit and disk storage. If a great deal of idle capacity exists in the form of main memory, processing power, and secondary storage, there may be sufficient resources for adding word processing software. At this time long-range data processing and word processing plans must be examined to calculate the amount of growth to expect on the various systems. The cost and difficulty of expanding the present computer system must be calculated.

If implementing word processing software on the computer system will degrade performance on all existing systems and require an investment in additional computer resources, it may be advisable to opt for an independent word processing system at the onset. If the need for expansion of the computer system is small, however, utilizing the existing facilities may be the cost-effective alternative.

The second step would be to examine the communications network currently in place. Would implementation of the word processing software involve the installation of thousands of feet of cables to connect additional terminals, or will the existing cable or dial-up systems suffice? Again, how much expansion would be required on the mainframe to handle more communication lines and more terminal activity on those lines?

This is the area that can pose the most difficult problems when implementing word processing software. The heavy editing performed on documents and the amount of text being transmitted to and from a remote terminal to support this editing requires considerably more resources than the inquiry or updating performed on data processing applications. If communications lines are shared, a great deal of line contention can occur when multiple terminals are sending and receiving data. Even if the lines are directly connected, there is some point at which the information must be received by the computer system's central processing unit, and bottlenecks can occur. Communications controllers can be purchased to solve this problem, but they are expensive. Again, the cost of any additional computer facilities must be included when calculating the overall cost of the word processing system.

Finally, investigate the types of terminals currently in use with the computer system, and the availability and cost of specialized word processing or multifunctional word and data processing terminals.

Determine whether the existing terminals are placed in locations convenient for word processing applications and whether they have idle time that could be utilized. Check to see if the keyboards and function keys are suitable for use in editing documents.

Additional terminals will probably be required when implementing a word processing system. If the functions of those terminals will be primarily word processing applications, an attempt should be made to acquire terminals designed specifically for that function. A wide variety of these terminals is available, with significant differences in price and quality. Be certain these terminals are compatible with the existing computer system and that an acceptable agreement for maintenance and repair of the terminals is available.

At the same time, investigate the cost and availability of letter quality printers to be utilized on the system. Typically most computer systems will not already have these, so they will become perhaps the first large equipment expense in implementing the word processing system.

EVALUATING THE SOFTWARE

Look closely at the word processing software being considered for the computer system. Keep in mind the productivity costs that will result from systems which are difficult to use or lack features essential for particular applications. After viewing a thorough demonstration of the software capabilities, have several individuals who will be working with the proposed system perform some common applications. The following steps may be used to evaluate features discussed earlier which may be found on the various types of word processing software systems:

1. Type the following two paragraphs, then correct any typographical errors.

   The First National Bank is planning to implement a word processing system. At the moment they are contemplating installing a system with communications capability to receive data from their main computer. They would like the capability to store their word processing documents on the computer hard disk.

   Currently several types of systems exist which will allow communications between word processing and data processing systems. A dedicated word processing system may have communications capability and therefore can be connected to a computer system via telephone lines or direct cable. Additionally, a computer system may have word processing software, so the single system can handle both data and text manipulation. The First National Bank must evaluate the tradeoffs present in these systems.

   Check the prompts given to the keyboarder when creating the document and the levels of menus or questions that must be completed before actually starting to key the text. Evaluate the ease of the system, including the availability of function keys, the presence of status information, and facilities of word wrap-around and automatic hyphenation. Check the ease of moving the cursor and correcting errors in the text.
2. Change the name of the bank to the 'People's Bank'.

   Check for ease of changing text and immediate screen formatting capabilities. A 'search and replace' command should be available to change multiple occurrences of the bank name. What effect does the underlining have on this change?

3. Insert the centered heading 'SELECTING A WORD PROCESSING SYSTEM' before the first paragraph.

Notice how difficult it is to insert text into the document and whether an automatic centering command is available. Does the heading appear centered when viewing it through the video display tube, or is there simply a code present which will cause it to be centered once the document is printed?

4. Move the second paragraph to appear in front of the first paragraph.

Check for the presence of special function keys, and the necessity of defining the parameters before the 'move' command is issued. Are the available operator prompts clear and helpful? How many keystrokes are required to perform the task and how long does the keyboarder wait while the 'move' is being performed? Is the text adjusted immediately, or is a separate command required?

5. Widen the margins of the first paragraph, and change to double spacing, leaving the format of the second paragraph unchanged.

Notice the complexity of the formatting commands and the flexibility of the system. Is the text reformatted immediately, or is a separate command required? Must each paragraph be reformatted with a separate command? Is there an option to reformat the entire document with a single command? Check the appearance of the text on the screen. In an effort to display more text, many word processing systems will not show variations in spacing on the screen, though some will offer a choice of showing the double spacing or simply indicate the spacing via the status line. Whichever method is used, is the difference in spacing between the two paragraphs clear?

6. Print two copies of the document.

What kind of information must be entered when requesting that a document be printed? Are defaults available, and can they be easily changed and stored for each document? Can a document be created or edited while another is being reprinted?

7. Make the name of the bank a variable, and use the merge function to print copies of the document with the following names: People's Bank, First National Bank, and First Women's Bank.

Check for clear system prompts, ease of creating the merged file, and number of keystrokes required. Check whether it is possible to merge partial files (such as using only the first and last names).

SUMMARY

Recent advances in the development of word processing software for mainframe computer systems have made the option of using existing computer capabilities as a base for implementing word processing very attractive to some offices. Evaluating the feasibility of this alternative involves identifying the word processing requirements of the organization and determining the suitability of the present computer facilities to be expanded for word processing use.

When examining the current computer facilities, special consideration should be given to potential uses of terminals and the existing terminal networks, the central processing and central storage resources available, and the cost and availability of letter-quality printers for word processing use. When evaluating word processing software, features may be lacking or cumbersome to use on central computer-based word processing systems as compared with dedicated word processing systems. The relative importance of these features must be weighed against the potential cost savings that may result from investing in a system that does not offer them.

Finally, it is important to look at the effects which the combination of software and hardware characteristics will have on the organization as a whole. Training requirements, personnel productivity, security and integrity of information, detrimental effects to the existing computer system, and future expansion potential must all be evaluated.

REFERENCES AND SUGGESTED READINGS

1. Bentley, Don D., and Duffy, Jans: Word Processing Interfaces with other Technologies. *ARMA Records Management Qtrly*, **16**, No. 4, 32–38, October 1982.
2. Wohl, Amy D.: Beyond Word Processing. *Computerworld*, **17**, No. 8A, 25–27, 30, February 23, 1983.
3. Coffey, Margaret, and Dunphy, Dexter: Towards the Paperless Office. *Work and People (Australia)*, **8**, No. 2, 3–9, 1982.
4. Wohl, Amy D.: A Whole New Set of Rules for Word Processing. *Office*, **95**, No. 1, 97, 182, January 1982.
5. Martin, Josh.: Successful Office Automation Part II. *Computer Decisions*, **13**, No. 7, 108–124, 161–162, July 1981.
6. Blackmarr, Brian R.: Cost Justifying WP. *Modern Office & Data Mgmt (Australia)*, **20**, No. 10, 64, 66, November 1981.
7. Smith, Charles L.: Word Processing and Scientific Writing in a University Research Group. *Technical Communications*, **29**, No. 3, 13–17, 1982.

Section II: Environments

Advances in Office Automation, Vol 1
Edited by Karen Takle Quinn
© 1985 Wiley Heyden Ltd.

Chapter 5

DESIGNING A WORD PROCESSING SYSTEM FOR THE SMALL OFFICE

Elizabeth McGee

McGee and Associates

INTRODUCTION

In the early 1960s when IBM was hot on the technological warpath, introducing the first word processor and attempting to convince the world of the illustrious benefits of office automation, small companies quite predictably were overlooked in all the commotion. The costs of such technologically advanced equipment prohibited even the most adventurous of souls from entertaining any thoughts of obtaining a high and mighty word processor. However, since the advent of the first word processor, improved technology has resulted in not only a decrease in price but an increase in the capacity and variation of automated typewriting equipment.

What is word processing? Word processing is a system that is supported by equipment, people, and procedures which facilitate the production and distribution of written communications by the most effective and efficient means possible. The most important concept underlying word processing is that it is a system. It is not just a matter of replacing standard typewriters with more sophisticated word processors. Such a change would fail to utilize the potential of the word processor. Word processors can be as simple as an electronic typewriter or as complex as a computer text editor. An effective word processing system utilizes a machine that is capable of handling the type and amount of written communications generated by an office, and yet not be overly equipped with features that have no application and thus are not cost-effective.

While office automation equipment may seem at first to be best suited for the large firm, its possibilities are not exclusive of small firms. Given the proper equipment, personnel, and procedures, word processing can work as effectively in a small environment as it can in a large one. Whether implemented in a small office or multilevel corporation, the advantages of word processing are fundamentally the same: increasing production while decreasing costs.

Consider for a moment the cost of the average letter. Taking into account the author's time, the typist's time, nonproductive labor (such as waiting), overhead costs, the cost of materials, filing, and mailing, the average letter costs $5.59.[1] By examining several of these factors more closely, we can determine how word processing can reduce the cost of the business letter. The means by which a letter is originated directly influences its cost. Is the principal (the correspondence originator) depending on the secretary to transcribe the letter via shorthand? If so, valuable time is lost because this process involves the time of two people. Furthermore, studies have shown that it is faster to dictate and transcribe a letter than it is to type from a longhand copy. How is the office staff organized? Does the firm employ two secretaries to handle both the administrative tasks and the correspondence tasks? If so, such a work distribution may be taxing productivity because of the lack of specialization in each area.

While automated typing equipment may do little to alter the time involved in typing a short, single-page letter, if revisions are required then the turnaround time of the second draft can be reduced by 50 percent or more.[2] Furthermore, since labor accounts for approximately 90 percent of the cost of the letter, the time saved by each additional draft increases because word processing eliminates unnecessary typing.[1]

The amount of paperwork generated by a single office has escalated over the past twenty years. Since 1960, correspondence and other business related documents have increased by 90 percent.[1] The number of people involved in originating and producing each written document has also increased by approximately 90 percent.[1] That much of this paper work is routine or repetitive in nature makes necessary a more effective and efficient means of processing this material. A word processing system can fulfill such a need. In addition to cutting production costs, a word processor is capable of producing error-free copies of superior quality and of revising and editing text without retyping. Because word processors have the capacity to print at very high speeds, the time spent typing and outputting a document is further reduced. Furthermore, the ability of the word processor to store documents indefinitely makes it possible for the originator or typist to edit and revise at his or her convenience.

The primary focus of this report is on office automation for the small firm. What follows is a discussion on how to design a word processing system by determining what the needs are of a particular office and what word processor would suit those needs, and by familiarizing office personnel with how a word processing system operates.

Before we launch into a discussion on office automation, the prosective user should keep in mind that the word processing system must be able to accommodate not only regular personnel but temporary personnel as well. While word processing has done much to liberate the office from the burdensome dictating and typing activities, it can be extremely taxing if precautions are not taken to plan a back-up system. Unlike the large corporation where the work of an absent operator can be distributed to several operators, if the operator is absent in the small office, then the system shuts down. Provision should be made to enable the office to maintain operations if the operator is absent. Factors which help or hinder the word processing system in an office staffed by temporary personnel are discussed throughout the chapter.

THE FEASIBILITY STUDY

While word processing may look very impressive, it is not always feasible. Or rather, if care has not been taken to design a word processing system, the effects can be, at best, limited, and, at worst, an investment lost. However, the risks involved in such a plan can be greatly reduced and even eliminated through the aid of a feasibility study. By assessing the needs of a given office, and evaluating the current office procedures and functions, the feasibility study can provide information about the kind of equipment best suited to handle the workload and the secretarial support needed to operate the system. Furthermore, the feasibility study can determine whether or not a word processing system will facilitate maximum productivity, and, through an increase in accuracy and efficiency, be cost-effective.

While statistics and detailed analyses play a major role in the planning and implementation of a word processing system, the 'human' factor must also be taken into consideration. For example, the feasibility study will most likely indicate a need for change in office procedures and personnel organization. In some instances, a word processing system will require a complete overhaul of the old procedures and the organizational structure in order for the office to derive full benefit from the system. In a very small office of one secretary and one principal, the changes may or may not be so apparent. Yet in a slightly larger office, for example, one that employs two secretaries and three or four principals, the change in secretarial functions can have distinct effects. While the feasibility study may point to such changes, it will at the same time aid the office in making as smooth a transition as possible.

The feasibility study may be conducted by someone in the office, by a vendor, or by a consultant. The advantage of having an office member conduct the study is that he or she is likely to have in-depth knowledge of the existing system and its policies. Through conducting the survey, the researcher will gain valuable knowledge which would be useful if the office ever needs to upgrade its equipment. The disadvantage is that the person assigned to conduct the study often lacks the necessary expertise and knowledge about the various word processors to implement the system. Furthermore, the feasibility study is a full-time task; therefore, the member is unable to attend to his or her routine duties. The advantage of using a vendor's services is that such services are usually done free of charge for all prospective purchasers. However, the vendor is still a salesperson and his or her primary goal is to sell the manufacturer's equipment. It is not unusual for a vendor to neglect to point out the equipment's weaknesses or to compare the prices of his equipment with those of other manufacturers. A consultant, in contrast, is apt to be more objective than the vendor. A consultant is highly knowledgeable and can effectively research, design, and implement a word processing system. Unfortunately, consultant fees can be astronomical, therefore sometimes making a consultant's services unfeasible for the small office. One final alternative is to hire a consultant to guide a member of the office in doing a study. Many consulting firms offer this service at a reduced rate.

Conducting the Feasibility Study

The feasibility study involves three main phases: organizing survey materials, collecting the data, and analyzing the data. The time involved in carrying out the activities of each phase depends on the number of people to be surveyed, the degree of participation required for each test, and the expertise and experience of the researcher. In the case of the small office, it normally takes approximately a week and a half to organize materials and inform the personnel. The second phase, collecting the data, takes approximately two weeks. Phase 3, data analysis, may take between two and three weeks depending on the experience of the researcher and the extensiveness of surveys taken. It is unlikely that the small office would require the preparation and presentation of a report to quite the extent that the large firm would. However, if a report is needed, then this fourth phase would take approximately three to four weeks.

Preparation activities include informing each staff member of the activities which are to take place during the study and obtaining full cooperation in providing accurate data for the survey. With the small office, this orientation is best accomplished by a small, informal meeting.

Following this orientation, survey forms are prepared. The following forms are suggested for use in providing detailed records of secretarial activities: correspondence activity survey, administrative activity survey, and the time ladder. (See Appendix A for examples of forms.) While each survey queries a different area, any one may be used to gather data which will reflect the needs of a given office. However, using the tests in conjunction with each other will result in a more complete survey of the office's present situation and needs.

Form A, Appendix A, is an example of a form used to take a 'paper survey'. In addition to filling out the form for each document typed, the typist uses 'action paper' (a carbonless tissue or carbon set) for each page of every document. The action paper is then attached to the form which has been filled out with all the details about the document. A specific number of action sheets is usually given to the secretary and the remaining, unused sheets are collected at the end of the study to insure that the data will be an accurate measurement of the typist's activities.

A daily collection of work samples is carried out for approximately two weeks. At the end of this time, the forms and their accompanying action sheets are collected and the text on the action sheets is counted either by page, $\frac{1}{2}$ page, $\frac{1}{4}$ page, or by line (using a line counter). It is also suggested that the degree of difficulty involved be taken into consideration and that the counting procedure be adjusted accordingly.

Form B, Appendix A, asks the secretary to evaluate how much time is spent on various administrative activities. This information indicates how many secretaries are needed to provide administrative support. Because this survey is subject to a certain amount of guesswork, it should be supplemented by other studies, such as a time ladder (Form C, Appendix A). The time ladder form is filled out according to how long each task takes. The information is charted in 5 minute, 15 minute, or $\frac{1}{2}$ hour blocks.

Questionnaires are useful for obtaining information from both the secretary and the principal regarding the administrative and correspondence needs. The secretary and the principal are asked to evaluate the current system and to give recommendations for improving it. An example of a Secretary Questionnaire and a Principal Questionnaire are given in Appendix A.

The data are interpreted on the basis of productive and nonproductive labor, the kinds of documents produced, the means by which the documents were originated, and the rate of typing errors and false starts.

The pie chart in Figure 5-1, which represents productive time and nonproductive time, reveals how much time a secretary spends on typing tasks, administrative duties, waiting for work, etc. This chart essentially indicates what the company is paying the secretary for. If the percentage of waiting time is high, then the office activities are not coordinated effectively enough to insure a steady workflow. A word processing system, with its breakdown of duties into two divisions (correspondence and administrative) would allow the principals to provide the correspondence secretary with a steady flow of work and to delegate some of their more routine business to the administrative secretary. More information on the reorganization of personnel activities is given further on in the chapter.

The chart in Figure 5-2 illustrates what types of document an office produces. This information is important not only for buying a machine that will cover the

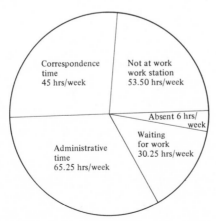

Figure 5-1.   Productive   and   nonproductive time.

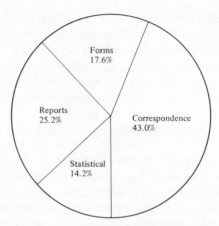

Figure 5-2.   Document classification.

minimum requirements, but also to help avoid buying a machine that has numerous and expensive options which may be unnecessary for a firm's particular typing needs.

Figure 5-3 illustrates the various modes of document origination. This chart indicates whether or not enough of the work is transcribed through longhand or shorthand to warrant machine dictation equipment. If the majority of the documents are those that have been previously typed and require heavy revisions, then dictation equipment would be more of a luxury than a necessity since its primary purpose is for correspondence work. In such a case, emphasis would be placed on word processing equipment rather than on dictation equipment.

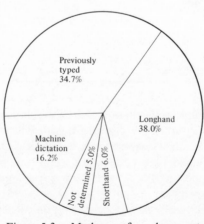

Figure 5-3.   Mode   of   document
                   origination.

The paper study is a good indication of errors and false starts. Because mistakes are costly not only in time but in materials as well, word processing equipment can provide a solution for an unnecessarily high rate of errors. Errors are counted per page and compared against the number of words typed. If the ratio of errors to the number of words typed is unacceptable by company standards, then a text editor would be a feasible alternative to the present system.

SELECTING A WORD PROCESSOR

While computers seldom make mistakes, they can be, nonetheless, imperfect according to human standards. The properly chosen word processor can handle major needs, but smaller details must often be compensated for. This fact is felt perhaps more acutely by the small offices that are without the funds to equip themselves with a word processor whose functions may come as close as reasonably possible to the ultimate system. Nor is the small office able to implement three or four different word processors in order to produce the desired effect. The feasibility study enables the prospective buyer to single out the office's major needs in order to find a word processor that will fit the match as closely as possible. The prospective buyer must then familiarize himself or herself with the various types of word processors to ascertain which one will best meet the office's needs. Equipment selection involves first evaluating the different systems of word processors within the word processing system itself, and then evaluating media, printing devices, and logic. The final aspect of equipment selection involves investigating machine dictation equipment.

Word Processors

The system within a word processor may be either a shared system or a stand-alone system. While both may look alike, the difference lies in the computing power from which each operates. With the exception of CPUs (Central Processing Units), and in some instances disk drives, the components of a shared system are identical to those found in a stand-alone system. Though both systems are used in the small office, the stand-alone is the more common system.

Shared logic refers to a word processing system which shares a common data base. The components of this system include CRT screens, printers, disk drives, and a CPU. The terminals which are used in shared logic systems are called 'dumb' terminals because they are dependent on the central computer. Hence, if the computer malfunctions, these terminals are rendered inoperable. In spite of this drawback, the shared-logic system can work quite effectively in an office which requires the support of two or more word processing operators.

A second shared system is known as 'distributed logic'. Rather than concentrating all the intelligence into one computer, the intelligence is distributed to the terminals, printers, and the storage center. The terminals used in the distributed logic system are called 'smart' terminals because each has its own computing power and relies on central support only for disk storage and output. If malfunctions occur, a system controlled by distributed logic may still be operable (depending on the nature of the malfunction).

Stand-alone systems, on the other hand, are fully self-contained units that do not require the processing power of a central computer. This system is ideal in the small office. It follows that if a firm requires only one operator, then implementing a shared system would not be practical, unless the office chose to tie into an outside computer. However, this is generally not practiced by small offices.

A stand-alone system may utilize either an electronic typewriter or a more complex word processor which is referred to as a stand-alone text-editor (or a stand-alone word processor). In addition, the stand-alone system may use peripherals, added pieces of equipment which upgrade the capacity of a particular word processor. Examples of peripherals are faster printers, OCR readers (Optical Character Recognition), and communications devices which enable text to be distributed from one location to another.

The electronic typewriter is considered to be the least automated of word processing equipment. It is, in essence, a more sophisticated electric typewriter. While still considered to be a stand-alone, the electronic typewriter's input and editing capabilities are limited. Its memory or storage capacity ranges from 7500 to 15 000 characters, or approximately six pages of text. The relatively inexpensive cost of these word processors makes them ideal for offices which generate simple documents that require a minimal amount of revising.

Stand-alone text editors may be further defined as either mechanical or display. A mechanical stand-alone looks similar to a standard typewriter. While the typist keyboards directly onto paper, the machine records every stroke into memory. This type of machine is also referred to as a 'blind memory'. The visual display text editor utilizes a CRT screen which is attached to a keyboard unit; the printer is a separate unit. The CRT screen simplifies the inputting process because it allows the typist to see exactly what the machine is recording. Because the keyboard and printer are separate, they are usually able to operate independently. With a system using an independent printer, it is not necessary to wait for the output of one document before going onto the next assignment; consequently, time is saved because the typist's action is continuous. An additional advantage of a visual display is found in the inputting and editing processes. While inputting with the visual display, the typist may proofread and make immediate corrections without printing out the document first. Revising on the visual screen text editor involves fewer steps and because the typist is able to see what he or she is working with, the 'goof factor' is reduced considerably. Since seeing is believing, the visual screen text editor is also easier to learn. The typist is not required to think like a computer in order to visualize the inputting and editing processes. These advantages and many more are the reasons why the CRT has become the most popular type of stand-alone text editors. Unfortunatly, CRT screens increase the price of the equipment. Yet while this initial fee may be steep, the time saved and added productivity compensate for the initial expenditure.

Media

The media most commonly used in word processors that are used in small offices include magnetic cards, magnetic tape cassettes, floppy disks, and an electronic memory. The main criteria for selecting media are how suitable it is for accommodating the most commonly typed documents, the length of the average document, and the degree of complexity involved in revising documents, as well as the length of retention.

The magnetic card holds up to one page of text. This results in a unique card to page relationship which makes it easier to identify specific pages of a stored document. Each card can be stored with its respective document if such a filing system is desired. In addition, word processors which utilize magnetic cards are usually easier to learn to operate. The disadvantage of cards is primarily centered around the revision process. The revision of a multiple-page document usually results in repaginating. With the individual cards, this can become a tedious and time-consuming ordeal. Furthermore, the possibility of deleting text increases with each 'manual' transition of parts of text from one page to another. A second disadvantage of magnetic cards is that this medium is becoming outdated. Hence, if a word processor is selected that uses magnetic cards, the possibilities for upgrading it are reduced considerably.

Magnetic cards work well for single-page items such as small documents and letters. This medium is less suitable for multiple-page documents and form letters requiring individual names and addresses.

Magnetic tape cassettes are capable of handling 15 or more pages of text per cassette. The advantage of this medium is that the cassettes are relatively inexpensive. Furthermore, because cassettes can store several pages, less handling is required, and filing and logging is simpler and less time consuming. The disadvantage of cassettes is the lack of universality. This medium is not as common as the floppy disk or the magnetic card, and therefore limits the prospective buyer in his or her choice of word processors.

Magnetic cassettes can handle single-page documents, letters, form letters, and larger documents which require a minimum of editing.

Floppy disks are the most versatile medium for use in small office automation. These disks can either be document oriented or page oriented. Document-oriented disks assign a space on the medium for the entire document and recognize it as a unit, while the page-oriented disks assign a space on the medium for each page and recognize each page as a unit. The advantage of a document-oriented disk becomes obvious with the task of making heavy revisions on a lengthy document. The document-oriented disk can repaginate a document automatically while the page-oriented disk requires manual repagination. Page-oriented disks are good for single-page documents and multiple-page documents requiring light revisions.

An electronic memory is characteristic of the less sophisticated word processors. While all word processors have a 'memory' of one type or another, some machines utilize an internal storage bin which is also called a memory. The memory is not considered a medium because it cannot be removed from the machine. The advantage of this kind of word processor is that since it is very basic, it is also very easy to learn. Furthermore, these word processors are less expensive than those which utilize card, cassette, or diskette media. One of the disadvantages of this system is that a document can only be stored temporarily. Hence, revising is restricted because the material can only be stored for a day or two in order to have space in the memory to handle new assignments.

The word processor with an electronic memory is suitable for short, single-page documents, and form letters with variable names and addresses. It also lends itself well to longer documents that require no retention. However, because the memory has a bin that stores a document page by page, the same revising problems encountered with the magnetic cards are also present with the electronic memory.

Printers

The printing unit in a word processor may be either an input/output terminal, in which keyboarding and printing is combined into one unit, or an output terminal, in which printing is carried out by a separate unit. The printing device within the printing unit may be either an impact printing device or a nonimpact printing device. An impact printing device may be a typebar, an element, or a printwheel. Impact printing devices print at speeds ranging from 175 to 700 words per minute. The typebar is found in only a few word processors because it is a relatively slow printing device. In contrast, the element (also known as the 'ball', 'golf-ball' or 'Selectric element') and the printwheel are much more common. Because the element and the printwheel are removable from the machine, it is possible to select a different pitch and/or style.

A nonimpact printer lacks an impact device, such as an element or printwheel. An ink-jet printer is an example of a nonimpact printer. The ink-jet produces characters by electrostatically spraying a very fine stream of ink onto paper or envelopes which are fed automatically into the printer during this process. The ink jet printer is faster than the impact printer; because of its high speed capability, the ink jet printer is ideal for accommodating tasks involving high volume form letters. However, because of its printing process, the ink jet printer cannot create carbon copies; furthermore, the automatic feed feature limits the range of paper types that the system will accept. The final disadvantage of this printing system is its cost; while an ink-jet printer is capable of printing very rapidly, it is cost-effective only if the firm outputs large volumes of text.

Logic

The final area to consider is the logic of the word processor. The logic of the machine is responsible for directing operations. The type and degree of complexity of documents generated by an office are the primary criteria in logic selection.

Below are listed four categories of documents, and the logic features which can accommodate the type of work in each category.

Simple documents—short, one-time, documents such as letters, memoranda, telephone notes, etc.

automatic carrier return—returns carrier automatically at the end of a line
automatic center—aligns titles and headings automatically
automatic tab grid—sets tabs automatically at machine designated intervals
backspace—also known as the strikeover key; used in correcting single-character errors
phrase storage—stores commonly used phrases such as those used in correspondence closings and return addresses
special keys—keys such as line delete, word delete; used for minor editing jobs.

Complex documents—multiple-page reports, documents which require heavy revisions, complex tables, mathematical or statistical reports, etc.

block—takes a section of text and stores it temporarily; for use in editing or creating repetitive letters
columnar interchange—switches whole columns around
decimal alignment—aligns decimal points in columns
dictionary—checks the spelling of frequently used words; dictionaries may be specialized, such as medical dictionaries, etc.
footnote capabilities—creates a bottom margin to allow for footnotes
global search and replace—searches through text for words or character and substitutes another character or words
graphic spacing feature—creates blank spaces for graphic art layout
headers and footers—places recurring information, such as titles, at the top or bottom of a page
justified right margin—aligns the right margin evenly
math pack, math edits—calculates column configurations or verifies already existing totals
pagination—automatically creates a page ending and numbers the pages successively
proofmarks—indication which alerts the proofreader to re-proofread only those areas which have been changed
repagination—automatically regroups text into new pages after editing and revising
scrolling—moves text that cannot be seen on the screen into view
subscript and superscript—moves numbers or notations $\frac{1}{2}$ line above or below the typing line
table of contents update—updates the table of contents as changes are made in a report.

Forms—form letters, contracts, leases, insurance policies, invoices, leases, purchase requisitions, work orders, job applications

document assembly—assembles previously stored paragraphs in a designated order
form packages—set up a grid for use in creating forms
merging capabilities—merges addresses with form letters.

Lists—mailing lists, catalogues

files capabilities—creates or updates a list and outputs a copy containing designated categories of items; i.e. in an address list, one could output the names of all the people living in Florida whose last names begin with the letter M.
sort capabilities—a selective feature which allows for the rearrangement of a file; for example, rearranging a file in alphabetical order.

Dictation Equipment

While not a piece of word processing equipment per se, the machine transcription device is a very important part of the word processing system. While many typists lament that it is more difficult to transcribe an orally dictated document because the initial problems encountered when switching from a sight to a voiced cognizance process and principals balk at the idea of talking their thoughts into a microphone, machine transcription has proven to be more effective than longhand and shorthand. A machine-dictated document takes one-third to one-fourth the originator time of shorthand and one-tenth that of longhand.[3] Machine dictation also facilitates a faster turnaround time. Machine dictation units can be one of the following types: desk-top, portable, or central units. The desk-top and the portable devices are the most feasible for the small office. Desk-top devices can be either an individual or a combination unit. If it is an individual unit, the principal dictates on a desk-top *dictation* unit and the typist transcribes on a desk-top *transcription* unit. The combination unit uses the same machine for both transcription and dictation. While the combination unit is less expensive, it is also less practical since the unit can only be used by one person at a time. Features such as telephone and conference recording capabilities, automatic volume control, electronic cueing (used to indicate the end of a document), and speech compression (a device which allows the dictator to omit pauses) make desk-top units highly versatile devices.

The portable machine dictation unit is a battery-operated unit which is usually used by the principal when he or she is away from the office. The portable unit can also be used in the office, in which case the typist would transcribe the dictation from a desk-top transcriber.

The portable and desk-top dictation/transcription units use one of the following types of magnetic recording media: standard cassette, mini-cassette, micro-cassette, or disk. In the case where the office wishes to purchase a desk-top dictation/transcription unit and a portable unit, the media should be compatible.

PERSONNEL REORGANIZATION

Once an office has conducted a survey to assess its correspondence needs and has chosen a word processor which will fulfill those needs, the next step is to reorganize personnel activities. In the traditional office, a secretary provided both administrative support (filing, mail, photocopying, collating documents, telephone calls, appointments, etc.) and correspondence support (typing, transcribing, and proofreading). The concept underlying office automation is one of specialization. To make word processing cost-effective, it may be necessary to reorganize secretarial services.

Provided that the small office has more than one secretary, the automated office would consist of an administrative specialist and a correspondence specialist. The advantages of the dual-support system are numerous. Because of the variety and wide scope of duties that a secretary performs, it is unlikely that he or she is able to operate at top efficiency in all of these areas. A division such as the one suggested above allows for people who are more inclined toward one or the other area of specialization to be placed in that area, thus matching his or her skills with his or her duties. Furthermore, the amount of manpower required to run an office is reduced since these functions have been delegated more effectively. For example, consider a firm of four financial advisors who are supported by two secretaries. There had been discussion of hiring a third secretary to ease the workload between the two secretaries. If this office were to implement a word processing system, the two secretaries could provide the needed support without the aid of a third secretary. Furthermore, when one secretary is designated to handle correspondence tasks, the turnaround time is reduced because the secretary is no longer required to divide his or her time between administrative and correspondence tasks. The administrative secretary, on the other hand, would be able to assume more duties, allowing the principals to attend to more productive tasks.

The word processing system requires that the principal take an active part in understanding the equipment's capabilities and limitations. He or she must cooperate in the correspondence secretary's attempt to process words rather than merely type them. The principal must have enough knowledge about the equipment to provide the secretary with relevant instructions in word processing terminology (such as instructions on storing, retrieving, dumping, etc.), and to know the proper procedures for editing and requesting revisions for previously input documents.

It is a joint responsibility on both the part of the secretary and the principal to know the word processing system and its concepts as well as the actual mechanics of machine operation. There are many tools which the secretary and the principal can use in order to learn more about this rapidly growing field. Articles in trade and professional journals offer valuable advice on word processing equipment for use in specific professions. Many word processing organizations such as the IWPA (International Word Processing Association) and the Word Processing Institute offer seminars. In larger cities there are often regional word processing associations, some of which hold monthly meetings that consist of a dinner and demonstration put on by a visiting vendor. Trade shows are another way to learn more about word processing. Sales representatives from various companies come together to exhibit their latest developments and to demonstrate some of the equipment already out on the market. Finally, visits to other offices and firms that use word processing equipment can give the prospective buyer some otherwise unobtainable information about equipment and procedures, most notably how dependable equipment is, how easy it was to learn, and how satisfied the users are with the product.

The secretary takes this orientation in word processing one step further by training on a particular word processor. If the installation date is delayed, he or she may be able to enroll in a class which offers training on the word processor he or she will be working on. The secretary should investigate in-class training programs while plans for a word processing system are still in the early stages. Due to the popularity of such classes, there is usually a waiting list or a priority schedule.

In the event that there are no classes that offer training on the kind of word processor which the office will be installing, the secretary should still consider enrolling to gain experience with operating a word processor. The logic master-minding word processors varies little from machine to machine. It is the process of learning to think like a word processor that accounts for the greater bulk of the training program. It is also this same process with which so many trainees have trouble. After the secretary has cleared this first hurdle, picking up the actual mechanics of another machine usually requires no more than briefly reading the machine's reference manual and spending a day or two experimenting on the machine.

If possible, the secretary should train on a machine which is similar to the type of machine the office will be installing. For instance, if the office is installing a word processor which has a 'blind memory' then the operator should also train on a word processor that has a 'blind memory'. While it is helpful if the secretary who is to operate a 'view screen' can learn on a word processor which is also a 'view screen', it is not always necessary. The transition from a 'blind memory' to a 'view screen' is not nearly as difficult as it can be the other way around. As mentioned earlier, most 'view screen' text editors are easier to learn than 'blind memory' text editors.

While most word processing classes use the same training materials furnished by the manufacturer and the student trains in the same way he or she would train in the office, training in a class does have many advantages over self-guided training. The first advantage is the availability of an instructor to provide instant help when problems arise. While vendors can provide the same service over the phone, a phone call is not always convenient, nor is the person on the other end able to see what has gone wrong and to step the trainee through the application to correct the problem.

In classes with a well-developed curriculum, students learn more than just the mechanics of operating a word processor. Word processing concepts and career paths are discussed to orient the student with the word processing system. Machine transcription training is also available in many classes, as well as refresher units in written communication skills.

Secretaries may also train by using the manufacturer-supplied training manual. These manuals are individualized kits that consist of a book which orients the operator with the machine and takes him or her through its different applications step by step. In addition to the manual, some manufacturers' training kits include lessons on cassette tapes. Some training kits include a manual and pre-programmed media, such as magnetic cards, cassettes, or floppy disks, depending on which medium the equipment utilizes.

The time involved in self-guided training is determined by the complexity of the word processor. The simplest machines take from 15 to 20 hours to learn the fundamentals while the most complex machines take from 40 to 45 hours. The training time for machines falling between these two extremes is approximately 25 hours.

Procedures

Developing procedures to accommodate the automated office constitutes the final phase in designing a word processing system for the small office. While some procedures such as the filing and the logging of the media will be new to the office, other procedures such as proofreading and document production will require modification. Procedures for filing, logging, and retrieving are vital to the success of the word processing system. Without these procedures, too much time is wasted in re-keyboarding lost documents, or, at best, trying to relocate haphazardly filed documents. In addition to the standard procedure of filing hard copies, the word processing system involves two additional filing procedures: internal filing and external filing.

Internal filing refers to the filing of an index of the documents stored on the media. While some media, such as magnetic cards which can accommodate one page of text per card, require no internal filing system, other forms, such as diskette media, heavily rely upon a system since over 60 pages of text can be stored on a single disk. This index is customarily output and stored either with the disk or placed in a binder of other filing system of sorts, thus creating a partial external filing system. Each time a document is created or deleted on a particular disk, the change is noted on the disk index as well as on the external index. The index format usually includes the code (explained further on), the date, the author, the typist, the name or description of the document, and instructions relating to storage: retain indefinitely, temporary, etc. Some word processors are equipped to automatically organize an internal file and output a hard copy of the file. While such a feature is a timesaver, most word processors are limited in their ability to create an index that includes all of the information necessary to identify a document in detailed form. In most cases, the typist must supplement the index with additional information.

In addition to the filing of the output indexes, the external file also involves filing the media. The three most frequently employed systems are setting up a disk for each principal, setting up a disk for each client, or using an all-purpose disk and reserving an archive disk for those important principal or client documents which must be stored permanently. If there is one author, then every disk will be his or her disk in a sense; therefore, an alternative must be found to file the material in the most effective way possible. One possibility is to reserve a letter disk, text disk, table disk, and archive disk. If clients are numerous, it would not be cost-effective to reserve a disk for keyboarding documents which pertain to each client. Bear in mind that the objective of any filing system is organization. The less complicated and more universal the system, the more organized it will be for not only the regular personnel but the temporary personnel as well.

Proper filing procedures also include dumping unnecessary material from memory or storage. Because media are expensive, the typist and the principal should review at frequent intervals what should be kept and what can be dumped.

Whatever filing system is used, a coding system must be implemented to enable the typist to relocate a particular disk when given a hard copy to revise or output.

Most codes include the principal's initials, the secretary's initials, the date, the page number, and index number. The code is typed at the bottom left- or right-hand side of each page of a document, or in the case of a letter, under the typist's initials.

For example:

$$AR/1m/01\text{-}82/1\text{-}2/8\text{:}B10$$

Author's initials	Date	Location of text on media* Disc number

| | Typist's initials | Page one of two |

* Not applicable for magnetic cards or electronic memory.

The media and index sheets are then filed according to the code number. Then, when the typist needs to locate a stored document, he or she refers to the code number on the document and locates it on the external index (also called a log sheet).

While it may appear as though all of this information is too lengthy to be included every time, it is still necessary since temporary staff do not have the working knowledge of documents processed months or even weeks before coming to a particular work assignment.

In addition to coding documents, text of a repetitive or 'form' nature also receives a code. Such standard text items are normally stored on another disk, cassette, or group of magnetic cards and filed individually with a separate index.

As mentioned earlier in the discussion on dictation equipment, a document may be originated through shorthand, longhand, or dictation. The document may also be given to the typist in the form of a rough draft; however, the extra effort involved in typing a rough draft is feasible only if the word processor is equipped with an OCR reader (Optical Character Recognition) which enables the machine to 'photograph' the page and record the characters it 'sees' into memory. Unless lengthy documents are the rule rather than the exception, this option is usually too costly and unnecessary for the small office.

If dictation equipment is used, the author should familiarize himself with the guidelines provided by the vendor or manufacturer. Successful dictation is contingent upon instructions provided by the principal to the typist concerning the recording (the spelling of names and synonyms, punctuation, etc.). The dictation equipment's guidelines can help the principal to decide what and when to clarify while dictating. Because transcribing machine dictated material requires more skill, the typist must also prepare for dictation by familiarizing himself or herself by reviewing the formats and the use and spelling of technical terms, as well as familiarizing himself or herself with the operation of the equipment.

For an office which has more than one principal, a priority schedule is suggested. Principals are informed of the best time to submit material for the fastest turnaround time. Furthermore, documents are labeled either rush, routine, or confidential to enable the typist to process these documents in the most efficient and effective manner possible.

Document production involves three main activities: inputting, proofreading, and revising. The most important aspect of input procedures is that of standardized formats. Not only do standard formats reduce decision making to a minimum and thus facilitate a faster turnaround time, but the added bonus of a universal format is a great advantage to orienting temporary personnel and for training incoming personnel.

Word processing makes proofreading an easier task than ever before. Because the entire document is not retyped after each revision, it does not need to be re-proofed in its entirety; only those areas that were revised need to be re-proofread. However, word processing does have one problem not encountered with standard typewriters. Because the operator will often fail to add a necessary machine instruction (such as to retain hyphens during playback), he or she must scan the hard copy for such errors whenever the document margins have been readjusted. Furthermore, since document revision is usually followed by an automatic adjustment of margins, spacing and indentations must also be double-checked. With time, though, the typist becomes accustomed to the 'personality' of his or her machine and is able to detect problems without necessarily having to proofread the entire document again.

Quite often, especially when working with long documents, a principal may send a previously input document back for revisions. The typist then makes the changes, outputs a new copy, and makes an erasable notation on the page to inform the principal of the areas that need to be read over again. As noted earlier, some word processors have a feature which will mark the point on the page where the principal should start proofreading.

The greatest pitfall for principals and typists unaccustomed to revising on a word processor is unnecessary retyping. For this reason, the revision technique of cutting and pasting is not advisable since the operator must know where to locate the previously typed paragraphs. Both the principal and the secretary can be spared of retyping by using the coding system which allows the secretary to retrieve a specific document in order to revise it. Unnecessary typing is also the result of the secretary's failure to store all of his or her work until he or she is absolutely sure that it can be dumped. Furthermore, the secretary often makes the mistake of not storing a document because it appears to be too routine, or else not a likely candidate for revision. A 100-word letter may look short, but in the end it results in added time when the document needs to be revised. Even documents which are temporary in nature should be stored in case a typographical error is found later or the principal makes a last minute change. Since taking such matters on chance can be costly, everything should be stored. Nowhere else is the need for storing work as noticeable as it is during the revision process. In offices using word processing equipment, it is not uncommon for principals to become 'editing happy', but with good reason. Principals now have an opportunity to produce not only an error-free document, but a document which is a finer piece of craftsmanship. It is a luxury which many principals should, and do, take advantage of.

To review, word processing is a system comprised of people, equipment, and procedures. Designing a word processing system for the small office involves evaluating the current office system and assessing which practices warrant change. This initial phase is followed up with the implementation of new equipment and procedures, and the reorganization of personnel duties. Word processing allows the small office to meet the increasing demands of industry and yet still retain its unique and independent position in the business world. The widespread success of word processing is certainly an indication that technology has provided us with the means to increase an office's productivity while decreasing its costs. Office automation neither seeks to replace people with machines nor impersonalize the work environment. Rather, it frees the workers from the more tedious and time-consuming tasks in order to use their most valuable resource: human ingenuity.

APPENDIX A

Form A

CORRESPONDENCE ACTIVITY SURVEY

Please fill in the form as it pertains to each document typed with action paper. Attach form to the action paper before returning to the researcher.

If the action paper attached to this form represents a false start, check here_____

Part I

       Time Started_____   Time Finished_____

       Document Origination

       _____Shorthand
       _____Longhand
       _____Machine Dictation
       _____Typed

       Document Description

       _____Letter
       _____Form letter
       _____Document
       _____Table
       _____Other*

* Please describe_____

       Document Treatment

       _____Rough draft
       _____Final copy

       Additional Typing Required

       _____Envelopes
       _____Labels
       _____Other*

* Please describe_____

Part II

Was this document previously typed by you or another secretary? If so, please attach the document as it was returned to you by the principal for revising.

For Researcher's Use Only

Part I

Counting Unit:_____ Line_____ 1/4 page _____ 1/2 page _____ Full page

Errors Per Unit: _____

False Starts Per Page _____

False Starts Per Document _____

Part II

Number of revisions noted per page of the original copy _____

Description of revisions:

_____ New text/delete text

Frequency: 1   2   3   4   5   6   7   8   9   10 or more

_____ Typographical error

Frequency: 1   2   3   4   5   6   7   8   9   10 or more

_____ Word or punctuation change

Frequency: 1   2   3   4   5   6   7   8   9   10 or more

Form B

ADMINISTRATIVE ACTIVITY SURVEY

Secretary _____   Date _____

Principal(s) _____

_____

Please estimate how much time is spent on the following activities each day:

            _____ Telephone calls
            _____ Filing
            _____ Photocopying
            _____ Receptionist Duties
            _____ Mail
            _____ Bookkeeping, record keeping, calculating
            _____ Errands
            _____ Non-business related (coffee, watering plants, etc.)
            _____ Composing original correspondence
            _____ Researching
            _____ Personal
            _____ Other*

Total
Administrative
Hours: _____

* Please explain miscellaneous administrative activities _____

_____

_____

How does this work load alter during a peak or slow season? Please list which duties are placed lower on the priority list due to additional assignments. Also, please describe what these additional assignments are.

_____

_____

_____

Form C

TIME LADDER

Seceretary _____ Principal(s) _____

Date _____

Please monitor the time you spend on each activity listed below and fill in the blocks accordingly. If you spend less than 15 minutes on an activity, mark the box with a slash. Please do not record the time taken for lunch under 'Personal'.

	15	15	15	15	15	15	15	15	15	15	15	15	15	15	15	15
Typing																
Proofreading																
Mail																
Telephones																
Photocopying																
Errands																
Dictation																
Coffee, watering plants																
Record keeping, calculations																
Waiting for work																
Personal																
Non-routine*																
Other*																

* Please describe these activities and the time spent on each _____

_____

Comments: _____

Form D

PRINCIPAL QUESTIONNAIRE

1. How much correspondence do you originate every day?

    _____ 1 to 5 letters
    _____ 5 to 10 letters
    _____ 10 or more letters

    How is correspondence originated?

    _____ Shorthand
    _____ Longhand
    _____ Machine dictation

    Do you ever originate work away from the office? _____ Yes _____ No

2. Would you prefer to revise and edit letters more thoroughly? _____ Yes _____ No

3. What is the average turnaround time for each letter? _____

4. Is the quality of the outgoing letters satisfactory? _____ Yes _____ No

    If no, please describe how the letters could be improved. _____

    _____

    _____

5. How often are original repetitive letters sent out? _____

    How often are form letters with fill-ins sent out? _____

6. How often are multiple-page documents composed? _____

    How much editing and revising is involved in each document? _____

    _____

7. How often are statistical tables typed? _____

    Do any of these tables contain repetitive material? _____

    _____   _____

8. Do some tables need to be retyped in order to be updated? _____

    If yes, how much revising and editing is required? _____

9. Do any of the documents produced by the office require error-free copies? (i.e. contracts, etc.) _____ Yes _____ No

   How often is this type of document generated from the office? _____

   _____

10. Do you often compose documents that contain 'stock' paragraphs or tables? _____ Yes _____ No

11. Is the turnaround time for any of the documents mentioned above longer for some documents than it is for others? _____ Yes _____ No

    If yes, which documents have a slower turnaround time? _____

    _____

12. Would you be able to delegate some of your more routine activities if there was enough secretarial support to aid you? _____ Yes _____ No

    If yes, please describe what duties could be delegated. _____

    _____

13. What future needs of the company do you anticipate? _____

    _____

    _____

14. What do you feel that a word processing system in your office should accomplish? _____

    _____

    _____

    _____

Form E

SECRETARY QUESTIONNAIRE (VERSION A)

Please evaluate the current correspondence system, including typing assignments, typing activity, and distribution. Include comments on the difficulty of work, deadline requirements, peak seasons, frequency of backlogs, and the amount of revising done by the principal.

_____

_____

_____

_____

_____

_____

_____

_____

Please evaluate the current administrative system, including the types of duties carried out, the time involved in completing these duties, the frequency with which these duties are performed, which duties take up the most time, and the degree of assistance from employer or other office personnel.

_____

_____

_____

_____

_____

_____

_____

_____

_____

In what ways might you be better able to provide correspondence support for the office?

_____

_____

_____

_____

In what ways might administrative activities be carried out more effectively and efficiently?

_____

_____

_____

_____

Do you feel that you could assume additional responsibilities if your typing load was reduced? _____ Yes _____ No

If yes, please describe the activities you feel you could assume. _____

_____

_____

_____

_____

SECRETARY QUESTIONNAIRE (VERSION B)

Please indicate the equipment you are currently working on:

_____ Manual typewriter _____ Electric typewriter _____ Transcription equipment

Do any of the people for whom you work travel? _____ Yes _____ No

If yes, how often? _____

Do you work overtime? _____ Yes _____ No

If yes, how many hours per week? _____

Please evaluate the current correspondence system, including typing assignments, typing activity, and distribution. Include comments on the difficulty of work, deadline requirements, peak seasons, frequency of backlogs, and the amount of revising done by the principal.

_____

_____

_____

_____

_____

Please evaluate the current administrative system, including the types of duties carried out, the time involved in completing these duties, the frequency with which these duties are performed, which duties take up the most time, and the degree of assistance from employer or other office personnel.

_____

_____

_____

_____

_____

_____

In what ways might you be better able to provide correspondence support for the office?

_____

_____

_____

_____

In what ways might administrative activities be carried out more effectively and efficiently?

_____

_____

_____

_____

Do you feel that you could assume additional responsibilities if your typing load was reduced? _____ Yes _____ No

If yes, please describe the activities you feel you could assume _____

_____

_____

_____

_____

REFERENCES AND SUGGESTED READINGS

1. Casady, Mona J.: *Word Processing Concepts*, South-Western, Cincinnati, Ohio, 1980.
2. Datapro: Applications In Industry. *Datapro Reports on Word Processing*, McGraw-Hill, Chicago, 1977.
3. Datapro: How to Choose a Word Processor. *Datapro Reports on Office Automation*, McGraw-Hill, Chicago, 1978.
4. Bergerud, Marly, and Gonzales, Jean: *Word Processing: Concepts and Careers*, Wiley, New York, 1978.
5. Bergerud, Marly, and Gonzalez, Jean: *Word/Information Processing Concepts, Careers, Technology, and Applications*, Wiley, New York, 1981.
6. Cecil, Paula B.: *Word Processing In the Modern Office*, Benjamin/Cummings, Menlo Park, California, 1976.
7. Meroney, John W.: Procedures, Equipment, and People. *The Balance Sheet*, November 1981.
8. Fielden, Rosemary, and Rosen, Arnold: *Word Processing*, Prentice-Hall, Englewood Cliffs, New Jersey, 1977.

Advances in Office Automation, Vol 1
Edited by Karen Takle Quinn
© 1985 Wiley Heyden Ltd.

Chapter 6

THE ADVANCED OFFICE SYSTEM (AOS) CONCEPT—MINICOMPUTER-HOSTED AND MICROCOMPUTER-ASSISTED

Audrey N. Grosch

University of Minnesota

INTRODUCTION

It seems that the concept of an advanced office system began in the 1960s, with the introduction of the IBM Magnetic Tape Selectric Typewriter (MT/ST). At that juncture systems specialists believed that the most important aspect of modernizing the office was the improvement of typing operations. Primary attention was placed on improving the productivity of the individual clerical employee, particularly the typist, in spite of the later studies which showed that only about 20% to 35% of the average office employee's time was spent in keyboarding activity. In retrospect it seems perfectly natural that early office systems should concentrate on typing productivity since this provided a natural evolution to office systems paralleling the data processing application evolution. In data processing, through the initial keyboarding of vast amounts of accounting, order processing, and inventory data, batch processing mode application programs improved the efficiency and control of many business activities. The acceptance of data processing was also similarly pervasive because it affected the lower-level clerical positions initially. The acceptance of applications in data processing which have direct affect on the managerial or professional employee have now just provided a roadmap to the introduction of advanced office systems as an encompassing concept in which all office personnel will be involved and will reap productivity benefits. Therefore, although the creation and manipulation of text documents will still be a significant activity of the office, the advanced office system (AOS) really must weld together on-line interactive applications targeted at personal productivity improvement with more traditional data-processing-oriented transactions and data-base-driven computer applications. With an estimated 6 million secretarial and 20 million managerial personnel, it is apparent that the productivity payoff will come by efficiency gains in this more highly-paid latter category. Therefore, although increasing the capital equipment investment for the knowledge worker above the $1500 to $3000 range has produced some productivity gain, it is clear that the emphasis of the AOS must turn to a product serving the manager and executive.[1]

Just what is this AOS concept? Is it somewhat of a Phoenix rising from the ashes of purely word-processing-oriented systems designed for clerical use? Possibly for some individuals, but for most of us it should be looked upon as a much-needed tool—much as the typewriter or telephone were becoming almost a century ago. The AOS concept views the office itself as a system, much in the manner of viewing applications in data processing. This system has resources which, if properly directed, perform certain operations and these in turn produce certain end products or results. The resources are the human intellect and experience, communications, and interpersonal factors which create the individual dynamics of the organization assisted by today's technologies. These operations involve the practice of certain professional skills: for example, a manager performing budget analysis and business plan development, coupled with the communication of these by passing his results through the appropriate organizational structure. The ability to communicate via voice and digital data coupled with the integration of information generated and controlled in corporate data bases within the computer resources of the organization are key aspects of the development of the AOS. The concept, although it has been variously defined by many writers in the data processing and office automation fields, really rests on three technologies. These are computers and associated software, communications, and the human/system interface.

Although many AOS aspects can be, and indeed have been, created using mainframe systems, it is this author's belief that current technology makes for more practical AOS systems if they are hosted on large minicomputer systems which can be used to power intelligent workstations and, in turn, communicate with mainframes and other computer nodes within a network. Moreover, these intelligent workstations are themselves computers, i.e. microcomputers, which may be preprogrammed to perform certain functions in concert with software executed on the minicomputer or downloaded to the workstation by it. Or, in some cases they may be microcomputers which support purely the work of one professional and when necessary become intercommunicating devices to the minicomputer host for AOS functions and/or to other computers within the network for other applications.

It is apparent that companies which provide computers, communications, and software products have declared war in order to try to win the empire of the office worker, or 'knowledge worker' which is a better title for this group of individuals. With the move to distribute computer resources nearer to the end user (distributed data processing) coupled with the development of a variety of local area network (LAN) technologies to complement digital data transmission nationally and internationally, we now have the basic technical ingredients to support the applications software development which will be required. Consequently, it is natural to see this first generation of minicomputer-hosted AOS products concentrate on the communications, filing, and document creation aspects of the concept, with the beginnings of inter-computer communications making possible some level of office system integration with the data-base-oriented applications within the data processing area of an enterprise.

This chapter concentrates its discussion on minicomputer-hosted AOS and attempts to show how microcomputers can be incorporated into the concept in order to bring specially individualized application support to the individual knowledge worker. Although there are mainframe-hosted software products which perform many or almost all of these office functions, such as various IBM, Honeywell, and UNIVAC products, it is our contention that future AOS implementations will involve a distribution of processing and file storage closer to the immediate end user, a further need for maximization of mainframe resources to large data base and computational problems, and a continuing need to maintain or improve user response times in interactive systems.

Since AOS applications often demand both hardware and software resources which are also demanded by other data processing applications it is more practical to use a LAN technology, either a broadband or baseband version, not only to tie several computers together but also to interface dissimilar devices such as facsimile transmission units, electronic memory typewriters, or graphics generation and support systems into a unified system. Larger and smaller institutions can easily be served by modular configurations suited to their workstation needs for both data and advanced office system applications. Smaller organizations will reap large benefits from this distribution since many traditional business data processing applications have already been hosted on medium to large minicomputer systems and even some of the more powerful multi-user microcomputers. Newer computer architectures such as the redundant processors and devices used in the Tandem Computers NONSTOP systems, when scaled appropriately, can provide even greater on-line interactive file processing on very large data bases at lower cost than many of the mainframe systems in use today. It is this author's contention that in the near term the AOS solution will revolve around the minicomputer-hosted system, with the introduction of a professional class of microcomputers having enriched software to aid the executive in communications, data analysis, graphics generation, text creation, and time and personnel scheduling. Today's personal computers such as the IBM Personal Computer, the Osborne I, Digital Equipment Corp.'s recent trilogy of micros, the Xerox 820, and others will be the foundation devices for the 'Executive Workstation' which will embody capabilities in its software and microprogrammed facilities which go beyond the normal intelligent terminal and timeshared computer. As an initial view of these capabilities one need only examine the Xerox STAR workstation product which really started the move toward human engineered software and hardware for the knowledge worker. Later in this chapter we will examine this development to show some of the underlying principles of the knowledge-worker-oriented system.

In a recent study for the National Bureau of Standards, Arthur D. Little, Inc. stated that in the 1990–1995 period:

> 'Most computer systems will be integral parts of larger systems which handle distributed processing and office automation functions as well as complex telecommunications functions. The operating systems of the computers will be completely self sufficient, operating the computer systems without requirement for human intervention except for management-level priority setting.'[2]

Figure 6-1 shows a schematic of this future general purpose computer system as forecasted in the above study. If we put credence in this view, then it is clear

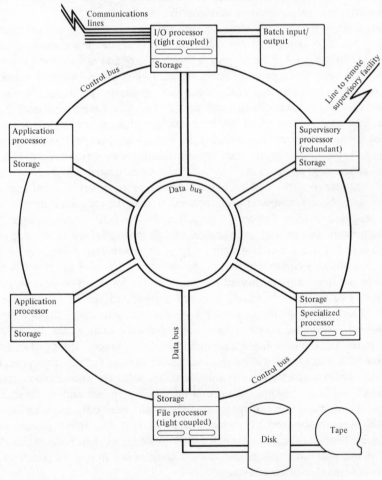

Figure 6-1.   Schematic of future general-purpose computer systems.

that microcomputers will advance to become these increasingly functional personal working tools to support localized needs of the individual while the large minicomputer will focus on applications which need much larger, faster main memory, faster instruction execution speed, and very large shared mass storage handling. This will mean that the user interested in implementing AOS support as it now is available and which has the most probable graceful growth prospect will seriously consider upwardly compatible minicomputer-hosted systems supporting intelligent workstations and/or communicating microcomputer systems possibly augmented by shared storage and file servers as used in the Xerox Ethernet. In other words, it is not a question of whether to micro, mini, or maxi, but rather it is a question of bringing appropriate computer/communications and software resources to the knowledge worker to serve his or her needs reliably, cost effectively, and responsively throughout a period when software and hardware will be evolving and yet an initial investment must be utilized for a period to show a return on it.

THE ADVANCED OFFICE SYSTEM CONCEPT TODAY

Today, an increasing number of the employed population spend their working lifetime in an office setting. They originate, analyze, process, and manage an increasing store of data which enables our modern business, industrial, governmental, and educational institutions to function in such a way that they may conduct their affairs in an orderly fashion, and comply with the various legal and regulatory aspects of operation of any organization today. Therefore, as in non- or partially-computerized organizations, the AOS today revolves around improving capabilities in the following areas:

- Communications, i.e. message and document transmission.
- Electronic filing systems.
- Resource scheduling, i.e. personal calendaring, etc.
- Text/document creation and revision.

Other software, such as graphics production packages and statistical analysis packages, is often also available to the user of a minicomputer-hosted AOS. Let us examine some of the facilities an AOS must have in order to support the four basic areas shown above.

First, an AOS must have a powerful text editor which is easy to learn to use and which will enable a progression of simple to complex editing, merging, arranging, and entry of text and data. It should be appropriate for use by both occasional and frequent users. Managerial and professional users who use the AOS for simple messaging or proofing of draft documents entered by clerical users do not normally use the advanced text editing facilities needed in a word processing activity in which proposals, reports, or other long formalized documents finally will be produced. As an aid to error-free text production, the AOS should have a spelling and hyphenation or even a translation dictionary facility if a business uses several languages in its communications. These dictionaries can be simple spelling checkers or they can be hyphenation drivers in conjunction with text formatting software. Several types of dictionaries can be used in some systems. A basic English language dictionary of 20 000 to 40 000 terms is normally found, with special vocabulary dictionaries for legal, medical, engineering, or scientific terminology also available in some systems. A third dictionary type encountered in some systems is that built by the system user to contain terms frequent to the user's institution, including product names or services. Other systems permit the single basic language dictionary to be modified and updated by users with terms as they are encountered and found not included in the dictionary.

Secondly, output formatting facilities also range from the simple to the very elegant depending upon the facilities needed by a particular organization. For example, if scientific reports are to be produced, a system must be able to handle multilevel mathematical equations and also possibly the incorporation of graphics. A legal office support system must have the ability to handle footnoted text in order to prepare legal briefs, depositions, or other court documents. If a large number of proposals are generated, then the ability of the system to merge text from different files containing boilerplate material coupled with custom-generated information for that individual client will be required. Also, the ability to perform column arithmetic to handle statistical tables may be a necessary feature. Therefore, it is important to know the type of text products to be generated by an AOS in order to judge whether sufficient capability exists in the systems under consideration.

Thirdly, the AOS requires communication support software to enable it to transfer data files as well as job execution commands to other computer systems in an organization's network or to other workstations attached to processors serving the AOS users. Conversely, it may be necessary to transfer portions of a data base or file for use in the AOS. Ultimately, it is to be expected that this communication support will integrate voice messaging via digitized speech with text and image generation messaging. For example, Wang's Digital Voice Exchange (DVX) system which currently operates as a stand-alone voice mail system shows some of the future possibilities in this aspect of integrated messaging. In this system, up to 200 telephone users can access the DVX by calling its special telephone mumber and leaving his or her analog voice message which is then digitally encoded as a 'voicegram'. This 'voicegram' is stored and the destination or receiver can be either a single user or a designated set of users with the time of actual delivery of the 'voicegram' specified by the sender. Although this capability has not as yet been integrated into the present minicomputer-hosted AOS, one can expect such integration to occur.

Fourthly, in most AOS implementations using minicomputers, filing parallels the manual concept of a filing cabinet with individual drawers and folders within these drawers. However, in manual filing, unless multiple copies of documents are made, location of documents becomes one of determining the one category under which it should have been filed and then hoping it has not been removed from the file. In this automated filing, users can determine multiple categories at the respective filing levels in most systems and in some systems designate key words or phrases which can also be searched. Some systems also permit searching of the document text itself or words or phrases in order to locate documents. Most automated filing systems allow the filing of electronic mail messages (letter length) and longer text documents just as one would find in the typical filing cabinet. In the case of messaging, the sender, receiver, date created, and subjects of the message are also readily accessible as search aids. Therefore, although not perfect, retrieval of filed items is enhanced beyond typical manual filing.

Finally, other applications are usually found in current AOS minicomputer-hosted offerings. These include facilities for maintenance of an individual user's daily calendar, meeting scheduling, telephone message logging, reminder or tickler files, address/telephone directories, desk calculator facility, possibly a spread sheet planning facility like VisiCalc or Multiplan, and the ability to create and maintain individualized files for the user. Some systems targeted at specific professions or industries have other capabilities of particular need for that setting such as time and billing facilities for legal or consulting firms.

The AOS concept may vary in its specific applications supported, in the techniques and technologies employed, and the mix of various computer, communications, and other peripheral equipment required. In order to form a concept of the appropriate nature of an AOS for a specific institution the executive needs to understand the marketplace alternatives now giving impetus to this movement as well as the various factors within the specific institution which will impact on shaping this concept both in the short and longer term view.

The data processing community has learned that successful implementation of systems requires thorough planning and top level institutional management commitment which in turn requires an increase in direct user level involvement in the planning and installation. The AOS, because it uses multiple technologies and incorporates them in a variety of ways which will drastically change both the support and professional work environment, needs the strongest top level management support along with sound planning and user involvement in this process. Without this, an institution can expect to realize very little benefit from its increase in per capita employee capital investment.

Marketplace Alternatives

A veritable ocean of software and hardware products is now drowning most principals who are planning solutions to office productivity. Although there is still a large emphasis being placed on word-processing-oriented systems, increasingly the systems now emerging are being directed at the professional or managerial level individual. Institutions would do well to consider seriously their total picture and realize that systems, to be successful in the near term, must now be used to improve the productivity of this higher-salary-level employee group. Almost as a spin-off, such systems will also produce general clerical productivity improvements for secretaries, stenographic, filing, and administrative assistants.

Since most developed country institutions now have host computer systems ranging from larger minicomputers to a variety of mainframes, the first alternative which can be considered is to use the existing computer(s) for AOS implementation. Usually some hardware and peripheral equipment augmentation must be done to support larger file space, larger numbers of users active on the system at any given moment, and also permit the generation of increased amounts or specialized printed output from the system. Moreover, software packages to permit electronic messaging, message archiving, text preparation, text formatting, business graphics, or other capabilities will be needed. Some mainframe manufacturers have achieved some degree of integration in their software to support the AOS while some have not. In general these systems hosted on mainframes are not as 'user friendly' nor easily learned due to their need to operate in a manner to conserve central system resources. Although this may seem to be a low-cost alternative, relatively speaking, it will not often be so because of the higher overhead and the augmentations to the system usually required. This approach will have most merit in situations where excess mainframe capacity is available, where workstation augmentation is small, where users are already largely accustomed to use of the computer resources, and where the stream of jobs on the system will not overtax the processor or disk-bind the system.

A second possible alternative is to employ a minicomputer-hosted approach and if other computer systems are to be integrated use a suitable communications protocol and software to enable communication between these computers as nodes in a LAN. This means that an institution can choose to use this system as a stand-alone or as a network node depending upon their need. For institutions requiring from 24 to 128 workstations active on a system a single minicomputer-hosted system can offer good price performance. Multiple systems of this kind in a network offer redundancy and thus increase reliability. Also, there is no impact on other computers connected into the net, since for the most part AOS users will be connected to their own minicomputer. System response times can be kept at more acceptable levels when this application distribution is maintained. Also, in institutions where the normal data processing applications are already minicomputer hosted, depending upon the configuration, it may be possible more easily to add the AOS software to an existing system, with lower cost system hardware upgrading.

Related to both of the above alternatives and also for some institutions a distinct alternative in its own right is to employ professional level microcomputers such as the IBM Personal Computer, the Victor 9000, or the Billings 6000 system either as a single-user support tool or integrated into a network for communications. In a network mode, using a LAN and file servers/shared disks such as the Nestar Cluster/One in which up to 65 Apple II+s can share storage space, it is possible to provide some level of AOS support depending upon the software employed. The Nestar uses one station as a disk server for a 16.5 MB Winchester technology disk unit using a virtual floppy disk layout.[3] Undoubtedly, when these microcomputers are used in conjunction with the above approaches, they become the forerunners of the executive/professional workstation development initiated with the Xerox product called STAR.

Institutional Factors Affecting Choice of Alternatives

Our enterprises which could benefit from the AOS concept will have different demographics and characteristics which will distinguish their individual institutional personalities. These may be the following general factors:

- Management philosophy—centralized, federated, divisional.
- Size of revenues and personnel—Small or Fortune 200, 500, 1000.
- Facilities locations—single urban or rural area, multiple national areas, single building site, multiple building site, international.
- Past and present technological experience, interest, success.
- Present computer/communications/technology resources.
- Office personnel demographics.
- Task interrelationships and job definitions.

Management philosophy will be a significant factor in whether an AOS will develop in an orderly, planned, and successful way. We previously mentioned the top-level management support which is necessary to the planning and implementation effort. If the institution is large, with relatively autonomous divisions exercising their own planning, but with little or no coordination or standards being set at the institution level, it will be difficult to achieve any satisfactory degree of compatibility between the systems installed at the division level. For example, in some large corporations acquisition of microcomputers and their software by individual professionals must be done under the guise of ordering a word processor or a calculator. In other business settings, the MIS or Data Processing top management has adopted the philosophy of serving as an education, service, and support center for personnel wishing their own micros. This does not mean that users can procure only one type of machine, but rather that some standards for price/performance and quantity purchasing advantages will be added to more effective utilization through user education. In the area of standards, it may be deemed advisable to make sure that all machines acquired in the 8 bit class can run CP/M version 2.2 operating system in addition to their own operating system so as to increase program sharing; or if programs are created in-house, to maximize the number of micros on which they will execute without reprogramming. Moreover, software libraries for micros can be maintained on a host computer accessed by micros with communications interfaces and distribution of software done by file copying down to a floppy at the user's micro. With federated management relationships, wherein wholly owned subsidiary companies remain relatively autonomous, the parent organization as a minimum still needs to insure that these subsidiary systems can communicate with the parent through some established communications protocol and network.

The size in employed workforce and revenues will also be a factor in which approaches are deemed most feasible. Small institutions will want AOS systems which are affordable, readily maintainable, and growth responsive as their business grows. These institutions will concentrate on micro- and minicomputer-hosted approaches. In fact, these organizations probably already use a medium to large mini as a host data processing system and might either augment this system or network another machine dedicated to the AOS function. Larger institutions have more flexibility and may choose to combine all three approaches, but will face the struggle of many mundane but nonetheless annoying problems of interfacing noncompatible devices, such as making two word processors from different manufacturers talk to each other. This is because most larger institutions have already acquired office system products geared to clerical work productivity improvement, such as word processors and automated centralized dictation systems.

Geographic location of an institution's various office sites will affect the need for local or long distance communications facilities. The expected message traffic and devices to be accommodated will determine the needed bandwidth of these facilities. This will affect a choice of technology such as routing all types of voice, data, and image communications via a Digital PBX or using some local area network such as Ethernet, Wangnet, DECnet, or the Ungermann-Bass Net/1 approaches for digital and image communications while leaving voice traffic to be handled through existing facilities. Since various studies performed at a number of companies have indicated that most communications occur between principals within an institution, the choice of a LAN will be a significant factor in the eventual AOS implementation design.

Past and present technological experiences, interests, and successes or failures will also give either positive or negative impetus to any AOS effort. Heavy and past successful data processing systems experience will tend to have positive reinforcement in the acquisition and installation of further systems while the reverse tends to be true where there has been either system failures or merely a lackluster interest in operational modernization. Competition will undoubtedly weed out such firms in time, unless they change their philosophy, and bring in needed planning and technical consulting help and generally follow through with the advice given by office systems and data processing consultants.

Current and near term planned data processing resources such as processors, communications equipment, software, and peripheral devices will also impact planning for an AOS, particularly in terms of capacity estimation and compatibility considerations. Consequently, there must be a high degree of coordination and cooperation between MIS or data processing management, general management, and user groups of both present data processing and planned AOS capabilities. For example, if AOS applications are operated in a separate minicomputer node with network communications to the computer serving database-oriented applications, it may not be necessary to upgrade the processor serving the data base as quickly nor may there be severe resource contention situations occurring with the introduction of the AOS applications.

Location of personnel and their relative office to non-office deployment will also affect the planning for an AOS. For example, if personnel are located in a single building which can easily be cabled, a more simple and less costly communications system will result. Even multiple nearby buildings are easier to handle than a vast network covering message traffic over the U.S. or the world. Another situation might be a small firm with 100 professionals and clerical support staff located in a single building installing an electronic messaging system to avoid 'telephone hide-and-seek'. In this situation mostly short communications of memos, employee announcements, or letters might be the message mix. However, what if suddenly this unified group moves from the single office site to three smaller and separated distance sites across town from each other? It is now more than ever likely that use of the electronic messaging system will increase and will also show a different message mix, with more longer report items being transmitted to keep each site informed. This might occur because, even with the telephone, personnel who used to communicate one-on-one now are separated by distance and will fall back to the easiest communication methods—the telephone first and then the electronic system when a formal record must be filed and distributed or a group product produced.

Finally, the relative dependence or independence of application tasks will determine how much distribution of computing capability to employ. For example, present desk-top microcomputers can handle many application needs for professionals in business and scientific fields to off-load some work from more powerful computer resources. In fact, with appropriate software in the micro and also with the ability for the micro to be used as a terminal to other computers, many individuals with largely independent tasks can be supported. However, if work tasks are relatively dependent upon others, such as a product development group, there may be more need for sophisticated messaging and scheduling facilities or high volume and quality document production facilities. It is in this latter area that the minicomputer-hosted systems offer advantages. Microcomputers will complement this approach in many situations where relatively independent tasks are to be performed.

Let us examine some of the recently offered minicomputer-hosted AOS systems as they have been implemented at this time of writing. Most of these systems offer a per station cost of about the same or slightly higher than most plain vanilla stand-alone word processors. Consequently, there is more cost–benefit potential in these systems since they are largely targeted at the professional or managerial level user as well as the clerical employee. One can surmise that in the not too distant future these stand-alone word processors geared to clerical use will become as obsolete as the veritable punched paper tape Flexowriter. Also since minicomputer configurations can be expanded relatively easily without software impact, these systems can begin relatively modestly and grow as needed rather dramatically in their hardware. Following this, let us discuss how the micro-computer approach complements the use of these minicomputer hosted-systems.

Minicomputer-Hosted Advanced Office Systems

These systems offer a broad integration of text, file, and communications oriented applications targeted to both clerical and professional personnel. Their hardware and pricing environment will be attractive to organizations requiring integrated office support for 16 to 128 users on a single system, with multiple-networked systems possible for serving even larger numbers of users. Some systems in this class are offered directly by the minicomputer manufacturers— IBM, Data General, Prime, Datapoint, Wang, and Digital Equipment being the major current competitors. Others have been developed and are offered by independent systems houses. Interactive Systems Corp. with their IS/1 and Computer Consoles, Inc. with their OFFICE POWER System, both of which are UNIX operating system based, are major entries in this latter category. Let us now examine some of these products to show their functions and design philosophies as these can be considered representative of the current state of these systems.

IBM CORPORATION

As a complement to their mainframe systems, IBM offers two minicomputer-hosted office systems in addition to their recent IBM Personal Computer entry. The IBM 5520 from the General Systems Division is an integrated system for text processing, electronic document distribution, and file processing. It is based upon separate software releases implementing these functions. It uses a menu-oriented interactive session design in order to appeal to both clerical and professional users. An individual account holder can customize this system through menu changes, different default display formats, and several input/output profiles which govern system operation. Although the on-line 'help' facility is quite good, there is little provision for by-passing the menus and directly entering commands, a facility really appreciated by a production or frequent system user. Text editing functions in a page orientation. Another perceived weakness in this system is its use of a single document directory or catalog instead of separate directories for each individual user library or file. Consequently, all document names must be unique within their 30 character length in a given system. Also, as the directory becomes longer and longer, response time to access and search the directory lengthens, sometimes beyond desirable limits. Supporting hardware for this system consist of the IBM 5525 system unit (processor) in Models 20, 30, 40, and 50 with Winchester type disk storage. Model 20 features 29 MB, Model 30 features 65 MB, while the latter two models provide 130 MB of mass storage.[4]

The other minicomputer-hosted product is the IBM 8100 Distributed Office

Support Facility (DOSF) introduced by their Data Processing Division. It is essentially a competing product of the above system and is also the successor to the IBM 3730 Distributed Office Communication System. The IBM 8100 computer is commonly encountered as part of a distributed data processing network communicating with various IBM mainframes. As a data processing system, under the DPPX (Distributed Processing Programming Executive) operating software it can also act as an autonomous computer. Under recently announced enhancements, a DPPX driven IBM 8100 can now also access another IBM 8100 using the DPCX (Distributed Processing Control Executive) operating software. It is this DPCX software under which the DOSF applications operate. One can see from the above the strong network prospects offered in this system for users requiring this integration of data processing with their advanced office applications. In all probability it will only be a matter of time until the necessary software will exist to permit IBM's Personal Computer to communicate with these other members of the IBM family.

Unlike the previously discussed system, the IBM 8100 DOSF employs individual user directories or catalogs but uses fixed allocations of disk space for each user for permanent or archived storage. Users perform text entry and editing on a copy of a document moved to a 'working' or ACTIVE storage area which is pre-allocated and shared by all users. One limitation is that the user cannot have two separate documents in working storage at once and move text between them; however, IBM has announced a forthcoming enhancement in which a user can have a primary and a secondary working storage area, enabling switching from one to the other for editing. But it still will not be possible to perform merging operations using the screen 'windowing' found in multiple-screen-type text editors. Later in this chapter one such facility will be described as part of the Interactive Systems Corporation IS/1 product.

Operational features of this system are well described and analyzed in the Seybold Report on Office Systems article, including an overview of the hardware.[5] One of the strongest points of this system is its spelling verification and hyphenation dictionary facility using a general dictionary of 115 000 words, a medical dictionary of 90 000 words, a legal dictionary of 20 000 words, and a user-defined dictionary of arbitrary length. When this system locates a text word that it cannot find in these dictionaries, it displays four lines of surrounding text with the non-matched word in high intensity display on the CRT. A list of 8 candidate words, listed statistically in most likely choice order, also appear selected from these dictionaries. The user may choose one of these as correct to provide yet another substitute word. This substitute word can also be optionally added to a 'unique word list' pertaining just to that document. If the word will apply to more than one document, the user can add words later from these 'unique word lists' to the user-defined dictionary. Hyphenation is equally sophisticated.

In addition to document creation and output, the DOSF with its limited disk capacity can provide remote document filing on an IBM mainframe connected via

System Network Architecture (SNA) communications and running the Distributed Office Support System (DIOSS) software product on both the host IBM mainframe and the IBM 8100.

It is this author's opinion that the IBM 8100 DOSF is at its best when an integration of text and data processing applications between several networked processors is the solution. However, presently other minicomputer hosted AOS offerings offer more integration of other office support functions within a single system and therefore may appeal to users not requiring as much integration of data and office support applications. Let us now review some of these systems.

DATA GENERAL CORPORATION

Their office system is built around their Eclipse line of minicomputers and is called the Comprehensive Electronic Office (CEO) System. This application software operates under either their AOS or AOS/VS version operating systems and integrates a number of professional and clerical support applications. Also, to support electronic filing aspects of the system their INFOS II file management software must be installed on the host system. Currently, five software components, when totally implemented, provide the following functions:

- Electronic mail.
- Electronic filing.
- Administrative support.
- Word processing.
- PRESENT (TM) Information Presentation Facility.

Let us examine each of these independent and yet functionally integrated modules since they can reside alongside traditional data processing applications within the same host minicomputer.

Electronic Mail

This program product allows users on a single computer or on a local or global network of computers to create, edit, send, and receive mail. Each recipient of messages has an electronic mail inbox to which all messages are sent for reading. The user interface is menu driven but frequent users are provided with ways of bypassing menus and directly entering commands. Access to a user's inbox is owner controlled so that a principal can designate others who might be permitted access. For example, a private secretary might be permitted access to the principal's inbox. When messages are received, the recipient is notified at log-on of messages which have not been read. Users can arrange inbox messages in order by sender, date or time, and subject for display or for printing. Confidential mail can also be sent to a user's inbox, and only the owner of the inbox will be alerted to its presence. Also, an urgent message category is provided. Messages can also be sent certified, where the sender will receive verification back that the receiver has actually read the message. Or, if the recipient deletes the message without reading, the system will verify back to the sender that the message was refused. Users can carbon copy, including blind carbon. Four distinct types of mailing lists can be set up by any user. Also, messages or documents extracted from other files can be sent as mail. Another useful feature is a provision for up to three aliases for a user which can be employed to segregate messages to a user's job title or department, thus easing personnel transitions or changing personnel responsibilities. The filing of these messages also uses the INFOS II software. Under Data General's X.25-based XODIAC networking, mail can be sent to other network-connected processors.

Electronic Filing

This module supports all CEO filing, invoking services provided by the INFOS II software. It is functionally designed around the common office concept of the filing cabinet, with file drawers, folders, and documents. Even a 'wastebasket' facility for the disposal of discarded documents is provided. The emptying of this 'wastebasket' is controlled as to its frequency for all users by the individual who acts as the system administrator. Until emptied, discarded documents can be retrieved. A similar menu-driven user interface to the electronic mail program is used with direct command entry provisions. Except for the physical disk storage limit of a given system, this software imposes no length restrictions on any part of the filing system. Text, graphics, tabular data, or any other system-stored database information can be filed. If the location of a document is known, i.e. the folder, drawer, and cabinet, the user can directly specify this path to retrieve a filed document. However, most accesses to the electronic file will undoubtedly be conducted using categories such as keywords, document or sender name, subject, date of creation, document type, or other user-defined parameters. Between-range searches on dates also help retrieval. All levels of filing can be controlled as to either public or personal. The user can also control the order of display of retrieved documents. A file owner or those granted access by the owner can only access or change personal files whereas a public file can have read-only access, append access (permitting reading and adding new documents), or unlimited access (permitting reading, appending, modifying, and deleting documents).

Administrative Support

This general area covers several applications designed to improve professional and managerial productivity. Telephone messages can be logged to a user's electronic mail inbox. Of course, this implies that the Electronic Mail software is also installed. It also permits maintenance of electronic desk or appointment calendars. These calendars are considered private unless the owner grants access to others. Calendar entries can be marked personal and cannot be accessed or read by anyone else, including secretaries who may have been granted access to another owner's calendar. Coupled with the electronic mail facility, a meeting organizer can notify others of a proposed date, place, and time of a meeting. Once an attendee confirms it is satisfactory, the meeting will be added to his or her calendar. Maintenance of meeting room schedules or other corporate resources such as video equipment may also be carried out with this portion of the CEO system. The system manager defines holidays or other days not to be used for scheduling as well as any corporate resources to be handled in the scheduling.

Word Processing

This program enables easy document creation to anyone from typist to manager. It, too, is menu driven but with command by-passing possible. When typing text the system automatically continues text at line ending, avoiding typing carriage returns. Errors can be corrected by moving the cursor to the beginning of the error and typing over the error or using the command FIND/REPLACE which can operate globally throughout a document or on specified individual occurrences of a text string. A wide range of other text manipulation is provided such as INSERT, DELETE, MOVE, and COPY. Placemark positions in a document for later reference are provided, as are index building and marginal notes. A view mode allows display of documents on the screen in page output format prior to printing. Output can be set up with centering, discretionary, or mandatory page breaks, boldface, underscore, sub- and superscripts, indention, and pagination. Output printing can be fully user-controlled including merging documents such as form letters with mailing lists, setting of margins, and discretionary hyphenation. An optional spelling facility uses two dictionaries. One is based on the American Heritage Dictionary and contains 75 000 words. The other is a user-defined dictionary. The word processing facilities are good enough for most general purposes, but hardly of the quality of the specialized word processors or those found in sophisticated publication systems such as the ATEX system[6] evaluated in another issue of the Seybold Report and used in many newspaper and publishing houses. The CEO system word processing functions much more like a line-oriented text editor such as the Waterloo Wylbur facility found on many IBM mainframes. For those used to page oriented, cursor movement type editors, this line and command editor will not be appealing. However, it is minimally consumptive of system resources to take this design approach in a system intended to co-exist in a minicomputer having a fair mix of data processing applications in addition to operating the CEO applications. Even so, this area is probably the one that will receive the most criticism from office system specialists.

PRESENT (TM) Information Presentation Facility

This module integrates a data selection and retrieval capability with data manipulation and output formatting for files maintained under Data General's

DBMS software or in standard AOS or AOS/VS file formats. It uses an English keyword command language in which users may also build 'macros' of command sequences for later re-use to generate an updated but similarly formatted report. Bar, line, and pie charts may be generated through the use of a companion graphics software package called TRENDVIEW (TM). The report writing features handle automatic pagination, title headings, columnar headings, right spacing control, underlining, subtotalling, and totalling. Automated log-on procedures implement an added file security layer beyond that provided under the DBMS facility. Four interactive 'Help' features provide on-line documentation. PRESENT can function as an integrated part of the CEO system or as a separate program within a given Eclipse computer configuration.

Considering the performance tradeoffs which must be made in this system when attempting to operate almost any conceivable mix of interactive applications within a given processor, this is a functional system which should appeal to present users of Eclipse systems particularly. However, its weakest component is its word processing facilities, yet it still beats an electric typewriter!

PRIME COMPUTER, INC.

This computer firm has been well known for producing relatively powerful and effective minicomputer hardware and systems software for large data base and demanding computational applications, such as graphics display generation and digital image enhancement. Many systems houses here and on the other side of the Atlantic have incorporated Prime Series 50 computer models into turnkey application systems. For example, Molecular Design, Ltd. of Hayward, CA uses a Series 50 Model 750 large minicomputer for the host system for their chemical structure/graphics system used by a number of chemical and related industries. This application involves not only a large data base, but also a lot of processor-intensive computational activity to generate the structure/substructure graphic presentations.

Prime's overall concept of an AOS probably represents one of the very best systems in the minicomputer manufacturer-developed category. Their AOS offering is called the Prime Office Automation System (POAS). It is a system with strong network communications and a very smooth integration of the office type application with data processing/DBMS oriented applications. The systems design emphasizes 'friendliness' in order to appeal to both managerial and support staff users. It is menu driven. For text creation, the PT 65 CRT terminal keyboard is set up with labelled function keys as the administrative terminal for this system. Their PT 45 block mode CRT terminal is used as the normal managerial workstation. The PT 65 is able to be downloaded with programs from the host computer, thereby appreciably lightening its load and improving performance in text editing. This terminal has 32K bytes of memory able to be used either for programs or display. This memory can contain full 158 character by 66 line text pages which can be vertically and horizontally scrolled by the system. Up to 63 users can be supported by a single processor model system. The software operates under the PRIMOS operating system on all Prime Series 50 models. Larger systems can be built via networking of two or more processors and using their network communications software to pass file data, messages, etc. between nodes.

Figure 6-2 shows the functional organization of the POAS. The functions under the management communication and support module are an extension of, and work in close relationship to, the word processing module. The degree of integration between data and word processing is heightened by the system's relatively smooth way of accomplishing the transfer of data from an application DBMS file. For example, a query to a human resources data base to derive all employees with foreign assignment experience could be made, the resultant list sorted and formatted, then passed over to a working storage area, merged with a text document

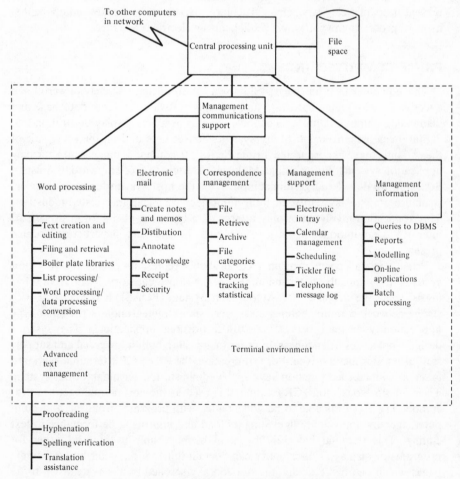

Figure 6-2. Functional organization of POAS.

such as a form letter, and the final product printed on a letter quality printer. Of course, other systems will permit such an operation but most systems require more commands and much more complex human involvement to do tasks such as this one.

The word processing portion of this system is stronger than that of the Data General CEO system. The other functional applications are also well conceived, flexible, and easy to learn. The Advanced Text Management Module features are treated as an extension of the basic word processing module and this increases ease of stepwise learning of this system in modules according to need. This capability features multiple dictionaries for spelling, proofing, and hyphenation. Hyphenation points are stored in these dictionaries and automatic hyphenation is done at output time so that the original text document is preserved intact. All dictionaries used in the system are able to be updated by the user. The basic dictionary is a 60 000 word English version. Other dictionaries are designed to help office personnel produce text in different languages. For example, when a user does not know the translation of the native word when creating a foreign text, the user can request a translation of the word by typing the word in the native language and pressing the appropriate 'LANGUAGE' key on the keyboard. The system will then display one or more translations, the choice left to the user depending upon his actual textual content. Business environments where multi-lingual personnel in the U.S. produce Spanish or French or German language documents will appreciate this built-in system assist. It is not an automated translation system, but if the user is composing a French language letter and cannot remember the word for 'church' the user could invoke the French dictionary and type the English word 'church' and find 'l'eglise' to be the proper term in French. In this author's opinion, Prime should be a leading contender in the minicomputer-hosted AOS and could possibly steal away some of the market share from IBM and Wang, the current market leaders in the office systems area.

DATAPOINT CORPORATION

In 1977, Datapoint introduced their Attached Resource Computer (ARCnet) network. This enabled their products to communicate and share resources. These products range from single-user 8 bit architecture micros to medium sized 16 bit minicomputers. Today, Datapoint is one of the most diversified suppliers of office automation systems. With the introduction of the Integrated Electronic Office System (IEOS) software, Datapoint entered the competition in the more general integrated advanced office system. In addition, their introduction of the ISX digital PBX system offers data and voice communications within the same network. Color graphics, laser electronic printers, and facsimile communications interfaces are other products designed to be incorporated into their office support systems.

The IEOS system operates under their Resource Management System (RMS) operating system, which is their main operating system for individual Datapoint computers either operating independently or as part of an ARCnet installation.

Processors used range from a single user, Z80A micro to the 16 bit Datapoint 8800, with up to 1024K RAM memory and up to one billion characters of disk storage to support up to 24 workstations. Their new 8600 Master and 8220 Attached Terminals are used as the predominant workstations. These emphasize good ergonomics, including amber screen displays through use of an amber-colored filter bonded to the face of a white phosphor tube.

This system is also menu driven, with commands entered on a reserved command entry line at the bottom of the screen. Consequently, an extensive array of labelled function keys are not used on the workstations. A HELP command when coupled with any other command will bring an explanation of the command, its options and its required or optional syntax. This system permits document creation, editing, and formatting as well as the maintenance of document filing. It also permits, via its ARCnet communications, electronic messaging. Datapoint has also integrated a version of the popular electronic spread sheet planning program called 'Multiplan' into its software but it does not operate under the IEOS editor facility. According to Joseph L. Ehardt, this would have been a more desirable way to incorporate this tool.[7] This author agrees with the strengths and weaknesses he found when examining this system.

One of these strengths is particularly worth explanation since it involves a method of searching for filed documents unlike that found in most systems attempting to emulate manual filing approaches. In IEOS, under the RMS operating system each disk can contain up to 10 000 files. Keeping track of these is done by a catalog or 'environment' which shows the logical names of the ARCnet network, a processor, a filing cabinet (disk name), a catalog (filing drawer), and one or multiple passwords. This latter feature gives IEOS added security above any other AOS offering within the minicomputer-hosted category. Within a catalog, a user can define any number of 'Libraries' which can be best conceptually viewed as file folders. In addition to accessing these catalogs and their library entries by name, a library can be constructed with an index built using a proprietary facility called the Associative Index Method (AIM). Through AIM, a user can search for user-defined text strings to locate documents and these terms can be from 3 to 79 characters in length. Operators logically define what the search action results should be. A space operator means the search terms must be two adjacent items. An ampersand (&) means the terms must exist in the same line while a plus (+) means they must exist in the same paragraph. A vertical bar (|) means they must exist in the same document.[7]

Although the strengths of this system far outweigh its weaknesses, some of these weaknesses may limit an organization to deriving less than maximum benefit from their purchase of this system. These are mostly in the word processing aspect of this system and some of these missing features are:

- No automatic or system assisted hyphenation of words.
- No widow and/or orphan line detection.
- No automatic footnote placement.

- No spelling verification.
- No automatic paragraph numbering, nor word index or table of contents generation.
- Difficult handling of input for multilevel mathematical expressions.

For some users the reliance on mnemonic commands rather than merely cursor positioning or entry of a number of a command from a menu list may be a weaker user interface; however, most users familiar with other interactive data processing systems will probably not perceive this as a problem.

WANG LABORATORIES, INC.

Long a leading manufacturer of minicomputers for business and scientific use, Wang currently shares the market lead with IBM for the office systems dollar. Their major minicomputer-hosted system consists of their Alliance software designed to run on their OIS Series minicomputers coupled with their Wang MAILWAY electronic mail and messaging system. Alliance, unlike the Wang-writer word processor, is designed for managerial level appeal as well as supporting staff. It is composed of many separately priced software modules which flesh out its basic document creation and filing/retrieval capabilities. These are a calendar maintenance facility, a ticker file/short note message system, an audio workstation which can autodial telephones via an online Rolodex, dictation storage, and forwarding and short digitized voice messaging.

With its introduction of the Wangnet broadband local area network, Wang has a way in which to integrate its myriad products into a distributed system. Moreover, in mid-1981 Wang introduced their DVX, digital voice storage and forwarding system. Wang systems, although offering some excellent capabilities, are not cheap, but they are generally very good! Even so, currently IBM and Wang lead the suppliers in office systems market share.

INTERACTIVE SYSTEMS CORPORATION

Interactive was formed in 1977 to provide support to users of the Bell Laboratories developed UNIX operating system software and to provide application software developed under UNIX. The major hardware host systems are the Digital Equipment Corp. 16 bit PDP-11 and the 32 bit VAX-11 series super minicomputers. Unix also operates on a number of other computers and potentially any of these could serve as possible host systems. Although Digital Equipment Corp. itself is a leading supplier of a number of office system products and software these do not run under UNIX. Due to the excellent functional integration of the two UNIX based AOS systems, both of which in this author's opinion surpass Digital's RSX-11 or RSTS/E based software solutions, it is appropriate to examine these in some detail. Certainly those organizations now running RSX-11 or RSTS/E operating systems on their PDP-11 models or the

VAX/VMS software on their VAX-11 models can find a wealth of text processing and electronic messaging software to complement these systems. Here, rather, we will examine the more integrated approaches of the Interactive System/One (IS/1) and then the OFFICE POWER system. Since the UNIX environment is quite different from that of the other systems presented in this chapter, UNIX itself warrants some comment before discussion of the IS/1 modules.

Because of the use of UNIX in many educational and research environments, there are many very confirmed users of this system. These users have almost established a cult-like adoration for this operating system due to its ease of use and transportability. UNIX itself is coded in a programming language called 'C' which had its early roots in another language called BCPL developed originally at London and Cambridge Universities. This Language is very efficient in execution and virtually obviates the need for lower-level language programming, making a good language for interactive use. It also is well adapted to string manipulation and other routines used in advanced office system applications and many other computer tasks. Secondly, the file structure employed under UNIX has been described by Robert E. Jones[8] as a large river with many tributaries, then with smaller tributaries running into these larger ones. Each main tributary is a list of files and directories, with smaller branches either a file or a directory. Any file can be accessed by its name and users can change their current directory in this hierarchy. This means that a very flexible and effective file system for text document organization and storage can be created, maintained, and secured against unauthorized access. Thirdly, some functions normally handled as operating system services in other systems are instead considered as user programs under UNIX. This affords easier maintenance and more flexibility, including the great ease of portability across different computers, a hallmark of UNIX. Three modules make up UNIX. The KERNEL module is the resource scheduler and data storage manager. The SHELL module converts and interprets the commands typed by users, either one at a time or in a series called a 'pipe'. The UTILITY program module provides routine and maintenance functions such as sophisticated text editors, spelling/hyphenation dictionaries, desk calculator, electronic mail, equation and table creation, photocomposition driver output for electronic typesetting, etc. For readers interested in further details of UNIX, Thomas and Yates[9] have published a concise and very understandable description. This brief introduction of its structure will enable our examination of IS/1 and later in this chapter the OFFICE POWER system.

The IS/1 system is composed of a series of programs which can be used individually or as a package to provide rather elegant text services, messaging, and network connections to other computer systems for other services. These programs are:

- INed, the Interactive Text Editor.
- INword, for word processing.
- INmail, for electronic messaging.

- INroff, for output formatting.
- INremote/HASP, the file transfer and remote job entry facility to other computers.
- INtwx, the interface to TWX/Telex messaging services.

Let us examine each of these programs since they all afford some rather different features from the systems thus far presented.

INed

This text editor is a multiwindow one designed to be used with Interactive's specially microcoded INtext terminal which is a modified Perkin Elmer OWL 1200. Due to these microcoded features few processor resources are used in editing sessions. However, the terminal itself could stand some ergonomic improvement for operator comfort! This editor allows the screen to contain from one to ten editing windows, thereby permitting up to ten files or documents to be manipulated. For example, with this system cut and paste operations for form letters or proposals is one of its greatest features. This editor does not automatically wrap words onto the next line, but generates an audible tone when the 'hot zone' is entered; then, as with a typewriter, a carriage return must be used at the end of each line. Also, INed allows the existence of two files for a given window, with this second file called the alternate file. One can switch back and forth between the two by merely pressing the USE key on the keyboard. Thus, an operator can quickly, if needed, leave one job to perform another, yet return to the previous task. Another significant feature is the virtually unlimited horizontal scrolling (up to 10 000 characters) which makes it an easy task to create horizontally long documents beyond most other systems. This editor is also able to use various auxiliary programs such as FILL which takes particularly ragged text lines and performs word wrapping such that they will appear of equal length. Indentation and justification are similarly handled. Even column numeric data can be totalled for a report.

INword

This facility is designed for the office assistant, employing files and documents built through use of INed. It will produce formatted documents of considerable sophistication. For example, footnotes can be automatically positioned on the proper page. Automatic hyphenation is another flexible feature. Headings can be automatically numbered, even and odd pages can be differentiated so that larger margins can be properly supplied for binding typeset products. New pages can be forced and a particular page can be extended by a few lines beyond the default bottom margin selected by the user. This program can virtually do almost any formatting done by the more complex mainframe hosted output formatting and publication programs such as SCRIPT which runs on IBM mainframes.

INmail

This program implements an in-house electronic messaging system in which each user has a private mailbox file to which messages are sent. The system has a 'confer' facility that enables designated users logged on to the system to conduct an elementary teleconference. A user can store mail messages in one or more files for retrieval by sender, subject, data, product name, or any other keywords depending upon that user's preference. This mail system is not the most sophisticated this author has encountered, but it certainly would be adequate for most internal electronic message users.

INroff

This module extends the formatting available under INword to handle complex tables, mathematical expressions, and multicolumn formatted documents. It will drive almost every known phototypesetter and laser printer, providing accents, diacritical marks, equations, table of contents generation, italics, multifont printing, and many other special output requirements. A file containing macros controls the formatting for a specific document. Manufacturing, engineering, consulting, and publishing organizations will appreciate all of these features for the production of technical manuals, design specifications, client reports, directories, and even books.

INremote/HASP

This software supports extension of the IS/1 system to a remote job entry station to another computer system using HASP such as an IBM or compatible machine. Also Univac and Burroughs protocol versions are available. This makes it possible to transfer files between the IS/1 and mainframe or execute jobs on the mainframe just as through any other remote job entry station.

INtwx

This subprogram makes it possible for the IS/1 terminal user to send and receive Western Union TWX messages as well as various other international carriers using the InfoMaster computer system. Thus, telegrams, telexes, and international telexes are possible. Messages sent to an IS/1 system are appended to a designated mailbox under INmail. INtwx operates as a subsystem to INmail. The system will also prestore TWX or telex numbers under a name and allow use of the name, automatically providing the corresponding TWX or telex numbers. For organizations using these messaging services frequently, this is an excellent way to invoke them.

Just how desirable is this system as an advanced office system product? The Seybold Report evaluation[10] pointed out a few weaknesses related to the generally passive nature of UNIX systems, i.e. they take some action and are not too talkative when something goes wrong. There is no extensive on-line help facility. The separation of editing from formatting in an office environment is also viewed as less friendly. However, this author does not perceive this to be a weakness. Of more serious concern is the INed limitation of handling approximately 18 000 text lines in a file, which would require segmenting book length manuscripts into two or three files. These then would be processed in turn to produce the final product. However, this must also be done on most floppy disk storage equipped word processors or microcomputers used as word processors. The strengths of this system far outweigh its weaknesses. These are the strong text and messaging features. The scientific and engineering community will especially appreciate this system as should Universities, research institutes, and government agencies. While a better ergonomic terminal could improve the user interface as could some 'help' facilities, the INed features are surprisingly easy to learn and are very powerful. Gillogy[11] and Yormark[12] have written technical papers which give a good view of text processing under this system.

A closing comment might be made on the pricing of this system. When IS/1 and a suitable mid-range hardware configuration are employed, for example a PDP-11/70 system with 32 terminals, the per workstation cost of this system is approximately $12 000, which is a bit higher than most single-user micros and low-end word processors. However, in functional performance this system is very competitive with the most sophisticated word processors and other minicomputer-hosted AOS offerings, especially where heavy photocomposition is needed. Also the general data processing strength and program development environment of UNIX will give added impetus for some users to examine this system closely. Present UNIX users for data processing or systems development might also wish to consider adding several or all of these IS/1 programs to their systems.

COMPUTER CONSOLES, INC.

Another UNIX-based OAS product is the OFFICE POWER system. When it was first introduced it was running under UNIX on a Digital PDP-11 series system, although the software can run on any computer which can run UNIX, including the IBM and Amdahl mainframe versions of UNIX. In this early implementation the developing company, Office Power, Inc., used Digital's VT-100 CRT terminals, so that in contrast to the IS/1 system above no special terminals were required for the use of the OFFICE POWER software, including the text editor. This developer merged with Computer Consoles in mid-1981 and now this product has matured into an excellent competitor to the IS/1 system, and even possibly the other minicomputer-hosted systems, due to the new turnkey packaging of this system around Computer Consoles' Model 5001 computer which will run in an ordinary office environment. In fact, due to the hardware modularity of this system the system sizing can range from as few as 8 terminals to around 64.

This company has a 'never-fail' computer system on the development track as well as larger configurations which will support very large numbers of terminals.

The user interface to this system is more friendly and more office terminology oriented than the IS/1 system. Also, this system addresses many other applications than the IS/1 system, but does not support the variety of electronic photocomposition output units, rather concentrating on typewriter quality low-speed devices and an interface to an IBM 6670 laser printer. On the horizon may be a new low-cost laser printer specially developed for this system. OFFICE POWER uses very nicely laid out menu screens, with options for a user to enter a command driven mode and by-pass these screens. It also features a relational approach data base management system software module called YARD which has a nonprogrammer interface so that users can easily build and maintain their own data processing files and make inquiries to them. OFFICE POWER's main menu functions are:

A. Calendar   — cal
B. Electronic mail   — mail
C. Telephone   — phon
D. Reminders   — rem
E. Name/address list   — list
F. Word processing   — word
G. Folders   — fold
H. Computation   — comp
I. Archival file system — arch
J. Miscellaneous   — misc
K. Administration   — adm

By positioning the cursor over a letter on the above list and pressing a corresponding letter labelled function key on the terminal the desired category is entered. Each user has protected access to this system, first through a unique log-on password and then next at the 'folder' level. All record sets, i.e. calendars, mailboxes, archival files, are stored in electronic folders, some of which the system establishes and others of which the user defines. The owner of each folder can indicate read and write permissions. In the same way read/write permissions can be established for record sets or documents within a folder. A third level of protection, allowing only the file owner access, is encryption wherein individual records or even individual data elements within a record can be encrypted. These security features apply both to word processing nature data and traditional data processing files.

The records-based applications above labelled A through E and G through K all use a uniform user interface with a uniform display of information in a series of summary lines which can be expanded to display the full record. The functions are also uniform with suitable subfunctions such as SEND for electronic mail. The editing procedures are also identical to the searching of files by pattern matching on a character string. In all categories, records can be sorted on any data field or group of fields.

For executives whose major time is spent in scheduled meetings, the calendar management facility is one of the best seen by this author. Calendar entries can be public or private. When displaying a calendar, the cursor points to the next scheduled appointment. Calendars can be viewed as a serial list of daily appointments or in a block graphic mode, so that open dates for scheduling trips, retreats, or similar multiday events can be easily seen. Complementing this feature is the electronic mail capability. Both short and long messages or documents may be sent and received, which have been generated via the word processing or data processing facilities of the system. Another related feature is the automated telephone log with call forwarding to improve speedy managerial delegation. Similarly, the reminder facility will serve to give the executive a good way of pre-organizing a day's activities, particularly if the executive uses the OFFICE POWER portable CRT terminal in his home or on trips before arriving at the office.

Further enhancing the above features is a four-function desk calculator, but now in development is an electronic spread sheet or 'VisiCalc' type program. It is clear that this system intends to compete with many of the applications found now mostly on the personal microcomputer.

The archival file system provides an index for each archive giving a long document name, author list, and a series of user-defined keywords which are all searchable fields. Each archive has controlled access to enable viewing, retrieving a document to copy to a word processing folder, storing a document from a word processing folder into an archive, and administrative access which enables deletion of a document from an archive. This latter access class also enables that user to update the access control list governing all of the above accesses for that archive. Those users having access to folders can create, delete, or set access permissions for their folders. The miscellaneous category in the main screen menu is used to control system related functions such as user's passwords or changing the group with which that user is associated.

Word processing is provided on three levels, each designed for a particular user group. The first level is simple text preparation usually used for creating typed drafts for a principal or for preparing memoranda. This level requires very minimal training for effective use. The second level adds some sophistication to permit final copy of short documents, business correspondence, or memoranda. The third level is a full text editing and final formatting capability for complex large documents such as proposals, book-length formal publication submissions, reports, or technical manuals. Unlike the previously described IS/1 system, this system features automatic word wrap so that carriage returns do not have to be entered in order to enter the next line of text. Also this editor is not a multi-window type but documents can be cut and pasted or merged using appropriate commands. Output formatting is generally commensurate with the IS/1 system.

We previously mentioned the computer hardware now offered in the turnkey system version with its ability to operate in a normal air-conditioned office environment. This essentially operatorless operation is a big factor in this system. Another very positive factor is the terminal OFFICE POWER uses. It has a very nice keyboard, and all the ergonomic features now becoming standard in the latest terminal offerings. On the other hand, the IS/1 system could use an improved ergonomically featured terminal.

To conclude, both IS/1 and OFFICE POWER, although both based on UNIX, are products oriented to differing users. In the opinion of this author OFFICE POWER is easier to learn and more versatile in its handling of advanced office applications beyond the text preparation area, while IS/1 will appeal more in its current state to those users already having digital computers or very demanding printed product requirements. The office user who is a manager or clerical user will probably prefer the OFFICE POWER system. Research and academic users will probably prefer the IS/1 system. System sizing may yet be another factor in choice if both hardware and software are to be acquired since the present OFFICE POWER turnkey system is not yet of a digital VAX-11 size system.

MICROCOMPUTERS—HOW DO THEY REALLY FIT THE AOS?

There is little doubt that out of today's procrustean bed of microcomputers targeted at the professional will rise a distribution of substantial computer power under individual control. Even IBM itself, long a mainframe prophet, responded to this potential, entered the competition with its Personal Computer, and then quickly rose to the occasion of the competition with its own announced improvements—memory and storage size increases, for example. To see this distribution in a powerful fashion, one only needs to examine the previously mentioned Xerox STAR professional workstation.[13] This microcomputer-driven unit developed out of the combined experiences of researchers who developed their own tools and were eager to explore new ideas about how humans use computers. Aside from the many ergonomic features of this terminal, the CRT screen is a bit-map display with 809 × 1024 dot addressable points (pixels). This is almost 75 dots per inch, making possible some exceedingly clear and yet complex displays. Some current microcomputers use bit-mapped displays; for example, the Fortune Systems 32:16 offers as an option a 640 × 480 or an 800 × 1480 dot addressable point controller for its displays. These microcomputers will clearly have an edge in the professional microcomputer field and the prospect of better software which will turn them into this long sought 'executive or professional workstation'.

Another STAR human interface development is the use of a 'mouse', which is a small movable unit which is hand held and moved on an adjacent work surface. The device contains a small ball and circuitry to read the rotation of this ball, with a 1/200 inch move on the surface moving the display screen cursor 1/100 inch in the same direction. This is an exceedingly easy way to control the screen cursor. Yet, aside from some laboratory experimental systems and hobby gaming uses, this device has seen no general application to either computer terminals or microcomputers and their associated displays.

Perhaps the most significant feature of STAR which will point the way for today's microcomputers to become tomorrow's executive workstations is its software. It is known that humans more easily deal with concrete objects than abstract or vaguely defined concepts. In present computer systems it is sometimes difficult for noncomputer professionals to visualize the idea of files, folders, or documents from the manner in which they are stored within a computer. Consequently, the STAR software gives everything with which a user deals a concrete pictorial representation or icon. This technique is carried to a maximum extent. Coupled with the 'mouse', the man/machine interface is vastly more friendly as a result. Some software created for other computers such as the Three Rivers PERQ and the Victor 9000 are now incorporating icon techniques. The bit-mapped displays on these microcomputers aid in clear icon generation. All of the potential applications such as document preparation, distribution, messaging, and analytical or statistical data manipulation can be enhanced for ease of use through this technique.

Therefore, present bit-mapped display equipped microcomputers will be the best potential precursor to a truly multifunction workstation which can provide localized individual support while extending its data base and communications to a variety of other computers operating in a network. This is why mass storage expansion capacity will also be an important factor in choosing a microcomputer having some growth prospect. It has been variously estimated that the truly multifunction workstation will require somewhere between 5 MB and 25 MB of mass storage. Consequently, the best prospect for this storage beyond the floppy disk capacities will be the Winchester technology disks in the 5.25 and 8 inch sizes due to their easy packaging into desk-top units. Meanwhile users choosing double density, dual sided, 5.25 inch floppy disks can achieve in a two-disk configuration about 2.4 MB. Ultimately, the prices for these multifunction workstations are going to have to come into the S5000 area from their currently much higher threshold. This will undoubtedly occur in the next few years if one uses the CRT terminal market as a potential indicator.

Even more powerful 32 bit microcomputers will undoubtedly provide cheap mainframe systems for data-base-oriented applications, as compatible network nodes to super minicomputers or as file servers for shared network storage to a number of 8 or 16 bit workstations. The literature recently has been saturated with predictions of demise for the minicomputer. However, this author agrees with the view of Paul Nesdore.[14] He believes that micros will undoubtedly push the low end minicomputers from the scene, much in the same fashion as the minicomputer pushed the small mainframe the way of the dodo bird. Peripheral device cost is virtually all that is holding back the micro from further inroads into the larger super minicomputer area. Because of this, the microcomputer typically will still need file storage services from other computers for some applications. It would appear that super minicomputers and mainframes will play this role so that a wider integration of data processing applications with advanced office systems applications can be facilitated.

Probably more business microcomputers were purchased to enable their owners to use Visicalc or similar electronic spread sheet software than any other single application. Until recently, such an application was strictly a microcomputer-hosted one. However, in 1982 several of these programs were implemented in minicomputers and this author predicts that virtually every minicomputer in the next several years will acquire possibly several such program products both from the minicomputer manufacturers and independent software houses. This demonstrates that there will be increased competition in software resources for the minicomputer market and this will further encourage the larger minicomputers to stay in the competition. This upward software migration has rather dramatically changed the nature of earlier software migration which was from a mainframe version to a minicomputer version and then possibly a microcomputer implementation. Now the reverse is also happening, and more frequently, too. It is clear that the microcomputer will form this multifunction executive workstation when it is equipped with the right software and peripherals and priced right.

CONCLUSION

Today's executive will continue to face a rapidly changing scene in AOS development. Independently of the size of the executive's institution, the key ingredient to success in this undertaking will be broad-based planning in data processing, communications, and the working environment itself. Out of this planning and a good understanding of present developments in the AOS implementation area, it will be possible to evaluate newer developments and their appropriateness to the executive's institution. With such planning efforts done well, management will have a sound foundation on which to foster their self confidence that the right decisions have been made and the commitment to total office productivity improvement will come naturally out of this foundation. However, if this commitment is one only affecting lower level employees in the organization the whole AOS concept will have little chance of real success. This chapter cannot supply that planning and implementation commitment, but its author has attempted to provide foundation technological information important to the determination of alternatives for institutions when they arrive at that stage in their efforts. It is this author's belief that minicomputers will provide many host services within local networks of an advanced office system and at the same time incorporate the personal microcomputer as a multifunction workstation. We would hope readers would view these as complementary developments rather than mutually exclusive or competing ones.

REFERENCES AND SUGGESTED READINGS

1. Armstrong, Anne A.: Courting the Executive, Focus in Office Automation Shifts to the Executive. *Bulletin of the American Society for Information Science*, **7** (6), 12–16, August 1981.

2. Arthur D. Little, Inc.: *The Effects of Future Information Processing Technology on the Federal Government ADP Situation.* Prepared for the National Bureau of Standards, Contract No. CA 0405, September 1981. NBSGCR 81-342. PB 82-138181. Available from NTIS.
3. Tomorrow's Office, Today's Technology. *Mini–Micro Systems,* **14** (6), 155–158, June 1981.
4. The IBM 5520 Administrative System. *Seybold Report on Word Processing,* **4** (2), 1–15, February 1981.
5. The IBM 8100: Is it an Integrated Information System? *Seybold Report on Office Systems,* **5** (1), 1–17, January 1982.
6. The ATEX System at the Supreme Court. *Seybold Report on Office Systems,* **5** (2), 1–18, February 1982.
7. Datapoint Integrated Electronic Office. *Seybold Report on Office Systems,* **5** (4), 1–17, April 1982.
8. Jones, Robert E.: UNIX—New Avenues in Research and Development. *Hardcopy,* **10** (10), 36–38, 61, 78–79, February 1982.
9. Thomas, Rebecca Ann, and Yates, Jean: UNIX. *Computerworld,* **16** (2), ID19-32, January 11, 1982.
10. Interactive System/One: Built from UNIX. *Seybold Report on Word Processing,* **3** (2), 1–19, March 1980.
11. Gillogly, James J.: *Word Processing with UNIX.* MIDCON 78 Electronic Show and Convention, Midwest; Dallas, TX, 2nd, 1978. Technical Papers. El Segundo, CA.: Electronic Conventions, Inc., 1978. 3 pp.
12. Yormark, Beatrice: *Advanced Text Processing using UNIX.* MIDCON 78 Electronic Show and Convention, Midwest; Dallas, TX, 2nd, 1978. Technical Papers. El Segundo, CA.: Electronic Conventions, Inc., 1978. 3 pp.
13. The Xerox Star: A Professional Workstation. *Seybold Report on Word Processing,* **4** (5), 1–19, May 1981.
14. Nesdore, Paul: Minis vs. Micros, the Next Five Years. *Small Systems World,* **10** (7), 24–26, July 1982.

Advances in Office Automation, Vol 1
Edited by Karen Takle Quinn
© 1985 Wiley Heyden Ltd.

Chapter 7

AN INTEGRATED OFFICE SYSTEM

Paul C. Gardner

IBM Corporation

This chapter is based on an August 1981 IBM Systems Journal article, *A System for the Automated Office Environment.*[1] Major portions of the text have been extracted from that source. (Copyright 1981 by IBM Corp.)

INTRODUCTION

In the following pages we will attempt to outline the near term office automation functions that will soon become pervasive across business. We will then briefly address our views on the needs of the business decision maker and the primary systems tools needed to support this key business activity. Following that we will discuss the difference between office automation and an office system with the intent of highlighting the need for an integrated office system. The body of the chapter will describe our experiences in developing and using such a system and conclude with an assessment of the impact and benefits being realized from the system by a large professional user community.

OFFICE AUTOMATION

The automated office environment of the 1980s should generate significant improvements in the quality of the professional work product. Decisions will be made in a more timely manner through on-line access to information data bases. Internal communications will be more effective with better tools for enhancing text creation and display capabilities. Color graphics, on-line terminal access to data, inter-office communications, event scheduling, and text processing are some of the potential benefit areas to be explored.

Office Automation will help managers perform their jobs more effectively. The quality and effectiveness of the professional work product will be improved as a result of improvements in four major areas of the office environment: communications, document preparation, scheduling, and personal services.

The process of automating the office will be an evolutionary one but due to the speed with which the new technology is becoming available the changes may cause revolutionary pressures. It is imperative that the direction to be taken and the reasons for that direction are clearly understood. Let us look at some of the specific changes that will be brought on with office automation.

Communications

Electronic mail should replace the current hand stamped, addressed envelope as the primary business memo and document distribution methodology. Considerable savings will be achieved in the mail process as well as in secretarial cost and postage when off-site distribution is eliminated. Distribution time for mailed items will be measured in minutes and even seconds rather than the days now often experienced. This means faster inputs to the decision-making process and more prompt resolution of business issues.

Messages and notes will be exchanged in an on-line interactive mode in place of the many phone conservations now required. Automatic note filing will provide a self documenting record of many conversations thus building an historic record of information sources and dates; this will contribute toward more effective support for the decision-making process.

Document Handling

Managers and professionals may find it more convenient and productive to review and edit memos and documents among themselves, thus reducing the need for secretarial support.

The office terminal may be used interactively to take computer-aided instruction courses without traveling to a remote location.

Document preparation efforts will be streamlined by having all typing performed on soft copy where editing changes can be made more easily. Soft copy storage reduces the need for filing space and permits search and retrieval of historic information, thereby reducing secretarial and administrative workload.

Scheduling

The ability to schedule conference rooms electronically will result in considerable savings. Today most conference room calendars are maintained by the secretarial/receptionist staff. Arranging for a conference room at a convenient time and location often requires numerous calls to both the conferees and conference room support staff. On-line schedules for all conference rooms within a site will eliminate the secretary/receptionist intermediary, thereby greatly streamlining the process.

Maintaining all personal calendars in an on-line data base accessible to others will simplify scheduling of meetings. Automatic meeting scheduling facilities will be implemented that will allow the 'system' to schedule meetings among users of the office systems tools. In addition such data will aid in activity report generation and comprise a convenient historic record acceptable for legal use.

Personal Services

Personal electronic calendars and note pads become the means by which actions can be tracked, things-to-do noted and drawn upon as source material for follow-up documentation. Note-pad items will be copied directly to activity reports, saving much time in monthly preparation. Electronic event reminders will improve promptness in meeting schedules and commitments.

The Needs of the Decision Maker

Along with the changes brought on by office automation, the enhancements in interactive service systems are changing the user attitudes regarding the usefulness of EDP support for the business office. We can see a new type of information system user emerging: the people who run the business. They are the decision makers, the professionals that make the business work. Some may be programmers, some of them engineers, but for the most part they are the management and the professional staff that keep the business moving. It is this community of users that will be looking for the integrated office system.

Before we discuss our main topic of office automation let us develop some perspective on the other aspects of the integrated office system.

How may we support the decision makers? First, we must put in place fundamental tools such as basic computer services. This is the major building block of an integrated system. The EDP function's primary responsibility is to ensure that the fundamental computer service is as effective and responsive as possible. Improved service level is perhaps the main element in the user service equation. The basic component in any integrated information system is to provide effective computing capability.

Data for Decisions

The next significant service to be considered is the capture and management of data used in the decision process. Management support activities to date have emphasized the automation of existing paper procedures. This has been done through the automation of the data collection and the generation of production reports. These reports are of significant value in drawing data relationships but often the real information is obscured by the volume of data.

Most businesses have many data bases on line that present a significant opportunity. With this in mind we may want to consider the implications of data dictionary facilities: the capability of cataloging all on-line data so that it becomes readily available for new or expanded application use. Such tools will enhance our ability to create and maintain inventories of data assets by defining those data bases and data elements. An information resource may soon be a visible and recognized element in a company's list of assets.

We should visualize a data inventory such that when the users want information, it can easily be located. We may be amazed at how much data we have on-line that is not being fully utilized because its existence is not visible to a potential user.

The true integrated office system needs to address data administration and the collection of the directory information by providing a generalized data inventory capability. We will then have the data resource under control and it will become a vital element in business decision making.

Focusing on Information

Following the data control emphasis the next focus should be on information display and what that can contribute to the decision-making process. The needs of the business decision maker go beyond the traditional batch processing capabilities with reams of production printout and stacks of fanfold. We are now well into interactive processing, but most of this activity generates printed reports as its final output step. We are still dealing with paper as the final decision support tool. The challenge is how to convert that printout to meaningful information—information that is available and can be used for decisions much more readily than the raw data. If data has been transformed from a tabular format into a visual display of information and thus into an information image, we have significantly enhanced its use as a decision support tool.

Information Images

The final objective will be to provide the decision maker with information 'pictures'. These may be defined as views of information that are structured to convey the maximum insight needed to assist the decision process. This last step may be a more difficult concept. To move beyond presented graphics to the philosophical concept of information images is a big stride. Progress is being made in the information presentation area. Here we have new hardware capability to address flip chart and foil making along with on-line 35 mm slide production. We can thus generate presentation business graphics from the previously extracted data reports to produce information displays.

The time of the integrated system for the office decision maker is fast approaching. Where we now need to be directing our attention is:

- To putting work stations on every decision maker's desk.
- Supporting enhanced information queries and personal data manipulation capabilities.

- Transforming the information displayed back to the user into a form of business graphics, charts, maps, or images.
- Presenting information so that it conveys the essence of what the decision maker is looking for, so he can make a decision and move along.

The implementation of such decision assist tools is a real possibility. We have the basic computer services, data bases, and query tools. We should be looking to better our understanding of what the correct tools are that allow the executive decision maker to effectively retrieve information from the I/S complex. We need to present an image of the information required to make decisions. This is still a concept, but we should work towards a better understanding of our ability to support this aspect of the business decision process.

With this brief overview of the information analysis and decision support elements of the integrated office system we can now look at the office support side of the issue.

OFFICE SYSTEMS

When considering the system environment needed by the above noted office applications and the support required by the business process it becomes apparent that there is a vast difference in scope between the concepts of office systems and office automation. The term office systems is used to represent the full range of information systems capabilities that may be appropriately used in a professional office. They include data base query, personal computing, special services such as business graphics, etc., along with office automation tools. The implementation of automated office tools should be recognized as being a component application in a total office system solution. The real meaning of office systems can be seen as the introduction of the full range of information systems capabilities into the office environment.

In order to better describe this difference we consider office automation in three fundamental categories. First, one may note the pervasive use of word processing equipment and related stand-alone devices supporting text-entry editing aspects of office automation. This activity consists of a relatively small set of applications that addresses the text-entry processing requirements of the office. The users of these tools are the typists and document support personnel whose responsibilities are generally limited to the typing and editing functions. They have no need for other system capabilities.

The second phase of office automation could be viewed as a structured systems solution. Here potential users are presented with a package of application functions that address the automation of various office procedures. Such a system is highlighted by its structured control and procedural operation nature. The users of this type of tool would most likely be part of a firm's operations support function, in areas such as administrative control which are highly proceduralized. In addition to the basic automation tools, users may have a need for structured access to the data bases or information query facilities. These added capabilities are available but usually are restricted to the specific support task at hand. There is little, if any, ability (generally no need) for individuals to expand the scope of their usage activities.

A third aspect of office automation would be the implementation of a functionally rich user environment. The intent would be to provide flexibility of use with a wide range of system capabilities. Such an office automation application, when coupled with other information systems facilities available on a host processor, introduces the broader application of office systems. This type of system would be applicable to the needs of professionals and decision makers, that is, those whose job responsibilities are best complemented by flexibility and richness in functions. It is believed that a professional decision maker should use a system with relatively open-ended capabilities as opposed to one limited to text automation functions. The environment described here is our view of an office system—an environment where the office application and the system needs of the professional decision maker are integrated.

Having established our views on the environment for the integrated office let us now focus on our experiences in developing and using such a system.

The Office Systems Environment

Selecting the system control program that will provide the overall structure for our integrated office system could have been an interesting exercise, but such an analysis was not done. We were running with VM/370 and were well along with our prototype before we thought to question the SCP in any great detail. Under VM/370 it appeared that an office automation application could be structured into a total systems environment, thus producing an office systems solution. When we took a look at VM we did note some very interesting observations. We will discuss some detail later but for now the net was that VM appeared to be an ideal environment under which to implement an integrated office system.

Early Prototype

Before discussing VM and the system architecture we may benefit from a brief review of the early prototype activity. Those efforts started in the early 1970s and were initially directed towards solutions for office support problems. At that time there was an obvious need to keep track of business correspondence, and controlling the local document files was a real problem. A primitive mail-logging facility was designed and implemented to address this requirement. All incoming documents were logged in a file called the mail log by entering index or filing records into an on-line display terminal. Each document was given a system-assigned index number. The document filing record contained this number, the author's name, recipient information, the subject, and various filing and status data. There was also some space for comments or keywords about the document and its content. The documents were then filed sequentially and were retrievable by the index number. This first tool helped the small programming groups cope with their document filing requirements and introduced the concept of office automation.

The mail-log application was followed by the development of a document-creation routine to assist the programming staff with the task of typing the necessary business correspondence. The technique of using the text formatter and CMS editor to ease the burden of creating a business memo quickly caught on. The application, called MEMO, controlled the format of the document using previously created format control files. It prompted the user for the various fixed field inputs such as subject and reference lines. The main body of text was entered free form. The application handled all paragraph and margin formatting, thereby freeing the typist to focus on the words being keyed. The user needed only to respond to the few prompts and type the text of the memo with no concern for format. A nontypist could create a formatted memo with little or no effort.

As a result of the early user experience many incremental improvements that enhanced the general usability of the document creation tool were made. A technique was developed to capture all of the necessary filing information from the user-prompted responses during the text-entry process. The filing record was thus automatically created and logged as a by-product of the user input. This process freed the user from the burden and concern of filing the newly created document. Automatic filing was a big benefit to the early users.

Once the technique of creating memos was mastered, it became obvious that the next step was to transfer copies of these documents to other users of the system. The virtual machine system allowed users to move a document file from their private storage area to the common system storage, known as the spool files. The specific document transfer process was initiated by users issuing a 'MAIL' command for a document that was stored on their local files. A copy of the document was moved to the system spool files. Recipients would read the document from the spool files and place the copy in their local files. The receiving function also updated the recipients' mail log with a copy of the document index record. The users' mail-log file would then contain index records for the various documents that they created or received. This process allowed copies of documents to be moved between users of the system. With this simple system technique the first attempt at electronic document distribution was set in motion.

Along with the new MAIL function, the document-filing application was extended to provide a search and retrieval capability. The basic capability allowed users to scan their local files by searching for author, distribution, time span, and/or keywords. The results of the search process presented the user with a list of filing records for documents that satisfied the search parameters. The user would then refer to the index number to retrieve the desired document from the file cabinet or locate it in the on-line storage files.

Assessment of Prototype Experience

By mid-1972 the set of functions had been expanded to include memo creation, local filing, document distribution, and search retrieval. The effort was beginning to take on the shape of a system and was referred to as Office Systems (OFS). The user reaction had confirmed the value of the functions and the general usability of the tools. The activity was at a point where a total assessment of the prototype experience was called for. The developers gathered all the known information on requirements of an office system, listed the problems and limitations noted in the prototype, and considered what had been learned from the exposure to the virtual machine environment.

The requirements, taken individually, appeared to be rather straightforward. The capabilities of the host virtual machine system were more than sufficient to implement all of the major requirements. The challenge appeared to be in structuring the application such that the various tools could be brought together as a total package. The initial assessment highlighted the development of an application architecture as being a key item. The intent would be to encompass the many elements of the application in a manner that added structure and control to the resulting environment.

The large number of individual user data bases was recognized as the main problem existing in the prototype. That implementation allowed multiple copies of documents to exist with each user managing copies on his or her own local files. This factor was consuming a lot of file storage and generating a definite records management concern. It was also clear that if an information source was to evolve from this collection of business documentation, a common file would seem appropriate.

Consideration of VN/370 and its implications as an office systems support environment prompted the most thought. VM/370, with its wide range of functions and capabilities, appeared to be an ideal operating base on which to begin structuring a total office systems interface. This underlying distinction between the potential scopes of each solution was and has continued to be a major distinction between the OFS application and other available tools.

Architecture Considerations of an Office System

After assessing the experiences with the prototype, work was begun to establish the architecture that would hopefully carry the application towards a future goal that itself was not completely understood. It was felt that there were a few fundamental concepts that the architecture should accommodate. One important consideration was to have the end user perceive his office as being supported by a dedicated 'mini' computer. This element was emphasized in most of the requirements statements that were reviewed.

The appropriatemess of a central shared data base had become obvious. The need to control the number of document copies and the desire to more readily share a common document file across a user organization became key objectives.

It was also clear that the application being undertaken would evolve over time, as functions were understood and included. This thought prompted a design that was sensitive to functional separation and allowed additions to be made easily.

The last element that guided the architectural decisions was a vision of where the computer hardware technology was headed. It appeared that the three basic office system functions of information creation, storage, and distribution would eventually find their way into specialized processors such as intelligent user terminals, document storage 'machines', and distribution control facilities. With these concepts in mind, it became apparent that the environment presented by the virtual machines was ideal for this application. It was also perceived that the VM/370 virtual machine control program facilities might be just what was needed to address the goal of an office system.

The individual users' CMS facility provided the desired personal computer image and, when used with the VM/370 communications facilities, allowed for interoffice communications. The need for a common data base could be solved by establishing a single data base virtual machine. This approach also created the possibility of a common searchable file, accessible by a large set of users. The same concept, of dedicating a virtual machine, applied to the distribution function. Separation of the application into these three main components would also provide a level of function separation that addressed the concern for ease of application change and extension. Finally, this configuration complemented the ideas on technology direction by separating the application along functional lines that would be adaptable to those possibilities.

FIRST SYSTEM INSTALLATION

A main element of the detailed system design was the extendibility of the various functions. The early system was jestfully referred to as the 'world processing' system to indicate the need for open-ended design. The general system perspective focused on the true office system as a link to the user's total information processing needs, a fully integrated approach. The idea was to have an interface that should present the user with a window into the information resources of the user's enterprise and perhaps beyond.

As previously noted, the office automation tools were considered an important subset of the much broader office system solution.

The significant elements of the initial production versions of the application were the common central data base and the controlled delivery of mail. The system controls were also adding structure to the user community, and the general interest level was picking up. The new system was first installed in October 1974.

Three Virtual Machines

As noted, in order to accommodate the various design objectives and take advantage of the VM/370 environment, the direction in which to divide the total

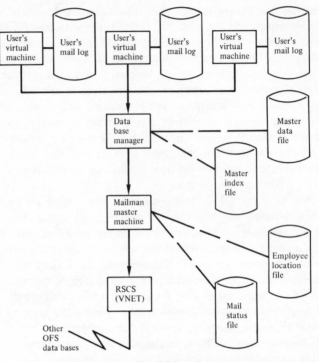

Figure 7-1.   The OFS environment.

application activities into three segments (Figure 7-1) was selected. In establishing the architecture, those functions such as text entry, editing, and data manipulation were designed to run in the individual user's CMS virtual machine. The second separate virtual machine was set aside as the data base function. It was called the Data Base Master Machine and was intended to control the common data files and manage the needed document security, authorization, and audit functions. The third component, the distribution manager, was referred to as the Mailman Master Machine. It was intended to handle the transfer of electronic correspondence and control receipts to guarantee electronic mail distribution. The latter two machines were to run continuously, in a disconnected mode, in order to provide service whenever needed by a user machine. With these basic architecture designs in mind, a more detailed review of the functions at the individual virtual machine level can be carried out.

User Machine

The individual user's virtual machine is intended to provide a general-purpose personal computing environment. As noted above, all of the users' interactions with the OFS application facilities take place within this virtual machine facility.

The document preparation routine is a major user application component that runs here. It provides for the control of all document entry and edit activities. Mail processing and the document disposition function are other key application elements that run in the user machine component. In addition to these primary features, all time management and personal service routines, such as suspended file management, meeting scheduling, remind functions, and message processing, are executed in the user machine.

Several application-related files exist in the user's local storage area. Most visible of these files is the user's mail log that contains the filing records for all documentation owned by the user in question. The user can add comments and/or action dates to this file to assist in the management and control of the correspondence that is being processed through the office. The search and retrieval function also runs in the user machine and uses the mail-log file to find the requested documentation. Documents are located by using a variety of search terms such as author, addressee, subject keywords, or date.

In addition to the office system application, a full range of other user applications is available through the general CMS environment. A typical OFS user may use the CMS file management functions to work with some job-related data on his or her personal file storage. Various utility-processing capabilities are available, and a user may find the need to run some specialized program function. As the users increase their familiarity with the new tool, they are better able to take advantage of this rich personal computing environment.

The CMS machine also provides users with a communications link to the rest of the information system resources of their enterprises. Using intervirtual machine communications facilities, a user may send files or messages to other users of the local system, or the user may also communicate with the networking facilities to initiate messages or file traffic across the communications network.

These basic system communication capabilities can be structured into applications that facilitate user interaction or access with local or remote data bases and execution processing. We can visualize users sending data to or retrieving data from various system nodes in the network. Execution processing can be done at the various nodes where specialized programs and/or facilities exist.

Additional facilities, known as terminal passthru, allow the user to access other interactive systems. Such access is attained by logically attaching the user's display to a virtual machine, serving as a terminal message-switching concentrator, which, in turn, is connected by communications links to remote interactive services.

The network facility rounds out the general system control environment available to the CMS user. With such a wide range of additional applications available, the user is able to execute a comprehensive set of local tools, transmit and receive files from other machines in a local communications network, and access remote machines for data base inquiry or retrieval. The user is given the image of being 'plugged' into the information network resources and can access or communicate across the facility as the need arises.

Data Base Manager

The data base manager (DBM) is a true virtual machine that runs as its own task manager under the CMS control environment. It performs numerous application functions such as updating filing records, storing and retrieving documents, assigning filing numbers to new documents, and validating user requests. The various tasks performed by the DBM are designed to interrupt themselves after various time increments and return control to the task managers. The amount of time is determined by the relative priority of the task to be completed. The task manager always gives control to the highest-priority activity. This technique was considered the simplest that would be independent of the system control program and would also provide sufficient task-dispatching flexibility to meet our anticipated performance requirements.

Most of the functions that would affect end-user performance execute in the user's CMS virtual machine. For this reason it was assumed that the data base performance considerations could be easily accommodated. Many of the time-consuming tasks done by the data base manager, such as storing a document or updating index files, are asynchronous from the user interface functions. It was felt that a user would accept a few seconds delay when retrieving a document from the data base manager. Other tasks, such as assigning numbers or validating authorization, items which were in-line processes with various user functions, should be responsive in the order of a second or less.

The data base manager controls two types of data files: the master index file and the actual document files. The master index file contains index records for each document that is stored in the data base. The records contain all of the document filing information and necessary system status indicators, along with retrieval authorization flags. The other file elements in the data base manager are the actual documents. They are individually contained in the master data base and managed as CMS files. The document files are stored in compressed and compacted form to save storage space and may be optionally encrypted for added security.

The data base is physically allocated across 'n' CMS mini disks, which may reside on separate real-storage devices. The data base is logically structured into 256 sub-data-base elements. Users are given authorization to access documents in some subset number of these logical data bases depending upon their organizational position. The authorization concept was based on a pyramid structure, where senior management in a given organization may be given access to the entire data base consisting of all 256 sub-data-bases. In the case of a department clerk, this authorization may be restricted to his or her department's individual sub-data-base files.

Retrieval access is structured into four major categories. General information or announcement notices are usually placed in sub-data-base (SDB) 0. Documents stored in SDB 0 may be retrieved by any authorized user of the system. Other business correspondence is normally stored in the user's default departmental sub-data-base where it can be retrieved by any user having access to that area of the files. If the author requires additional restrictions placed on the access the document may be filed under restricted distribution control. In this case an author, selecting restricted distribution, limits retrieval authorization to those users to whom he, and he alone, gives retrieval authorization. For this category of documents, chain mailing is not available.

The data base manager performs extensive activity journaling, maintaining records of all transactions on an audit trail file. This file is available to installation support personnel for both accounting purposes and activity analysis of the user population. Data extracted from this file can be useful to an organization in determining value-added benefits. The time between completion of a document to its delivery or the number of times a document is retrieved from the files are examples of elements that can be evaluated. Further analysis may be useful in projecting items such as a need for additional hardware facilities or perhaps even identifying the need for end-user education.

Distribution Virtual Machine

The distribution manager virtual machine controls the distribution of mail notices and manages the receipting of all such activity. The distribution process operates with two primary data files. The first file consists of distribution status records used to track mail in the process of being delivered. This file is controlled by the distribution manager. End users may query the distribution manager to determine delivery status. The system will provide the requester with a list of all as yet undelivered mail that they originated. The second file supporting the distribution process is the Employee Locator File (ELF) and is managed by the data base virtual machine.

The ELF contains user name and address information for all members of the local user community. Users are able to add their names to the file and make corrections to reflect changes in address information. The file can be queried to determine the electronic address of any member of the local user community or to look up phone numbers.

The ELF file can also be used to automatically generate notice records in response to a document mail request. This technique is currently being experimented with. The specific process involves retrieval of the detailed distribution list information from the mailed document by the distribution manager. This list is then compared against the employee locator file to resolve electronic addresses. Where matches occur, distribution notices are automatically sent. In the case of no match or multiple matches, the information is presented back to the user who is asked to supply additional mailing information or to authorize printing copies of the document on the local hard-copy output facilities. Effective use of the automatic mail distribution function is considered the key to promoting the concept of soft-copy distribution and having users gradually give up the habit of generating hard-copy output.

ELECTRONIC DOCUMENT DISTRIBUTION

Using the transmission facilities of the local communications network (VNET) as an intersystem file transfer medium, a comprehensive 'electronic mail' function has been developed based on the OFS application. A document distribution facility has been implemented that spans multiple real systems and provides guaranteed delivery with data-base-to-data-base receipting. The VNET communications act as the carrier, and OFS provides the user procedures along with overall control of the distribution process.

The VNET communications links establish a network environment where a single application program can span multiple processors. The OFS application environment consists of a distributed front end processing capability with a central shared data base. Figure 7-2 depicts the local mail process across configuration. The VNET links form the various real machines in the network into a total system environment. The single application distributes its component functions across the real machines in such a way as to create a single user interface encompassing this multiple machine configuration. In this configuration, OFS presents a good example of the concepts of distributed processing and shared data bases and how they can be implemented across a system complex interconnected by VNET links.

In the local OFS environment, consisting of several VM/370 systems, one

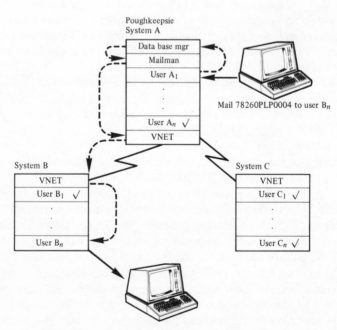

Figure 7-2.   Local mail process at Poughkeepsie site.

would find individual users working with the data entry tools from any one of the real VM/370 systems. Their individual virtual machines communicate with the single central data base virtual machine over the local VNET communication links. Any number of users operating off the local complement of virtual machine systems can store documents in and retrieve documents from the single shared data base virtual machine. The two VM/370 systems not running the data base virtual machine can be viewed as distributed processors. To consider the shared data base concept, we must look at the interaction of the distribution applications with other locations.

The distribution manager virtual machine controls the flow of correspondence across the total complex of local real machines. If mail is to be sent beyond the local application environment, the distribution function will communicate with a counterpart distribution function running at the destination location as shown in Figure 7-3. In this case, the application extends itself one level of distributed control. The local distribution facility communicates across the VNET link to a remote copy of the application. The two distribution managers can exchange electronic documents, update each other's data bases, and maintain total control of the process with full transaction receipting back and forth.

This combination of a central data base and distributed control creates an application environment that will span any number of real systems. The individual user sees a single application interface, regardless of which real VM/370 system he is running on. The intervirtual machine communications capabilities of VM/370 and the intrasystem communications supported by VNET make this possible.

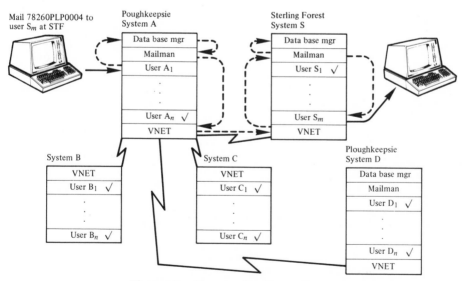

Figure 7-3. Process of sending mail to distant site.

CURRENT SYSTEM ENVIRONMENT

At the time of writing the local configuration consists of seven data base installations supporting over one thousand users across ten VM processors. This configuration represents the environment for a specific enterprise location. The major communication and information exchange is taking place within this site user group. The primary focus is therefore on supporting the needs of this affinity group but network connection to the many other corporate wide office system installations makes possible electronic mail on a much wider scale. This capability is now beginning to be explored.

Full Screen Support

Let us return to the development of the application. The need for full screen menus that would prompt the user and operate through program function key selection was apparent. The full screen support made the application more friendly. Instead of requiring a user to remember the long list of commands and the associated parameters, the full screen version presented the command functions for selection. The required user parameters were made visible by a 'fill-in-the-blanks' technique and use of the program function keys (PFKs) as shown in Figure 7-4. A user could step through many of the application functions by simply depressing specific keys.

The new support confirmed that the application could be more user friendly. It

```
                        DOCUMENT SEARCH                        D01

        Enter Desired SEARCH Parameters     Userid___(if not searching own)

            AUTHOR  gardner_____/_____/_____
        AND
            TIME   jan81_____/_____
        AND
            KEYWORD  ofs_____/office_____/_____
        AND
            ADDRESSEE _____/_____/_____
        AND
            IDENTIFIER _____/_____/_____
        AND
            DESCRIPTION __/__/__

        AND
            ACTION _____/_____/_____

        PF1  Search for items DUE
        PF2  Find documents that contain ALL of the keywords
        PF3  Replace (and) with (or) between parameters


        Press ENTER to initiate              PF9 Help   PF12 RETURN
```

Figure 7-4.   Fill-in-the-blanks technique.

was also discovered that it was easier to train new users and was more supportive of casual users. The application screens were able to present a broader picture of the system's range. The novice or casual user saw more and thus learned more. The end result of the first full-screen-oriented version clearly improved on the usability of the application, but, additionally, it provided insight to the next step.

An important observation was made when it was recognized that the screen should not only be easy to use but should convey information that would help the users to better understand the environment they were working in. This capability would become a key element when development progressed to the point of addressing end-user personalization. It was becoming increasingly clear that the format and content of the screen presentation was of primary importance. The ease with which an installation or individual user could customize or personalize the screen content would affect the acceptance and usefulness of the new tool. When users understand the environment and how the various functions and system capabilities work, they are better able to adapt these facilities to their individual needs.

In addition to the various usability items, support for scheduling meetings was introduced for the first time. This facility allowed individuals to maintain their personal schedules on-line and view one another's calendars. Secretaries and principals were able to schedule meetings by using their office display to find an appropriate time slot on the various attendees' schedules. Authorization structures were in place to control who could see the schedules and who could update any given schedule. The facility was well-received and generally considered a beneficial first step. Copies of the application were distributed to other IBM sites where it was given further user exposure and acceptability testing.

Process Flow Control

The first full screen version demonstrated the ease of use technique, but the application still was a collection of numerous functions that operated independently. Switching from typing a memo to searching for a reference document was a cumbersome task that required the user to keep track of various amounts of application data as they moved in and out of the desired functions. Adding a level of application process flow control was established as the main objective for the next release of the system. The flow structured control was a first attempt to provide for the structured connection between functions that would normally be used in some logical sequence.

The open-mail process is perhaps the best example of the improved flow control (Figure 7-5). Under the general control of the open-mail function, a user is able to view all incoming messages and documents, take action on the messages such as replying back to the sender (Figure 7-6), forwarding to another user, optionally filing the message, or passing over it for a later session. Formal correspondence can then be viewed, routed with a buckslip for action, left in suspense, or filed. All of the functions normally associated with the activity of going through one's in-

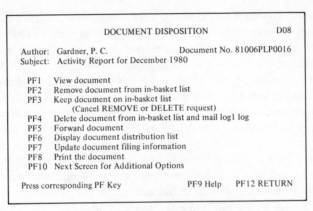

```
                    DOCUMENT DISPOSITION                    D08

     Author:  Gardner, P. C.              Document No. 81006PLP0016
     Subject: Activity Report for December 1980

        PF1    View document
        PF2    Remove document from in-basket list
        PF3    Keep document on in-basket list
                  (Cancel REMOVE or DELETE request)
        PF4    Delete document from in-basket list and mail log1 log
        PF5    Forward document
        PF6    Display document distribution list
        PF7    Update document filing information
        PF8    Print the document
        PF10   Next Screen for Additional Options

     Press corresponding PF Key           PF9 Help    PF12 RETURN
```

Figure 7-5.   Open-mail process.

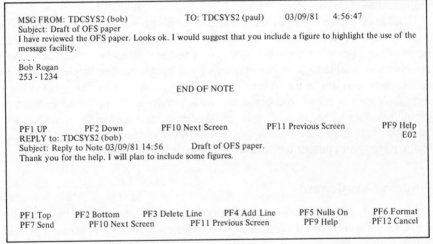

```
 MSG FROM: TDCSYS2 (bob)         TO: TDCSYS2 (paul)    03/09/81    4:56:47
 Subject: Draft of OFS paper
 I have reviewed the OFS paper. Looks ok. I would suggest that you include a figure to highlight the use of the
 message facility.
 . . . .
 Bob Rogan
 253 - 1234
                              END OF NOTE



 PF1 UP        PF2 Down       PF10 Next Screen      PF11 Previous Screen       PF9 Help
 REPLY to: TDCSYS2 (bob)                                                           E02
 Subject: Reply to Note 03/09/81 14:56      Draft of OFS paper.
 Thank you for the help. I will plan to include some figures.



 PF1 Top      PF2 Bottom    PF3 Delete Line    PF4 Add Line     PF5 Nulls On    PF6 Format
 PF7 Send         PF10 Next Screen        PF11 Previous Screen      PF9 Help     PF12 Cancel
```

Figure 7-6.   Use of general control of open-mail function.

basket are available in a logical sequence and initiated with program function key control.

Personalization

Once the general system facilities were in place, and the usability was at an acceptable level, the desirability of increasing the personalization of some of the new user tools came to the forefront. The first attempt at personalization was directed towards the initial application menu screen (Figure 7.7). With this feature the user is able to select, from a comprehensive list of application functions, those

```
┌─────────────────────────────────────────────────────────────┐
│                 PROFESSIONAL OFFICE SYSTEM                    │
│                                                               │
│   PF1    Schedule Appointments (PCG)          Time 2:58 PM    │
│   PF2    View In-Basket                                       │
│   PF3    Search and Retrieve          1981      MARCH    1981 │
│   PF4    Document Preparation          S    M   T   W   T   F   S │
│   PF5    File Hardcopy                 1    2   3   4   5   6   7 │
│   PF6    OFS Directory Information     8    9  10  11  12  13  14 │
│   PF7    Send Messages / Review Notes  15  16  17  18  19  20  21 │
│   PF8    Access Other System's (PVM)   22  23  24  25  26  27  28 │
│   PF10   Desk Calculator Facility      29  30  31              │
│   PF11   Away from Office              Day of year: 068        │
│                                                               │
│   Press corresponding PF Key       PF9 Help       PF12 EXIT   │
└─────────────────────────────────────────────────────────────┘
```

Figure 7-7.   Initial application menu screen.

elements that were viewed as most significant to their office operation. These key functions could then be identified as part of the users' application profile, which describe the content of the initial application menu screen. In addition to OFS functions, users can select any valid CMS program to be included in the list. Function and presentation syntax can be tailored by the end user. The users' initial screens would then be defined according to their unique office needs. This approach was the first attempt at structuring the individual user's view of his or her integrated office system, their window into the information system resource.

At a more general level, personalization has been implemented for the output-handling facilities. The users may describe to the system those printing facilities available to them and establish default output characteristics, such as special print parameters for variable font devices. At any point when hard-copy output is to be created, the user can select from the list of printing devices defined for his or her needs.

These few initial personalization techniques have clearly demonstrated the desirability of this approach. It is obvious that additional work in this area will continue to improve the usability and usefulness of the system tools. Recognition of the dynamics and individualities of the business office clearly highlighted the need to further personalize system applications in order to adapt them to these environments. In the final analysis, personalization may well be the key to making office system solutions acceptable.

CURRENT SYSTEM USAGE

Secretarial and Administrative Users

As noted above, there is a rather sizeable user community actively benefiting from the office automation tools. The secretaries that use them find the mail-log facilities and document creation functions to be the most valuable. Mail logging is done by using the system tools to control all incoming hard-copy documentation. Some secretaries have switched to a totally sequential filing system, relying completely on the search retrieval functions of the system to find hard-copy correspondence. Others have used the on-line mail log in place of hard-copy logging, but continue to utilize previous filing procedures. The on-line mail-log filing record can accommodate this practice through reference fields identifying the actual physical location of a given document and relating it to a project file or filing category.

The general consensus is that the technique of using the on-line mail log makes records more accurate and introduces some filing flexibility. The search and retrieve capabilities are of value to the secretaries, but the principals and professionals especially find it beneficial to be able to use the search functions independently of the secretarial staff. This facility is particularly helpful when administrative support personnel are not available.

The Administrative Service Centers have been able to implement procedures to better distribute the typing workload as a result of using the OFS tools. Documentation entered by one person can be temporarily stored in the common data base and worked on by other members of the department. Common departmental and organizational files are now possible, and the burden of record keeping has been greatly alleviated. Use of the document preparation facility, in conjunction with the on-line text formatters and editors, has greatly enhanced the productivity of the document creation workload. Initial assessments have indicated a productivity improvement of more than 25 percent in the document creation and revision process over the previous techniques. The use of output printers, installed directly in the Administrative Service Centers, has improved the turnaround time and is now allowing distribution of final output from one center to another. Delivery of a document created in one building is facilitated by having it printed on the output station in another building, with resultant savings in distribution time.

Professional Users

Use of the system by professionals has caught on well despite some early skepticism. The intent was for all professionals to utilize the system in such a manner as to support all of their individual administrative requirements. Documentation productivity was emphasized by requesting that professionals do their own typing (this was a concern to many at first). It was anticipated that the professionals, most of whom were familiar with the basic terminal keyboard characteristics, would be able to type information into the system with as much ease (potentially easier) as recording the same information on paper. The experience of the past few years has demonstrated this assessment to be true.

Through the prompting, formatting, and automatic filing capabilities of the system, the burdens of document aesthetics and related administrative concerns are removed from the process. It has been found that with a minimal amount of exposure to the system (using it for approximately a week or two), a professional can do his or her own typing with no increase in total work effort. In most cases, after an extended period of use (typically a few months), the benefits of the on-line editor and full-screen text manipulation start to increase overall productivity, thus making the process more beneficial. In both initial use and use after training, the end results are still immediate availability of a final document, clearly resulting in a dramatic improvement in overall turnaround time. Both of these points have resulted in a general acceptance of the system by the professional staff.

Numerous examples exist of how general organizational effectiveness has been improved through the use of the system tools. Improvements have been noted in the quality of business memos and activity reports. A noteworthy benefit is the timely distribution of weekly status meeting information to the large number of technical support personnel requiring its availability. In this example, the various status meeting chairmen are able to update status documents immediately after the weekly session and distribute clean updated documents to all involved personnel. As a result, the information is more current and meaningful than it had been in the past. Many other benefits are difficult to measure specifically but are of obvious value to the overall performance of the organization. It has been recognized that the meetings are requiring less time and are considered more productive. The accuracy of status information is also contributing to a general improvement in control.

Management Users

The management staff has been using the system as a principal-support vehicle. The on-line calendar and scheduling facilities are proving to be especially beneficial. Users are able to enter meeting notations and move or copy appointments from one date to another. With proper authorization a user can look at the calendar of another user and schedule time. The more meetings to be scheduled, the more useful is the tool. It provides a handy real-time way of looking at various individuals' calendars that in the past were inaccessible or required numerous phone calls to coordinate. In addition, consider the fact that calendars often reside physically in an office that is at some distance from the person needing the information. The task of arranging a meeting or locating someone can now be done directly through a principal's or secretary's terminal.

The use of the open-mail facilities and the ability to 'manage' incoming correspondence through normal in-basket processing is also a benefit. The major improvements are seen as better control and follow-up and the vastly improved speed with which action items can be moved through the organization. A number of the managers, who are frequently out of town or at meetings in remote buildings, have found it useful to periodically check their 'mailbox'. They communicate with the Poughkeepsie machine through the internal IBM communications network and gain access to their incoming messages and memos. Such tools are thus providing a valuable means of staying in contact with the day-to-day information flow of one's office and allowing a principal to continue participating in the management of the office while attending to other business at off-site locations. More importantly, however, the on-line mailbox and complementary message-routing facilities have speeded up the flow of important business-planning and decision-making information among the management and professionals of the organization that the facilities available.

The use of the informal message has caught on well, and it is used extensively by many of the principals having access to the system. Messages are used in place of telephone calls that often would have taken several attempts to complete. The tool is also providing an ideal means of communicating with off-shift personnel or as a means of initiating activity when working late in the evening.

General improvement in information availability is only now becoming understood. Because of the ease with which documents are generated, the professional users are being encouraged to document their activities more completely. This focus is resulting in a rather comprehensive project and activity file. The amount of detailed project reference material is increasing and resulting in more timely and accurate communications. Management is now attempting to better understand the usage techniques that will apply this new source of documented information to its business decisions. The task of administrative follow-up and closure on business activities is being greatly enhanced by the readily available memos and reports. The exploitation of this new information source may potentially hold the biggest benefit for the management decision makers.

CONCLUSION

We believe that the key to a successful office system is the integration of office automation tools with the evolving decision support capabilities. The size of the target user population and their anticipated interactions will dictate the appropriateness of an integrated approach over distributed stand-alone automation solutions. The real value to the business decision maker will come from the marriage of decision support tools with the office automation functions. Only through an integrated system can a large business organization realize the potentials of an office system.

REFERENCE

1. Gardner, P. C., Jr.: A System for the Automated Office Environment. *IBM Systems Journal*, **20**, No. 3, 321–345, 1981.

Section III: Essentials

Advances in Office Automation, Vol 1
Edited by Karen Takle Quinn
© 1985 Wiley Heyden Ltd.

Chapter 8

TRAINING THE OFFICE WORKER

Lena S. Menashian

BNR Inc.

INTRODUCTION

The key to successful office automation is training. Industry experts conclude that the successful use of automated systems is primarily dependent on user acceptance of the electronic office, rather than technological advances. With continuing advances in office systems, training takes on a new and vital role in the office. Even though many organizations, particularly those in high technology, have recognized the need of some management, technical, or continuing education for their employees, they will be required to provide more electronic systems instruction for everyone working in their offices.

Office automation (OA) training presently puts more emphasis on user applications. As people interface directly with the computer and other electronic systems, instruction is necessary to teach them how to effectively use these 'electronic tools' for necessary tasks.

Training, in the future, will have a greater impact on the office environment by:

● Helping to raise the productivity levels in the office. Training the worker how to use the various systems and teaching basic concepts of automation will give them a better understanding of these technologies.
● Aiding a successful transition to office automation. Workers will be more accepting of these technologies as a necessary and integral part of their work.
● Contributing to professional and personal growth. New learning experiences provide the potential for more work satisfaction and better work quality.

Management must come to accept training as an integral part of running a business. Often training is not given proper emphasis because of the expense and difficulty of measuring its cost effectiveness. Many training benefits are intangible, making it difficult to see a concrete return on investment. But an organization, when considering some form of training, must keep in mind the projected money savings of the electronic office. A Booz–Allen study estimates that information workers will show a productivity gain of 15 percent by 1985 which equates to a potential saving of $100 billion.[35] The price for training is small when compared with potential savings and the 'intangible' benefits for both the organization and workers.

Why Train?

A quiet revolution is occurring in the American workplace. The evolution of the Information Society is causing a significant change in various facets of the office. These changes are seen in the advances of OA systems, the nature of work, and workforce. Together these changes influence the corporate goals and expectations of the employees. However, there is a notable decline in productivity. Productivity has failed to keep pace with advances in office technologies. As the decade of the eighties progresses, it is expected that even more American workers will be touched by the electronics revolution. Projections by A. D. Little, Inc. indicate that by the end of the decade some 40–50 percent of the workforce will be involved with daily electronic terminal usage.[17] An SRI study projects that by 1990, 40 percent of today's clerical support staff will use OA.

A major factor in the push for automation is pure economics. For example, office costs are rising annually between 12 to 15 percent. Seventy-five percent of those costs go in salaries and benefits. These costs are expected to parallel the increase in the number of high-salaried 'knowledge workers', who are people who put knowledge to work, instead of doing manual or physical labor. In general, they have more education, are highly skilled, and expect a greater return for their work. The remaining 25 percent of the costs are spent on office operation expenses, which include capital expenditures. Significantly, the cost of OA is projected to drop at a rate of 10 to 20 percent annually. Consequently, office automation is becoming more important to business. In spite of the money being invested, the return on investment (ROI) has not been fully realized because of the declining productivity of the knowledge worker. Since the 1970s, knowledge worker productivity has decreased by 4 percent. This decrease may be explained by the interaction of the traditional office and the growth of information-related work. The traditional office is often based on routine work. Knowledge workers, on the other hand, rely on a variety of tasks to accomplish their work. This creates a conflict. As work becomes more information-based, the traditional office concept becomes a bottleneck to increased productivity. It cannot keep up with the dynamics of the changing work environment, since the processing, integrating, and analysis of information was never required of it. However, these are the tasks of knowledge workers and their efficiency is measured by how well they process information. Thus, business is in a bind. It is paying increased knowledge worker costs and not realizing a corresponding increase in productivity. To remain competitive, business is under pressure to increase productivity. Because of the decreasing costs of OA and the increasingly smaller portion that it occupies in corporate budgets, OA is the most cost-effective means of improving productivity. Investing more money into OA is the best alternative, since this directly impacts the information processing work of today's office worker.

The economics of OA presents a sound reason for increasing productivity: however, other important factors could have an impact on its return on investment. These are related to the cultural environment of the American worker. The American society has encouraged individual achievement. In reflecting this, business philosophy encourages individual accomplishments which, in turn, could influence a parallel increase in group productivity.

With this understanding, one can see further changes occurring in the workplace. For example, women comprise 40 percent of the workforce, often occupying clerical and other support positions. These women are becoming more career-conscious and assertive. There are secretarial shortages because of women abandoning traditional office jobs for higher paying, more challenging work. Those women in clerical support jobs find a classic supply-and-demand situation working to their advantage. This has encouraged the rise of the 'pink-collar' workers who are forming clerical unions and other bargaining-based professional groups to promote their interests. These workers, recognizing the value of their office skills, are expecting business to be more receptive to their individual needs in exchange for productivity increases.

Of the American workforce today, some 60 percent are involved in some kind of information work. This workforce is composed primarily of knowledge workers. Being part of a changing work environment, they need to utilize electronic technologies not only to perform their work, but also to raise their productivity. By using OA, repetitive tasks are minimized, freeing the office worker to pursue more complex tasks requiring more creativity, analysis, and decision making. Office automation will have a major impact on the way workers perform their jobs, since they must acquire additional skills to deal with the electronic tools. However, OA brings up another potential problem. Office automation can speed job obsolescence. The workers who fail to use these technologies fall behind in skills required to maintain or improve productivity, becoming less valuable to a company. Awareness of this forces business to consider how to keep worker productivity up while providing OA tools. It also forces consideration of how workers can be encouraged to use electronic tools in their work. All of this impacts the return on investment in OA. When office automation is not used to the fullest, productivity will not match the investment.

Thus, OA is causing higher expectations on everyone's part. Workers are expecting quality of worklife, while employers are expecting more productivity from their workforce for a given cost, which, in turn, affects their bottom line profits. Simultaneously, both are trying to cope with their own issues. Business is concerned with maximizing its profits, while workers are concerned with the value of their experience and knowledge as it relates to their own individual job growth and satisfaction. Office automation lets office workers do more of what they are trained to do best, that is, the application of their skills to given tasks. Workers become more valuable to the company. Business becomes more profitable with increasing productivity. This means a better return on investment for monies spent on OA and on staff. For the workers, it means greater job satisfaction resulting in more motivation and potentially more productivity.

Therefore, in today's working world, the problem becomes one of how to bring together all the various facets of the office environment. Often, when implementing OA, attention centers on issues of equipment selection, OA planning, and understanding office procedures and workflow. These are often the most easily identifiable solutions to the office productivity problem, since they are the most easily evaluated in terms of dollars. However, they fail to account for the most crucial element in the success of any OA effort—people. Paradoxically, OA acts as a boomerang. While it offers the potential of raising productivity, it requires business to find innovative ways to manage the human resources. If companies fail to manage this resource, there is a great possibility that OA efforts will fail. One of the ways to ensure the optimum use of human resources is through *training*. Training, in this context, is not just the imparting of new skills. It is, instead, a broad endeavor that seeks to develop human potential to coincide with business and individual goals.

Past Approaches to Training

Prior to the widespread use of OA equipment, training was limited to on-the-job experiences. Office personnel were hired for their immediately applicable skills, obtained through some kind of formal education or previous job experience. Additional training was given to instruct these people in the company's office methods and procedures. The actual basic skills required by the business remained relatively unchanged, since the technologies in use did not necessarily demand the acquisition of new skills.

The first applications of OA in the 1960s were limited to specialized tasks. People required to operate the equipment were limited in number, and were usually given special instruction by the vendors.

As more office automation was placed in business, the user base expanded, resulting in the need for a more universal upgrading of skills. It was no longer economical to rely strictly on on-the-job experience of the employee. Vendors, seeing their customer base growing, also became more reluctant to provide unlimited instruction, leaving instructional voids that the individual company had to fill. These included specific office procedures for which the equipment was being used.

As a result, training assumed a more important role within business. When OA became more widely used, training became a transitional vehicle, allowing business to move from a pre-automation environment to a semi-automated one. Once OA was established in a given business, training's role changed and was expanded to include employee development. Training had two goals: helping business with the transition phase of integrating automation into its environment, and providing an on-going process of continual upgrading of skills to meet new demands. Since business needs varied, different approaches to instruction were tried. This forced training to reflect those needs and, at the same time, it means that business had to gain a better understanding of training.

What is Effective Training?

Understanding the function of training requires a total approach. Business must overcome the temptation to just concentrate on money invested and the immediate benefits it can reap. Long-term planning must include employee development to assure the optimum use of all resources. It must adopt the philosophy of 'training as if people mattered'. This means that instruction is directed to personal growth and job challenge, in order to increase long-term employee motivation and quality of work. It is not sufficient to judge productivity simply by quantity. Office automation may improve the quantity of work, but it can never substitute for its quality. This is why the human element is so crucial.

The total approach to training considers both the business and human elements. Within the business element, training will:

- speed office automation acceptance
- increase employee motivation
- improve work quality
- impart new job skills.

The human side of training considers all of the business factors plus:

- behavior modification
- personal and professional development
- quality of work life.

All of these factors are interrelated. The common denominator among them is the human aspect. Each business environment consists of complex social interactions, with its own unique culture that has evolved over a period of time. Various coping mechanisms handle occasional crises. People have a familiar environment and know what is expected of their work and how they can accomplish it. This may not be an ideal environment, but at least its familiarity provides emotional comfort and security.

Office automation is a major change agent. Because it is an unfamiliar change agent, the initial response often provokes resistance, primarily from the fears and awe of its technology. People must learn the jargon, and transform their personal work habits and office procedures to permit the technology to work. Eventually, a restructuring of jobs in the office environment happens, affecting everyone. This restructuring of job tasks often provokes fears of an unwanted change in job status or employment. In addition, there are fears of failure associated with the unfamiliar, particularly in those people with low self-esteem. This change forces new ways of performing familiar tasks. Training can prepare the workers for this change and lessen their fears. Training helps the workers build trust for the new technologies. Once this trust is developed, they are more receptive to change, particularly as new or improved OA systems are integrated in the work environment. Eliminating these fears through an awareness process by training assures *the acceptance of office automation* and reduces the probability of active resistance of workers, including sabotage.

Training contributes to *workers' motivation*. Proper preparation through training to do specific job tasks gives the workers confidence in their abilities and therefore contributes to productivity. This benefits the business by raising the quality of work and the value of each individual's contribution. Simultaneously, the workers, by their accomplishments, gain a positive attitude towards their work.

Training contributes to better *work quality* by providing additional knowledge on how to best apply available OA tools to do a job more effectively. This encourages creativity, which in turn, generates new ideas. For business, the bottom line is a reduction of worker frustration, since a worker's capabilities are being challenged. Training gives the worker a sense of controlling the technology rather than being controlled by it.

The introduction of OA changes a business's operations enough so that its workers often feel like 'new employees'. Like new employees, they are confronted with the task of *learning new skills*. Training helps 'acclimatize' employees to the new automated environment by teaching them the new skills needed. This is necessary, since like any new employee, no one is an 'off-the-shelf' worker, who can be plugged in and expected to work immediately according to the company's ways.

Training also seeks to overcome the transfer of old behavior patterns to the new systems. People cling to old familiar methods and procedures in unknown situations. In the case of OA, the transfer of these methods impedes proper or full use of the equipment. People are forced to accept the idea that they have to change their work habits in order to perform their jobs with the new equipment. They must confront change directly through incorporating *change in behavior patterns*. Training provides understanding of change, making it less threatening. It seeks to make people feel comfortable about learning something new.

Training can contribute *personal and professional development* as well as being a deterrent to job obsolescence. As OA forces a redesign and restructuring of jobs, employees need assurance that they can still remain valuable to their company. Training provides a mechanism by which a company can contribute to the growth of an individual's knowledge and job skills, and, concurrently, retain good, skilled employees. Training also demonstrates to employees the commitment of a company to taking an interest in their welfare and professional future. It allows individuals to build on their existing skills, *enriching their work lives*. This directly translates into benefits for a company. As individuals become motivated and enthusiastic, they tend to share their new knowledge and skills with their co-workers. This encourages them to apply their newly acquired skill in job tasks and promote its use among others.

Planning for Effective Training

Training is only as successful as management allows it to be. Management must adopt the philosophy that training is an integral part of its operations. Too often in the past, training was given inadequate support. It was usually one of the first functions cancelled when business slowed down.

Once a decision is made to set up a training program or expand an existing one, a company must establish a plan based on its needs, both immediate and long-term. It must also determine how to measure training effectiveness. It must determine how to deliver the instruction and what methods work best for its particular needs. Finally, it must continually refine its training, to keep pace with the evolving technology.

Before beginning a training program, sufficient groundwork is necessary to efficiently use human and financial resources involved in training. The following are the basic concepts to be considered for a training program.

- *Identify needs* Two separate needs must be identified: the organization's productivity goals and the training needs of its employees. Both are interrelated. The goals reflect the objectives of the firm and provide a basis for decisions on the various tasks to which instruction is applied. The training needs of the employees are determined by their current level of performance and the styles of instruction that work best for them. Also included are previous experience and knowledge and individual goals. Trainee needs are determined through pre-training assessment measurements.

- *Determine training alternatives* Various training alternatives include developing internal training resources or relying on externally available programs, or a mix of both. Once the alternatives are identified, consideration must be given to the cost–benefit of each one. For internal training, costs include staff salaries, facilities, and equipment and materials costs. For external training, costs include vendor fees, consultant fees, equipment rental, materials cost, and travel expenses. In both cases, lost employee work-time costs must be added. Also, the costs of any substitute or temporary help to cover the absence of the trainee should be considered.

- *Design and develop a training curriculum* After instructional resources are selected, it is necessary to design courses to satisfy the organizational needs. This means working with the training staff, either internal or external, to determine the course content and to set benchmarks that will allow monitoring of course development and its effectiveness. This also includes the development of testing procedures that will realistically show student progress. The development of the curriculum involves coordination of all details associated with the production of course materials and the obtaining of equipment and facilities.

- *Implement training* Implementing training involves the actual scheduling of courses, attendance by trainees, monitoring their progress, and student feedback.

- *Evaluate training results* The evaluation of instruction is a necessary, ongoing process. Initially, training results can be evaluated in terms of how well the training met the original objectives as defined by the organizational

- Identify needs and goals.
- Assess instructional alternatives.
- Choose appropriate resources.
- Design curriculum.
- Implement program.
- Establish evaluation procedures to measure effectiveness.
- Compare curriculum results with training objectives.
- Redesign as necessary.

Figure 8-1. Checklist for effective training.

needs. Crucial to the success of training is the continual evaluation of the organizational needs. Training can only be considered effective if it meets the needs of the organization. Return on investment in training can be best determined if adequate cost–benefit measurements are available.

TRAINING ESSENTIALS

This section on training essentials focuses on the important concepts that promote the quality of any training program, independently of the resources used in the development and implementation phases. The essentials discussed here include learning/teaching concepts, training methods, instructional aids, and support and training costs.

LEARNING/TEACHING CONCEPTS

Adult learning and curriculum development can use various techniques to implement a sound instructional program.

Adult Learning

Before an instructional program is created, it is important to know the audience. This dictates what approaches will work, how material can be retained, and how behavior can be changed to accept new ideas.

Adult learners may:

- Be more self-motivated.
- Use learning as a coping mechanism (especially if other situations or environments are changing).
- Seek learning to meet a specific goal.
- Need additional support to promote greater confidence.
- Prefer self-directed over competitive classroom environment.
- Prefer variety of media in instructional resources.

Figure 8-2. Some characteristics of adult
learning.

The changing office environment is experiencing the growth of a student population of working adults who have different goals and expectations in their educational endeavors. In time, with the increasing application and usage of electronic systems, a majority of the adult population, from top executives to clerical support staff, will require some degree of instruction on the basics of the systems and how they apply to their jobs. This presents a challenge to businesses and their training programs to motivate adult learners so that the instruction will be well-received and applied. To facilitate learning and motivation, an understanding of the process of human, in particular adult, learning is important.

Research in the learning process reveals that people learn in a variety of ways. One way that this difference can be understood is through the concept of how the brain functions in learning. This concept, based on the brain dominance theory, divides the human mind into left and right hemispheres. The two brain hemispheres perform different human processing functions. The left brain does the verbal, logical, analytic, mathematical, structured, and sequential processing. Thus, reading, writing, planning, and organizational skills are left brain functions. However, the right brain functions primarily for spatial and visual relationships, intuition, holistic thinking, creativity, and imaging. Although, ideally, both sides should be working together in complementary roles, in reality one side often takes the lead for a majority of individuals. Consequently, brain dominance effects the learning patterns of humans. For example, teaching concepts and relationships with only pictures will make it difficult for left-brained individuals to assimilate the information. Similarly, approaching a right-brained individual with a purely logical and verbal teaching strategy may not work. In a heterogeneous student environment, instructional techniques addressing both brain functions should be used in order to facilitate the education process. These techniques and learning styles contribute to an effective education program.

Educators have found that adults have specific requirements and needs. In particular, adult learning must be self-motivated or encouraged through mutually benefiting incentives. Most adults, especially those who are formally educated, seek applicable education primarily as a coping mechanism for a life-changing situation (i.e. new job, promotion, marriage). This complements the developmental stages of adult life where their needs and values are constantly changing. Although love of learning can be a reason for pursuing more training, adults usually seek education for practical results in order to increase their skills and personal self-esteem. Since learning is often sought for specific purposes, the teaching of applicable concepts to relevant problems is preferred. Similarly, it is important that new concepts presented be integrated into existing knowledge to easily assimilate, retain, and use.

For the learning of new ideas and concepts, a familiar, comfortable environment is preferable, particularly to help relieve 'phobias' adults might have with the new technologies. Adults, initially, need more support ('hand holding'), to overcome any feelings of inadequacy when confronted with a new technology that affects their job tasks and work behavior. This support is important because adults tend to take errors personally which, in turn, affects their self-esteem and confidence. For this reason, they are more likely to use familiar methods to avoid mistakes, rather than taking the risk of learning something new. Furthermore, studies show that adults prefer self-directed and self-designed, straightforward learning experiences over group situations. This gives them more control over the process and allows the learning to be done at their pace, which ensures mastery of the subject.

Adults, in pursuing self-directed study, still want some support of other resources for feedback and exchange of information. In self-directed study, adults are open to using many kinds of resources to aid in the process such as textbooks, programmed instruction, computer- or video-assisted learning. A final benefit is that it enables them to practice new skills progressively as the subject matter is mastered. Overall, the adult students use learning opportunities for practical purposes, seeking the most efficient means to achieve mastery of subject that can be integrated with previous knowledge.

The concept of the 'learning curve' is also important in understanding the human learning process. The learning curve is simply an expression which states that learning occurs most rapidly when new material is first introduced, gradually levelling off as the material is assimilated. The importance of the learning curve derives from the understanding it gives of the efficiency of adult learning. Even though adults learn new material fastest in the beginning, they learn at different rates and with different levels of comprehension: thus, no one standard method of teaching is universally effective for all adults. Experiences and previous knowledge play a large part in a student's ability to assimilate new concepts readily. The important point is that a learning curve mirrors the experience of an individual to a given type of teaching method and material. Because of this, it is vital to vary instructional experiences in order to maintain optimal rates of learning.

Management Training

Executives and managers form a special class of adults in the office environment. They have to be convinced that tasks done manually can be completed faster at a workstation. This provides an incentive for them to be trained to use a new system. They also have special instructional needs. For example, they require less instruction since they use workstations only to access and communicate information that subordinates have processed. They tend to shun formal training and prefer quick nonpressured training that suits their needs. In addition, training is more effective if conveniently scheduled to take place outside of their offices, cutting down on distractions and interruptions. Follow-up instruction is important. The instructor should not be a subordinate of the executive. This avoids possible embarrassment and feelings of inadequacy. Specialized jargon should be avoided, since it might make the learning process more difficult. Training can take a building-block approach, stressing extensions of concepts that would allow easier teaching of different applications. Managers need to feel that the machines are there to serve them and accomplish their work. They need a

● Must be convinced of ROI before beginning training (this includes system usefulness and the time they are investing).

● Prefer quick, nonpressure, noncompetitive instruction.

● Prefer instruction away from office.

● Prefer to be taught by experts not subordinates.

● Prefer not to learn new specialized jargon.

● Prefer building-block approach.

Figure 8-3. Keys to successful OA training for management.

feeling of control over the systems, imparting confidence in their new skills. To avoid frustration, they need to be gently guided, should help be needed. User-friendly features, such as extensive user prompts, will promote systems use by executives and professionals and encourage them to become more receptive to the training needed to learn how to use the equipment.

The training process is ultimately a behavior modifier. If management can be convinced that a system is a valuable tool for their work, they are likely to accept OA and its benefits for themselves and their organizations.

Behavior Modification

Instruction helps to change the individual by increasing his skills or knowledge. To be effective, the instruction must be integrated into the individual's present knowledge and incorporated into new concepts or understanding of job skills and performance. This new understanding prevents an office worker from transferring old behavior and work patterns to new equipment and systems. It is important that each person trained understand how the new equipment will aid in performing his tasks. If integration is not effective, the individual under pressure to meet job deadlines will not apply 'partially integrated' concepts but will stick to familiar methods to accomplish the work. Unused new concepts and methods tend, over time, to be forgotten or poorly applied.

Feedback during the instruction period helps the student accept the change as a positive measure for increasing productivity and work satisfaction. This encourages new ideas and creative use of new skills learned. In order to keep this momentum, it is important that management be aware of these new ideas and provide feedback as needed. Finally, behavior modification can only occur if the individual is open to change. Management must provide incentives and workers must see that the accomplishments of training contribute to job advancement and personal growth.

Curriculum Development

A strong training program requires good curriculum development. The development effort involves instructional design, training profiles, and feedback and evaluation.

Instructional Design

Successful instructional design concentrates on three basic questions. What are the course objectives in terms of learning desired? What activities and resources are to be used to achieve the objectives? What quality measurements are available to evaluate the learning?

The first step in design is listing the topics to be covered. These topics can be determined by conducting an analysis of the skills needed or that must be developed in the workforce, and by a detailed study of the workflow within an office. Skills analysis focuses on an individual's productivity, while workflow relates individual productivity to the overall office productivity. The topics outlined form the basis of various instructional modules which have their own set of objectives, skills to be taught, and evaluation techniques.

Analysis of new skills requires a comprehensive evaluation of an organization's immediate and long-term goals. The immediate goals depend on what OA is in use or will be implemented, while long-term goals dictate the evolution of skills needed to keep pace with the organization's push into OA. Workflow can be understood as an organization's operational solution to how it wishes to accomplish its work. Workflow forms the basis by which individual skills and overall productivity are related.

Once the topics are determined through needs evaluation, they are subdivided into smaller units of study. This teaching strategy is known as modular training. Each modular unit represents an independent entity that can be combined with related units to form the basis of customized instruction, according to the type of student and level of proficiency desired. In addition, each unit varies in length and complexity, allowing a mix-and-match approach to tailor instruction to the needs of the student. The most effective modules are those which are self-contained and presented in short sessions, allowing students to learn the material before going on to more difficult concepts. More complex modules can be organized to have predefined segments which gradually introduce difficult material, progressing from introductory concepts to advanced material, followed by continued training. One advantage of modular training is its versatility. Various training modules may be assembled and presented to different groups as dictated by their needs. Another advantage is that modular training can be the basis for self-paced learning.

- Determine topics for each unit of instruction.
- State goals and outline expected results.
- Establish process to measure results.
- Develop subject outline for each goal.
- Determine related instructional activities to support goals.
- Choose training materials.
- Develop evaluation tools to measure student progress.
- Revise and improve training unit as needed.

Figure 8-4. Checklist for successful instructional design.

- Self-contained.
- Limited to short sessions.
- Mastery-based with building block approach.
- Difficult material introduced gradually.
- Basis for self-paced learning.
- Allows customizing instruction to fit individual student needs.

Figure 8-5.   Checklist for effective modules.

Instructional design provides the framework for individual modules. In applying instructional design techniques to module development, one can follow several steps. First, the subset of topics in a unit is determined. Then the goals are stated for the unit, outlining the results expected and the means of measuring the results. Next, a subject outline is developed for each goal. Once an outline is developed, related instructional activities are determined to support the goals. To ensure that the information is accepted, these goals must be understood by the students. The chosen activities determine the type of instructional materials and the training resources needed. A pre-test will determine the student's present knowledge and skills as they relate to the goals of the unit. This pre-test is a time-saver, since it channels the student's efforts directly to the new material. Once the student has completed a unit, an evaluation must be designed that will compare the student's performance with the unit's stated goals. Interviews of students completing a unit provide valuable feedback that can be used to revise and improve a training unit. The first students using a module serve as a gauge for determining adequate training times needed to complete the unit.

Training Profiles

Designing good training programs also requires an understanding of the student's present skills and knowledge. A training profile is a written assessment of an individual student that details his past training, present knowledge, and potential. To create a training profile, tests and interviews can be conducted. These should be viewed as an opportunity for positive reinforcement, which allows students to understand the design of a training program and to accept its goals. A profile can also be used by the instructor to direct the student to the proper learning materials to reach a given level of competency.

TRAINING METHODS

During the instructional design process, several training methods can be chosen. Some of these methods include: lecture, self-study, one-on-one, programmed instruction, interactive medium, buddy system, and hands-on. Each of these methods has its own strengths and weaknesses which can be overcome by successfully combining and using them in a training program.

Lecture

This widely used, traditional classroom method is particularly effective for teaching concepts, giving general overview or observation, reinforcing concepts, and reviewing materials. Since a group of people may receive the same lecture at the same time, the costs may be lower. However, this method does not provide individual pacing or regular student support and feedback. Little time is available to give personal attention to students or to answer questions in order to clarify concepts.

Self-Study

This low-cost method, requiring little instructor time, is best used for highly motivated students. Adults who prefer self-directed study on a specific topic find this method the most suitable. Correspondence courses are a classic type of self-study. However, learning is usually done in a vacuum, giving little feedback to questions and increasing the possibility of misunderstanding of the subject matter. Self-study complements other methods such as one-on-one or computer-aided learning, which inherently have some form of monitoring and feedback of the student's progress.

One-On-One

One-on-one instruction is often considered the most effective method. Although costly because of the large amount of personalized attention the instructor gives the student, it is very effective in monitoring the student's progress, providing feedback, and customizing the learning process to the individual's needs.

Programmed Instruction

Programmed instruction or self-paced study is a step-by-step building block approach to learning that permits mastery of the subject at the individual's own pace. It initially has high development costs but, if properly designed, it has great potential as a training method. Since this method requires very little instructor intervention, it is important that the students be self-motivated to complete the program. Otherwise, alternatives must be available for those who do not respond to this method. One disadvantage is that immediate feedback is not often available, raising the possibility of misunderstanding of the material.

Interactive Medium

This method uses some form of interactive medium such as computer-aided or video-assisted learning to automate the programmed instruction concept. A mastery-based technique, it allows the students to set their own pace while receiving immediate feedback and reinforcement. Little instructor time is required and progress is automatically monitored. Because this method is machine- and software-dependent, some frustration can be experienced, especially if the student is unfamiliar with the computer terminal or equipment, or if the software lacks 'user-friendliness'. Program development and capital equipment costs can make this method prohibitively expensive.

Buddy System

A type of one-on-one method, the buddy system gives the more experienced or knowledgeable employee the responsibility of training another worker. This flexible method often occurs on an informal basis and can be effective in teaching new skills to others. This approach, however, does not guarantee quality instruction and is best-suited to a low turnover environment. It is a low-pressure method where the trainee learns by doing the actual work required and where work disruption is minimized. Advanced or continued training can be given as required. This method is more comfortable for some workers and can be very effective for motivated, interested individuals.

Hands-On

Any training can be supplemented and reinforced by 'hands-on' experience. Although careful monitoring is required of each student's progress, this method is considered a low-pressure type of experience where the individual can learn in a self-paced, independent mode. Students learn best by having an opportunity to practice before they must put their newly acquired skills to productive work. It reinforces the new skills and gives the students added confidence. However, it is important that adequate support materials such as workbooks and reference guides be provided to guide the student through the learning experience. This is a flexible method where the training sessions can be scheduled to the office and worker's convenience.

In summary, these are a variety of methods available for use in training. They can be applied independently or in combination, according to the goals of the training program. As the training function becomes more widely applied, other methods can be developed to meet the continuing needs of the organization.

INSTRUCTIONAL AIDS AND SUPPORT

Instructional aids are the supportive materials of a course. They may supplement or be the primary means by which instruction is delivered. These aids include instructor's or trainee's handbook, textbooks, practice exercise books, equipment reference manuals, programmed workbooks, lecture support aids such as slides and charts, and multimedia or computer-aided learning packages.

Instructional support deals with the various facets of training program management. It includes guidelines such as organization goals, program plans and procedures, course objectives, scheduling, and evaluation forms. This also refers to the obtaining of equipment, providing of facilities, and controlling of environmental factors such as lighting and noise.

Training Costs

Training costs are the sum total of personnel, equipment, facilities, and material costs over the lifespan of a training cycle. The total cost alone is not useful unless compared with various training alternatives and their impact on business return on investment. Several models exist to evaluate training alternatives.[21]

Determining the impacts on return on investment requires study of various soft costs and benefits and relating them to the costs of each training alternative. 'Soft' refers to items that one cannot quantify. Soft costs include the costs of not being trained, of poor training, absenteeism, lack of motivation, and misuse of skills. Soft benefits include increased productivity, employee satisfaction and growth, and reduced turnover. Only when training alternatives are compared with regard to soft costs and benefits can a decision be made in selecting the best one. It is possible that the most expensive training alternative could be the most desirable, if it has the greatest positive impact on the ROI. Soft costs and benefits ultimately come from the goals of the organization and the needs of its employees.

TRAINING RESOURCES

There are four primary types of training resources a business can use in setting or enhancing a program for its employees. These are vendor-supplied, in-house training, consultant-supplied, or a combination of any of these. In selecting the best resource for a particular training program, a business must be aware that each of these resources can have some drawbacks that might influence their training effectiveness.

Vendor Training

Vendor-supplied training historically has been the most widely used method of instruction during the implementation phase of new equipment. When the expensive systems were first introduced, vendors, eager to accommodate the buyer, made training readily available and included this service in the equipment costs. However, with the continual reduction of equipment costs, this expense became too burdensome for the vendors who, in turn, either limited training or charged a high fee. Today vendors provide either off-site, on-site, or pre-packaged, self-instruction training programs. Their instruction concentrates on the basics of their system, detailing how their system operates and what its features and limitations are. Advanced or special-applications training is available, but usually at a high cost.

Off-site vendor instruction, often done in a classroom environment, assures the least amount of interruption in office operations, provided that temporary replacements have been found for the absent trainees or work can continue without them. The instructional approach, usually 'canned', stresses basics and is not directed at specific applications. Costs resulting from traveling expenses, temporary replacements, and instruction time can be expensive if high turnover dictates the continual training of new employees. An off-site, unfamiliar environment can be stressful for some students or simply not the best environment for everyone. This, in turn, might affect their learning process. Vendor training, standardized in approach, can be unpredictable in results and effectiveness since student learning styles are not 'standardized'. Some of the learning styles used include one-to-one, small group, self-paced programmed instruction, or interactive computer-aided learning.

Vendor on-site training is usually conducted in a more personal manner. Trainees tend to be more receptive and less resistant to learning new skills in their own office environment. Instruction is generally conducted with small groups or on a one-on-one basis, making it less intimidating for the student. A 'friendly' learning experience, which is more applicable to a specific office environment, gives students more freedom to ask questions, and to be creative and more positive about learning new skills.

Self-paced instruction packages are becoming more attractive to equipment buyers, particularly for customers who lack sufficient resources for providing education for their employees, and for some this is a better approach. Vendors, recognizing the need for providing some training, sell these low-cost packages to cover the basics of their system. These 'pre-packaged programs', often developed by independent training houses, are primarily for in-house, self-paced instruction use. The materials include workbooks, systems manuals, training manuals supplemented with audio/visual, interactive computer-aided, or video-cassette/disc media. One of the more effective types is audio-cassette-directed learning in which the student 'walks through' instruction that can be very specific. In comparison with other types of vendor training, self-paced instruction is a very cost-effective method which allows the trainee to assimilate the material at his or her own learning speed. Although this might seem a time-consuming process, it does assure better retention of the material studied and gives an opportunity to review or reference as needed. One important requirement of this type of learning is a scheduled, uninterrupted period of study for the student. Motivated individuals may study during off hours, at home after work, and while commuting. Self-paced instruction works well where there is less pressure and the frustration level is low. Some drawbacks to this method include the difficulty in gauging training effectiveness, and the overly general approach, which makes it hard for people to actually apply what they are 'attempting' to learn. Over-reliance on this basic approach limits the usefulness of the equipment.

Wherever the training occurs, it is important that any instruction of the new system be very close to its implementation time. Periods of over a week might cause frustration and stress for the employee who is under pressure to remember and perform new tasks with the new complex equipment. Also, proper timing can prevent misconception and incorrect learning and use. Studies show that the sooner the actual 'hands-on' experience occurs, the better the retention of the new skills. Thus, the worker becomes more productive, experiencing greater satisfaction.

Vendor training has some disadvantages. It can be too general and not directly related to specific job tasks; it may lack sufficient means to monitor the student's progress, and it may dwell more on the operation of the system rather than relating the system to a particular office's application. Sensitive to these limitations, vendors are redirecting their emphasis in customer training by giving more personal attention to instruction and orientation, providing more teaching aids, and being more aware of the user's lack of understanding of technical jargon and system features.

If the organization lacks the internal resources to develop its own instruction, vendor training can be the cheapest route. Surveys demonstrate that when an organization decides to purchase a commercially available training package instead of developing one internally, the following are often used as the selection criteria: the vendor's ability to customize its training according to the buyer's unique needs; its ability to deliver a quality product in a timely manner; whether the vendor's resources are adequate to perform the job contracted; and whether this is the most cost-effective method.

In-House Training

The OA marketplace is also forcing companies to consider internally-developed or in-house training programs as a means of providing instruction and understanding of the new electronic systems. When OA equipment was first introduced, vendors, eager to sell their products, included extensive training as a selling point. Initially, these expensive systems hid the training costs as part of the sale price. As vendor training costs increased, pre-packaged, self-paced instruction was often the only economical method. More of the training burden was shifted to the end user.

Increased system features, allowing multifunction office applications, are also affecting the training function. In addition, improved communications between various types of equipment allow multivendor environments as each vendor strives to meet a particular need within the office. The end result of these trends is that the user must assume more of the training responsibility. In multivendor environments, the best each vendor can do is to provide adequate instruction for his system. Integrated systems training is not filled by other resources.

Many companies provide in-house training as a cost-effective alternative. They are discovering that external resources for instruction are often inadequate or too costly for their changing needs, even though staff attrition and the continual need for the skills upgrading of current employees requires some form of training. In-house instruction permits the custom designing of programs to meet specific organizational needs. It can be more easily revised and expanded on an ongoing, as-needed basis to meet growing requirements. This customized approach is cost-effective since students learn about an OA system within their employer's operational needs and apply their skills in less time. A company also saves on the costs of sending staff to vendor training sessions. In-house programs can save on the costs of training and documentation of new applications and help minimize system under-utilization. Finally, instruction can be flexibly scheduled to work around deadlines, and can be provided in an ongoing customized program.

To be effective, an in-house program must be fully supported and properly planned and managed. This includes providing the right people to develop and manage the program. It is also wise to visit other organizations with similar programs to gain from their experiences and avoid possible costly errors.

Once the commitment is made to use internal resources, an organization must be prepared to carry the costs involved in establishing such a program. Some of these costs include training staff salaries, productive work time lost due to instructional sessions of students and instructors, initial lower productivity with new skills because of individual learning curves, equipment and supplies' expenses, facilities maintenance costs, and supplementary resources such as commercial instructional packages or aids.

Human resources are crucial to the successful design and implementation of an in-house program. Training responsibility must be assigned carefully, using experienced, knowledgeable professionals skilled in curriculum design, management, and communication. These professionals can be part of administration, personnel, or a separate training and development department. The role of the in-house trainer includes interfacing with the vendor support team and systems users. The trainers must know the new system features and how they can be used to directly teach new skills for office functions. As the trainers become more skilled and knowledgeable about the systems, they act as a valuable resource for the evaluation and use of new hardware or software. With their expertise, they can train others who can assume the training responsibility where necessary.

The development of any successful internal training program relies on the training essentials that were outlined previously. Briefly, these essentials include learning/teaching concepts, training methods, instructional aids and support, and training costs. Learning/teaching concepts deal with ways that adults learn, how behavior can be modified, the importance of training profiles, and how instructional design can be used to develop courses. Training methods are various approaches for instructing students. Instructional aids and support refer to the various material used in the execution of a program and its management. Training costs are the considerations that must be made to evaluate the cost-effectiveness of training over its lifecycle.

In-house training can be expensive. If an organization attempts to shortcut the costs, several problems arise. Sometimes use is made of lead operators who are expected to provide training for others. This works only if they are relieved of their other responsibilities so they can function as trainers. Most companies are

Does the organization or company have a commitment to training?
Will it provide continuing support and resources for training?
In-house training will usually offer the following benefits:

- Multifunction training.
- More cost effective.
- Greater customization.
- Directly teach new skills.
- Offer more flexible scheduling.

Figure 8-6. Checklist for in-house training decisions.

reluctant to dedicate their best workers to training because productivity suffers. In other cases, low-cost programs often are not given in quiet facilities that foster the learning of material, which results in inadequate instruction and retention.

The need for in-house training will continue to grow. Multifunctional equipment will become more widespread in the office, forcing companies to develop instructional resources to ensure that full use is made of the equipment. In the end, this may be the most cost-effective alternative available.

Consultant-Supplied Resources

In-house programs may not be possible for various reasons. A firm may lack either people or money to provide such a program. Or a company may not want to commit resources to training, especially if instruction is needed infrequently. An organization may have several kinds of systems and want to provide integrated instruction on their use. A consultant can be the answer.

Consultants, because of their wide exposure to various systems, provide the expertise for an integrated approach to training. If their services are needed infrequently, they may be the most cost-effective method of providing instruction. Finally, consultants' work could be more useful since it is their job to understand the workings of a company and how OA can best be used.

Once a decision is made to use a consultant, several issues should be considered. These issues fall into three categories: evaluation, selection, and assessment.

Evaluating consultants requires consideration of several issues. The primary issue is the amount of money available for consulting services. Once this is determined, a decision can be made as to the type of consulting service desired, such as a large professional firm, an individual, specialized consulting, or broad-range consulting. When the type of consulting approach is selected, a company can then investigate the possible consulting resources. The initial selection of consultants should consider the following: the expertise and professional backgrounds of consultants and their previous work; what reasonable fee arrangements for work can be made; the time needed to complete the project; and if a written proposal can be obtained that clearly defines objectives and work to be done.

The final selection of a consultant depends on these additional points: how closely the submitted proposal meets the specified training requirements of the organization; studying each proposal to see if a consultant understands the requirements; what experience and knowledge are available to solve the instructional needs; if specific tasks and milestones are well specified; and what are the qualifications of the personnel who will actually do the work.

A consultant should be willing to provide a consulting contract that outlines an agreement of the services that will be performed and their completion dates.

After a consultant is retained, several factors can be used to assess the effectiveness of the work. One important factor is how well a company can apply the work in future applications. A good consultant attempts to provide a company with the information and work needed to proceed on its own, if required. The consultant does not make a client dependent on his services. Another factor is how effectively and timely the work was in meeting the goals of the proposal. The progress of the work should be clearly reported, listing not only accomplishments, but also problem areas that need more attention.

Well-qualified consultants benefit an organization and meet its instructional needs in several ways. Being outside an organization allows them to objectively understand the training requirements. Their experience with various OA environments provides more approaches to solving a training problem. Their judgments are less influenced by vendor claims and more by vendor results. Finally, an important aspect of their work is to train and develop others who then assume the teaching responsibility in the future.

Mixed Resources

An organization may find that the combination of its particular instructional needs and resources requires more than one of the three training resources. For example, a company may lack the understanding of how its multivendor equipment can best be used, though it has people skilled in the use of individual equipment. In this case, it could use a consultant who can provide the necessary understanding and integrated training needed. The company can then proceed from this base to provide an in-house training program, making use of the consultant's work. Or a company may wish to use vendor packages to provide basic instruction and develop an in-house program for advanced training.

Summary of Training Resources

Training resources continue to evolve as new products are introduced. Because of increased computing power, memory storage, and the development of new applications, future machines could provide their own instruction by possibly using voice-response and recognition. A projected scenario sees the development of interactive computers which can conduct conversations with users by means of verbal instructions and feedback, replacing the manuals and instruction now provided. Machines could adjust their level of instruction to meet the needs of the individual. This feature will have a positive effect on the acceptance and use of office systems.

TRAINING TECHNOLOGIES

Educational technology is also undergoing a revolution, with electronic advances providing more flexible alternatives to traditional educational approaches. Educational technology, as used here, refers to using any medium that complements or supplements the effective delivery of instruction. Just as OA seeks to increase productivity, so can these technologies increase the productivity of the educational process.

The wide use of OA devices, and the need for a continually trained staff, have forced business to seek out more cost-effective means of providing instruction. In today's environment, two conflicting needs arise. First, the need to train larger numbers of people for a given amount of resources, and, second, the need for individualized instruction.

One traditional approach to the first need is classroom instruction. Although viewed as a cost-effective method, it does not readily support individual learning differences in the student population, since neither time nor resources allow personal attention to students. Classroom instruction typically teaches a wide range of materials, requiring the student to selectively remember material in order to perform a certain task. Another approach is to provide individual tutors. This is an effective means of addressing personal learning styles, but does not handle more than a few students at a time.

An alternative approach is to allow technology to aid in the training process. Today, these include computer-aided learning (CAL), computer-managed instruction (CMI), authoring systems, video-assisted instruction, and generic courseware. The technologies presented are the major ones in widespread use. Each has advantages and disadvantages that may make one more applicable for a particular organization's training program. It is best not to wait for the 'ultimate' technology to appear, because the advantages and benefits of using what currently exists would be lost.

Computer-Aided Learning

Computer-aided learning (CAL), also known as computer-based training (CBT) or computer-aided instruction (CAI), is a process by which instructional material is delivered by a computer. The essential element of this medium is its interactive nature. The computer responds to the students by taking their input to determine the next step in the lesson. The teaching process is one of continuous interactive dialog that includes questions, student input, evaluation, and progression that leads to mastery of the topic studied.

A major advantage of CAL is that it is mastery based. CAL provides students with patient, individual instruction, which advances them to more difficult material only after adequate learning is demonstrated. CAL also prevents the students from wasting time on familiar material. Giving the students a sense of control of the process contributes to a better learning experience, reinforced through instant feedback and active involvement.

CAL provides for distributed education. It can be used on a central computer accessed over a network, or it can be used on individual microcomputers that are placed at various company locations with course materials delivered to the site. In both cases, course materials are readily available, allowing flexible scheduling of instruction and savings in lost time from the job and travel expenses.

When considering CAL's advantages, it must be noted that one possible drawback is the initial high cost of developing courseware and providing hardware to implement this technique.

CAL can be adopted to most training needs and is more cost effective than other methods if the following guidelines are considered:

(1) *Demonstrated cost effectiveness* Because CAL often has high initial costs, it is important to apply it to areas where increased learning and retention can directly contribute to improved productivity. Long range planning and well defined goals for training must be clearly stated to assure the best return on investment.

(2) *Stable course content* Though CAL can adapt to changes in subject matter, it is important that course material content be stable ubject matter, it is important that course material content be stable for a long period of time in order to be cost effective. CAL would not be justified in areas that are subject to constant revision, such as law.

(3) *Wide applicability* CAL is often too expensive to justify for a small group of users since it is more cost effective when applied to a large user population. Its best applications are found in environments subject to rapid employee turnover, large expected employee growth, or continuing need for education as business requirements change.

(4) *Well designed courseware* User friendliness and instructional design quality of the courseware assure less user frustration and better use of the system. Course content is broken down into logical units that ease student mastery of the subject. Responses to student inputs are logical and consistent. Recording and evaluation of students' progress should be provided in order to determine the type of additional training needed. A technical expert is advisable to aid in the development of courseware that truly meets users' needs.

Traditionally, CAL has only been available on mainframes that were accessed by special terminals such as Control Data's PLATO or IBM's IIPS (Interactive Instructional Presentation System). Since it was difficult, costly, and time-consuming to develop custom software, users were forced to accept what was provided. However, the microcomputer brought a change to this situation.

With the application of the microcomputer, it was possible to design custom

- Promotes mastery-based instruction.
- Provides for distributed education.
- Allows student to progress at own speed.
- Allows instruction to be tailored to student's needs.
- Gives students a sense of control over the learning process.
- Allows instant feedback and active involvement with learning.
- Allows flexible scheduling of instruction.
- Allows use of microcomputer technology, as well as mainframes
- Gives students familiarity with successful use of terminals and computers.

Figure 8-7. CAL advantages.

CAL. This allowed flexibility for courseware development, course scheduling, and portability. Also, the costs of providing instruction decrease as hardware costs decline. When several microcomputers are available, it is possible for one to fail and not completely halt training. Many users prefer microcomputers because it gives them a feeling of control of the system. Gradually, more courseware is becoming available for either generic applications or special purpose training. Even PLATO is being expanded to run separately on a microcomputer. Furthermore, as the price of microcomputers declines, and the courseware increases, one machine can serve a wider audience for less cost.

A 'hidden' advantage to CAL is that it allows the user to become familiar with terminal-based interaction, either from a terminal connected to a mainframe or to a microcomputer. Gradually, as users become more comfortable with using computer-based technology in a learning mode, those skills directly contribute to improving their performance. Instruction can be made less boring by using a microcomputer that provides sound effects and graphics. This prevents CAL from becoming just an electronic page-turning mechanism.

A recent *Training Magazine* survey indicated that of those people questioned, 20% are using computers as a training resource. Furthermore, 60% of the respondents, who presently did not use computers, expected to do so within the next five years.[26]

The key to CAL's effectiveness lies in the development of user-friendly systems, immediately comprehended by students without extensive preparation. CAL designers should incorporate good instructional design principles and human factors engineering into courses to promote acceptance of the material and the medium.

Computer-Managed Instruction (CMI)

Computer-managed instruction (CMI) is the application of the computer to track student progress and mastery of course material. It controls the pace of instruction the student receives and provides tests to assure that mastery has been achieved. Testing is tailored to a given course's material and also can be extended to cover previously learned subjects. It is used as a tool to evaluate and guide the student's progress. Based on the information gathered through CMI, a training coordinator can make suggestions for remedial or additional instruction. Finally, CMI can be used to identify learning styles, as evaluated by the results of tests based on a particular learning technique.

Authoring Systems

An authoring system is a software system which a courseware designer uses to create an interactive CAL program. The computer searches and retrieves certain segments of video or text material. Presently, it cannot replace formal instructional design but can only facilitate its implementation. There are two types of authoring systems. One type is controlled by menu selection that does not require the learning of a 'programming language'. The designer chooses 'canned' functions from the menu and enters the required text. This easy-to-learn menu system allows the rapid creation of CAL courseware. The other type makes use of an authoring programming language. Its main advantage is the flexibility and power that it gives the courseware designers since they are not restricted to predefined functions which only partially meet their needs. The major disadvantage is the time required to learn the language and the extra time needed to program a CAL session.

Video-Assisted Instruction

Video-assisted instruction makes use of videotape or videodisk technologies for programmed instruction. Both devices provide high-quality color pictures, either still or moving, with sound. Both playback 30 frames (pictures) per second for 30 minutes of total playing time amounting to some 54 000 total frames. They differ in their method of information access, flexibility, and ability to be interfaced with a computer system.

Videotape players are the less expensive of the two devices. To be useful a videotape player must have the ability to record frame numbers so that, during fast-forward or rewind, a specific frame of video can be found. Normally, this is done using one of the two audio tracks to record the frame number. If course materials change frequently, videotape instruction is a better medium than videodisk, since a videotape can be edited, rerecorded, and reassembled. To accommodate changes for videodisk courses, a new master must be produced costing several thousand dollars. Videotape is also preferred in situations where course material is presented in a sequential fashion, as in a lecture.

Videodisk players, though more expensive than videotape players, have several major advantages. Microprocessors with small amounts of memory are incorporated into the videodisk player, allowing for some interactive programming of material. Videodisk players provide rapid access of videoframes while videotape often requires several minutes to search for a video frame near the end of the tape. This is especially critical when interactive instruction is required. Videodisk provides the students with the ability to vary the speed and order of course material to fit their individual learning pace. Generally, if the instructional material is fixed and if more than 75 copies are needed, videodisk is the cheaper alternative.

With the introduction of personal computers, video-assisted instruction and CAL have merged to form a very powerful educational tool. Instead of textual material appearing on the terminal screen, it is now possible to have color video, both stills or moving picture with sound, to introduce concepts. All of the advantages of CAL are retained, with the added advantage of being able to present either video, graphics, sound, or any combination to introduce or reinforce a concept. By use of pre-tests, the videodisk/computer can determine which portions of videodisk material the student must cover. This allows efficient use of resources and customizes the training material. For reinforcement of vital concepts and skills, videodisk/computer can be programmed to review only those segments that are critical, but infrequently used. Because of its versatility, the videodisk/computer's applications are limited only by the trainer's technical skills and creativity.

A possible future application for CAL would make use of a touch-sensitive screen to input user responses to questions, eliminating the need for keyboard input. This would differ from input by a light pen on a computer screen, since the users would be answering directly on a video monitor by touching a particular section.

Generic Courseware

Generic courseware simulates an electronic system by allowing a given piece of hardware to assume the characteristics of several related pieces of equipment, such as word processor keyboards. This allows concepts to be taught, instead of specific vendor-dependent functions. Since it is likely that an organization will have a variety of hardware, this method allows for cross-training of skills transferable to several types of equipment. It also encourages reinforcement of skills through hands-on experience. Learning time is reduced since the student concentrates on the concepts and procedures, rather than on equipment details.

CONCLUSIONS

Office technology is advancing in both computing and communications; this will have an impact on training needs and directions. Computing resources, including mainframes and microcomputers, will become more powerful, allowing more functions to be performed. At the same time, communications will improve, allowing different machines to understand each other. Applications will multiply which will require even more training. Future office workers will be more familiar with computers through home or school exposure. Training will be less directed to teaching fundamentals and overcoming resistance. Instead, instruction will emphasize understanding of office procedures and applications.

Training technologies are also advancing, making it important to keep abreast of the latest developments. One important resource is a local library/information center, which can provide access to technical literature and perform on-line literature searches on subjects of interest. Some key instructional technology sources include these periodicals: *Training*, *Training and Development Journal*, and *Educational Technology*. General information on office automation can be found in such titles as *Office Administration and Management*, *Computer Decisions*, *The Office*, *Computerworld*, and *Personal Computing*.

Training is the key to successful office automation. To insure success it is important that organizations be committed to training. The office environment is continually changing, and this will force some form of training in order to use electronic technologies. These technologies will not be readily accepted by users unless they are provided with training resources. As organizations become committed to training, their experience can be a valuable resource for developing new instructional approaches to meet changing office systems applications.

REFERENCES AND SUGGESTED READINGS

1. Abraham, Steven M.: Impact of automated office systems on the productivity of managers and professionals. In *1981 Office Automation Conference Digest*, AFIPS, Arlington, Virginia, pp. 165–175, 1981.
2. Baumbardner, Mary: Productivity improvement for office systems. *Journal of Systems Management*, 12–15, August 1981.
3. Bejar, Isaac I.: Videodiscs in education. *Byte*, 78–102, June 1982.
4. Billadeau, Thomas R.: Word processing training: Alternative approaches. In *Datapro Office Automation Solutions*, Datapro, Delran, New Jersey, pp. A37–200–201 to A37–200–206, 1980.
5. Brown, James W., Norberg, Kenneth D., and Srygley, Sara K.: Designing instructional systems. In Administering Educational Media: Instructional Technology and Library Services, McGraw-Hill, New York, pp. 125–139, 1972.
6. Carrell, Patricia: School days. *Computerworld—Special Issue on Office Automation*, 70–74, December 1, 1982.
7. Computerized training may finally be about to take off. *Business Week*, 88, March 28, 1983.
8. Connor, Ursula: Success of office automation depends on user acceptance, not high technology. *Computerworld*, 46–47, September 28, 1981.
9. Conroy, Thomas R., and Bieber, Jacque: Educating the manager to use new office technology. *Administrative Management*, 39–41, 85, November 1981.
10. Cushing, David: Can training unlock the potentials of office automation? *Training*, 22–31, July 1981.
11. Gardner, David W.: For executives, a boom in computer education. *Dun's Business Month*, 113–114, March 1983.
12. Fauley, Franz: When to use CAI in training. *Training*, 82–84, January 1981.
13. Friedman, Selma: Tools for training users of automated equipment. *Administrative Management*, 38–41, 56, July 1982.
14. Gaffney, Carol T.: Selling the office internally. In *1981 Office Automation Conference Digest* AFIPS, Arlington, Virginia, pp. 127–131, 1981.

15. Garon, Jacques T.: A stitch in time ... Feasibility Study: II. *Computerworld—Special Issue on Office Automation*, 21–27, September 29, 1982.
16. Guiliano, Vincent E.: The hidden productivity factor. *Telephony*, 30–36, 79, July 21, 1980.
17. Giuliano, Vincent E.: The mechanization of office work. *Scientific American*, 148–164, September, 1982.
18. Goldfield, Randy J.: Training for the office of tomorrow. *Computer Decisions*, 66, 68, May 1981.
19. Heller, Dorothy K.: Training is missing link in office-computer success. *Infoworld*, 17, 21, December 14, 1981.
20. Herrmann, Ned: The creative brain. *Training and Development Journal*, 11–16, October 1981.
21. Kearsley, Greg, and Compton, Terry: Assessing costs, benefits and productivity in training systems. *Training and Development Journal*, 52–61, January, 1981.
22. Kirk, John: Training at the management level. *Computer Decisions*, 74, 77, 228, September 1982.
23. Kleffman, Roger W.: Modular training—a new emphasis. In *AFIPS Spring Joint Computer Conference, 1972*, AFIPS, Arlington, Virginia, pp. 69–75, 1972.
24. Larkin, Marilynn: Hands-on training gets nod over 'conceptual'. *Infosystems*, 98–99, January 1983.
25. Lashbrook, Velma J.: New training programs: to buy or to build. *Training*, 52–55, November 1981.
26. Lee, Chris: Adding the new technology to your training repertoire. *Training*, 20–26, April 1982.
27. Lippitt, Gordon L.: Criteria for selecting, evaluating and developing consultants. *Training and Development Journal*, 24–31, June 1981.
28. Marcus, M. Lynne: The new office: more than you bargained for. *Computerworld—Special Issue on Planning Office Strategies*, 34, 38–40, 44, February 23, 1983.
29. Marx, Raymond J., and Wicks, Fredrick W.: Videodisc: Novelty or revolutionary medium? *Training and Development Journal*, 67–70, August 1981.
30. Matthies, Leslie: How to pick the top training methods. In Association for Systems Management (Ed.), *Peopleware in systems*, Association for Systems Management, Cleveland, Ohio, pp. 77–81, 1976.
31. McSween, Jua: Developing a word processing training program. in *Electronic Office: Management and Technology Section 002.0001.006* (17p), Auerbach, Pennsauken, New Jersey, 1982.
32. Menashian, Lena: Continuing education resources for electronic-based, high-technology R&D professionals. Part one: an overview. *Educational Technology*, 11–20, November 1981.
33. Menashian, Lena: Continuing education resources for electronic-based, high-technology R&D professionals. Part two: corporate programs. *Educational Technology*, 12–17, December 1981.
34. Noeth, Merrilly: Operator training in a multivendor environment: options. In *Electronic Office: Management and Technology, Section 002.0001.010* (14p), Auerbach, Pennsauken, New Jersey, 1982.
35. Poppel, Harvey L.: Knowledge worker performance: the missing link. In *1981 Office Automation Conference Digest*, AFIPS, Arlington, Virginia, pp. 41–44, 1981.
36. Poppel, Harvey L.: Who needs the office of the future? *Harvard Business Review*, 146–155, November–December 1982.
37. Rosenberg, Marc J.: The ABCs of ISD (Instructional Systems Design). *Training and Development Journal*, 44–50, September 1982.
38. Schwartz, Marc D.: Interactive video: tape or disc? *Educational and Industrial TV*, 68–70, December 1981.

39. Selden, Paul H.: How to avoid the headaches of CAI. *Training*, 26–32, September 1981.
40. Smith, George W.: Got a question? Just touch the screen! *Bell Laboratories Record*, 206–213, October 1982.
41. Weinstein, Laurence M., and Kasl, Elizabeth Swain: How the training dollar is spent. *Training and Development Journal*, 90–96, October 1982.
42. Young, Richard T.: New training, work analysis methods needed to manage office of future. *Industrial Engineering*, 66–68, July 1982.
43. Zembe, Ron, and Zembe, Susan: Thirty things we know for sure about adult learning. *Training*, 45–52, June 1981.

Advances in Office Automation, Vol 1
Edited by Karen Takle Quinn
© 1985 Wiley Heyden Ltd.

Chapter 9

ELECTRONIC MAIL

Raymond R. Panko

University of Hawaii

INTRODUCTION

Now that word processing is entering its mature phase, users are beginning to ask 'what comes next?' For many firms, the answer is electronic mail. After producing a document electronically, why deliver it by post or even courier? Why not deliver it electronically?

The biggest stumbling block for electronic mail in the past has been cost. A user could expect to pay $1.00 to $3.00 for each message sent, and this was a heavy premium to pay for rapid delivery.

But costs are falling rapidly, and by the late 1980s several forms of electronic mail should be *cheaper* than postage. For some companies, electronic mail is already cheaper than postage. Hewlett–Packard, for instance, sends more than 25 million messages each year over its internal message network, and the cost is under five cents per message. Most large organizations, in fact, can now build electronic message systems that are cost competitive with postage. As costs plummet, electronic mail should grow rapidly.

Even today, electronic mail is a healthy industry. As shown in Table 9-1, 750 million electronic messages were sent in the United States in 1979.[1] This represented one billion dollars in annual revenues. Traffic is growing very rapidly, but costs are falling, so revenues are growing more slowly than traffic.

Electronic mail still has a long way to go. Table 9-2 is taken from a large survey of corporations by Mackintosh International and Communications Studies and Planning, Limited. This shows that even in Germany, where electronic mail is developed, only 4% of the mail in the organizations surveyed was handled electronically.

Another problem, besides cost, has been the diversity of technologies available to electronic mail users. As shown in Table 9-1, electronic mail is really a grab bag of delivery technologies. Generally speaking, terminals in one category cannot talk to terminals in another. Even within a category, standardization is sometimes poor.

This diversity means that whatever alternative a corporation chooses may lock it into a technology that makes communication difficult with some users. Even

TABLE 9-1

Electronic mail traffic in 1979 (millions of messages)[1]

Electronic mail category	Traffic
Facsimile	350
Telex and TWX	128
Private teletypewriter networks	100
Electronic message systems	66
Telegraph	45
Mailgram	40
Communicating word processors	20
Voice message systems	1
Total	750

Note: The Yankee Group uses the term 'computer based message systems' instead of 'electronic message systems'.

TABLE 9-2

Total daily mail volume in four countries (millions of items)[2]

Category	France	Fed. Repub. Germany	U.K.	U.S.
Total	23.6	24.7	24.0	146.8
Facsimile	0.03	0.03	0.04	NA
Telex	0.32	0.91	0.48	1.0*
Intraorganizational	3.1	1.76	2.28	41.1

NA: Not available.
* Western Union Telegraph Company estimate.

within a firm, communication may be difficult, because most firms already have several kinds of electronic mail systems. So in selecting technologies, firms must assess the technologies already being used by frequent communication partners.

Another consideration in selecting technologies is that different electronic mail tools offer different functions. Facsimile, for instance, can transmit logos, graphics, and signatures as well as text. Electronic message systems, in turn, often have desk-top terminals used directly by managers and professionals. The characteristics of the various electronic mail technologies are discussed in some detail below. On the whole, comparing electronic mail technologies is like comparing apples, oranges, and box cars.

Fortunately, a good deal of progress is now being made in the standards area. As discussed at the end of this chapter, many electronic mail terminals from different categories should be able to 'interwork', that is, exchange messages nicely, before the end of the 1980s.

Sophisticated electronic mail systems, of course, will be most attractive to larger firms, especially those with extensive intracompany traffic which can be easily standardized. The Mackintosh/CSP study[2] found that 2% of U.S. organizations send 78% of all intracompany mail, while 55% send no intracompany mail at all. During the next few years, electronic mail should grow increasingly segregated. For large companies, we should see a trend toward corporate-wide integrated systems, so that information can flow from any part of the firm to any other. These systems will be complex and will represent major investments. This chapter focuses on the emergence of these advanced systems. In small companies and scattered offices in large organizations, however, we should continue to see brisk sales in 'convenience' devices such as Group II facsimile and Telex using very low cost terminals.

PUBLIC RECORD SERVICES

Historically, the telecommunications industry has distinguished sharply between voice communications and record communications. Record communication, as the name suggests, involves the delivery of printed messages. The telegraph, a record service, was the first form of electronic mail, but its more sophisticated successors, including Telex and Teletex, have made the telegram an anachronism that is only used today under special circumstances, usually as a delivery system of last resort.

Record services are normally public services, offered by common carriers and available to all users. In the United States public record services are offered primarily by the Western Union Telegraph Company, but new regulations have recently opened the U.S. market to other competitors. In Canada, the public telephone system competes with CNCP Telecommunications. In most other countries, a postal telephone and telegraph (PTT) monopoly controls public record services.

The telephone cut deeply into the record market, first for local calls and later for long distance and international calls. Yet public record services have continued to grow, albeit slowly, because of their ability to deliver printed records of the message. This has been especially important for international communication, where translation is needed. The 'hot line' between the White House and the Kremlin is a record communications line.

The Telegraph

Samuel F. B. Morse established the first telegraph line in 1844, thanks to a $30 000 grant from the U.S. Congress. Morse and his backers immediately tried to sell the telegraph to the U.S. Post Office, but the Post Office declined, seeing little future for the new technology.

During the next few years, the telegraph grew rapidly. At first there were many vendors, but after World War II, only Western Union Telegraph Company (WUTCO) and AT&T continued to compete in the United States. In 1971,

AT&T was forced to sell its TWX service (discussed below) to WUTCO, and WUTCO became a de facto monopoly for domestic record services in the United States. In most other countries, the PTTs have monopolies in the telegraph and later record services.

Record communications between the U.S. and other countries have been handled by the international record carriers (IRCs), including Western Union International, RCA Global Communications, ITT, TRT, and several other firms. Western Union International is a spin-off from WUTCO. When WUTCO acquired its last telegraph competitor, the U.S. government allowed it to do so only if it sold off its international operations. WUTCO and WUI are entirely separate companies, although both refer to themselves, vaguely, as 'Western Union'.

The Federal Communications Commission has recently reopened competition in both the domestic and international markets. WUTCO is likely to compete in the international markets soon, and a number of firms have already opened Telex networks (discussed below) in the U.S. market. Foreign governments, who have been used to dealing with a few stable IRCs, have protested strongly over some of the U.S. Federal Communications Commission's policies, particularly its free-wheeling pricing policies. In the past, international record traffic has been used in most countries to subsidize internal communications.

The telegram is a public-office-to-public-office service. When you want to send a message, you deliver it to a public telegram office or, in some cases, phone it in. Your message is then transmitted to a public office near the receiver, from which it is messengered or delivered via a telephone call. This is obviously an awkward service. Why can't companies have terminals right on their premises for sending and delivery? This was the idea behind the next step beyond the telegram, the public teletypewriter network.

Public Teletypewriter Networks

In 1931, AT&T established TWX, the Teletypewriter Exchange Service. TWX customers leased teletypewriter terminals that had regular typewriter keyboards plus a few special keys to control transmission. An outgoing message was usually prepared on punched paper tape before the transmission, then fed into the terminal during transmission. The receiving terminal printed the message on paper and usually also punched it onto paper tape, in case the printer jammed. Figure 9-1 shows a typical TWX terminal.

A nationwide TWX network similar to the telephone network but supporting much lower transmission speeds was also established. Over this network, any TWX terminal can dial any other. TWX is a circuit switched network. This means that the receiving terminal has to be free before a connection was made, just as in telephone calling. If the called terminal is busy, the sender has to try again later.

TWX was introduced in the U.S. and Canada. In Europe, however, a similar

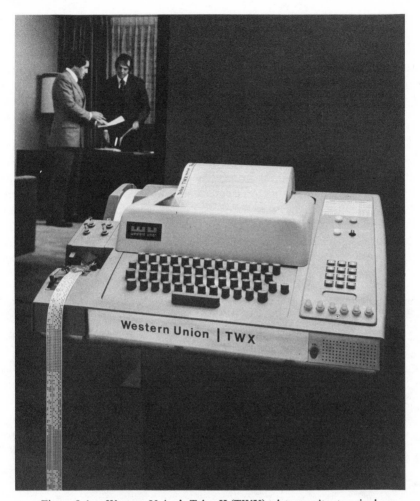

Figure 9-1.   Western Union's Telex II (TWX) teletypewriter terminal.

but incompatible system evolved, called Telex. Telex transmits messages at 50 bits per second, which was similar to TWX's speed and was roughly the limit of mechanical receiving systems at the time of its creation. It uses the limited Baudot code (CCITT Alphabet No. 2), which uses only 5 bits to represent each character. In 1958, WUTCO introduced Telex service in the United States. CNCP Telecommunications brought Telex to Canada.

When the Consultative Committee on International Telegraphy and Telephony (CCITT) settled upon Telex as the international standard, TWX's days as a thriving communications medium were numbered. Although TWX is still used in the U.S. and Canada, Telex has become the dominant international teletypewriter service.

Most Telex users send messages only occasionally, so they have a strong desire to keep terminal costs low. These users typically employ terminals that have changed only slightly since the earliest days of Telex and TWX, for example still using punched paper tape. New low-cost terminals with more sophistication are appearing, however, such as 3M's WhisperWriter (Figure 9-2). These cost about $1000 and have electronic memories and editing capabilities. Even these, however, are having a hard time against very low cost terminals based on ancient technology.

High-volume users, however, usually have more expensive terminals, often communicating word processors with optional Telex modules that allow them to act like Telex terminals during transmission. Even when a company uses communicating word processors (discussed below) as its main electronic mail network, it usually connects to Telex as well, to send messages to other companies.

Most users pay three separate charges for Telex. First, they must purchase, rent, or lease the terminal. Second, there is a flat monthly service charge for each

Figure 9-2.   3M's new Whisper Writer Package 83 Telex Communication Terminal connects to F1/F2 Telex lines and offers such features as keyboard dialing, automatic case shifting of figures and letters and 4K semiconductor memory.

terminal (usually called the access fee). Finally, there is a transmission fee for each message sent. The transmission fee may vary with distance, but the trend is toward a flat rate per minute or fractional minute, regardless of distance, at least for domestic (intracountry) transmission. Obviously, estimating the cost per message in a multitier pricing environment can be difficult, but a typical price per message is around $1.50.

Teletex

For many years, the technology of Telex has been recognized to be obsolete. During the 1970s, efforts to develop a next generation service developed momentum, and in 1980 the CCITT formally adopted standards for a new service, Teletex. The International Telecommunications Union, CCITT's parent body, accepted the standard in its 1980 Plenary Assembly. Telex will remain in place, but Teletex offers a higher level of service. Telex and Teletex are to be interconnected.

Teletex operates at 2400 bits per second—about 50 times faster than Telex. Calling times and the labor to handle calls are slashed from minutes to seconds.

The Teletex terminal is a communicating word processor, with full text-editing capabilities. In fact, most terminals are likely to be commercial word processors with optional Teletex modules. The Teletex system assumes that messages consist of one or more pages, either the $8\frac{1}{2}''$ by $11''$ pages popular in the U.S. or the A4 pages popular in Europe. Teletex uses a 7-bit extended ASCII code, which has a rich character set with over 300 characters for European languages, punctuation marks, monetary symbols, and transmission control codes.

A Teletex terminal can receive incoming messages even when it is being used to compose outgoing messages. This is obviously a major benefit if the terminal is heavily used. Teletex is often called a 'memory-to-memory' system, because delivery does not depend upon what the keyboard, screen, and other devices are doing.

Teletex was created within the ISO Reference Model of Open Systems architecture for designing standards. Specifically, the Teletex standard has two layers, corresponding reasonably well to the fifth (session) and sixth (presentation) layers of the ISO architecture.

For lower-layer service, the Teletex system will probably use X.25 or other existing standards. User groups and standards agencies, in turn, can design 7th layer (applications) protocols that incorporate Teletex for message transmission.

The Teletex standard involves automatic 'hand shaking' among terminals. When a session is established or a message transmission is begun, the two terminals first talk to each other, determining which optional features the other has, then negotiate the features that will be used during the session or message transmission. (Several messages, each with different requirements, may be sent during a session.) An example of information that must be determined during hand shaking is the available memory capacity of the receiving unit.

Teletex has been implemented by several European PTTs. Several companies, including WUTCO, have announced that they will introduce Teletex in the United States.

Private Teletypewriter Networks

A number of large companies with many sites have found that they can build their own internal teletypewriter networks for a fraction of what it would cost to use Telex.

Many of these private networks are Telex clones, using the same types of terminals as Telex and giving the same kind of service.

Other private teletypewriter networks are extremely sophisticated, using intelligent terminals and minicomputer switches. The Hewlett–Packard system, mentioned at the beginning of this chapter, is such an advanced system.

A company using private teletypewriter delivery normally leases transmission lines from a common carrier, then buys or rents terminals, multiplexers, and switches from a variety of vendors. Sometimes, a company will hire a third party to engineer the system, purchase the necessary components, and perhaps even manage the system on an ongoing basis.

For medium size companies that cannot afford to build their own networks, an alternative is a shared network, in which a number of companies share the use and cost of a system but still use it only for intracompany message delivery. WUTCO has a public shared service, InfoCom.

In contrast to electronic message systems, which are discussed below, private teletypewriter terminals are terminal-to-terminal systems, and terminals are not spread throughout general office areas, as they are in EMS.

Private teletypewriter networks are normally used mostly for sending sales orders, manufacturing information, and other information that is sent in business forms when postal delivery is used. Often, this information must be keyed into a computer after it is received, so a number of advanced private teletypewriter networks allow messages to be sent directly to computers. In such cases, the distinction between a private teletypewriter network and a transaction-oriented electronic data processing system becomes very tenuous.

Enter the U.S. Postal Service

The United States Postal Service has long regarded electronic mail as a potent competitor that could divert its most profitable traffic, first class mail, and so amplify its chronic deficit problems.

Rather than be left out, the USPS has made a number of tentative forays into electronic mail. The first was Mailgram, which it established in 1971 as a joint service with the Western Union Telegraph Company.

The sender delivers a Mailgram message to WUTCO in one of several ways, including phoning it in to WUTCO or sending it via Telex or TWX (which WUTCO now calls Telex II).

WUTCO then transmits the message to one of several post offices with special printing equipment, ordinarily the one that is nearest to the receiver's address. The message is then printed, stuffed into a special Mailgram envelope, then delivered with the next day's mail.

Mailgram combines electronic long distance transmission with the universal local delivery capacity of the USPS. The cost of a Mailgram is about half way between the cost of a letter and the cost of a telegram.

In January 1982, the USPS opened a similar service called Electronic Computer-Originated Mail (E-COM). In contrast to Mailgram, E-COM is operated entirely by the USPS.

While Mailgram will deliver a single message, E-COM will only process large batches of messages. Each 'input' must generate messages to at least 200 separate addresses. E-COM, furthermore, *requires* electronic input. Another restriction is that text must be limited to two pages, with 43 lines on the first page and 50 lines on the second. E-COM only has 25 serving post offices at present, and delivery may take two days.

The good news about E-COM is its attractive price of only $0.26 for a one-page letter or $0.31 for a two-page letter. Although there are other fees, the E-COM Service is attractive when compared with other bulk mailing services.

E-COM offers a number of service options. The simplest way of using E-COM is to send a stream of individually-addressed letters. You can also send a 'common text message', broadcasting the same message to many addresses. Third, you can send 'text insert messages', which allow you to insert one up to 36 different pieces of text in various parts of the body, thus allowing limited individualization. E-COM does not yet allow fully individualized inserts, for example putting the amount owed by a particular person in their bill.

The USPS did no marketing research before setting up E-COM,[3] and initial volumes were only five percent of the volumes forecast. Since the USPS has virtually unlimited borrowing capacity, massive losses can be sustained for long periods of time, but the future of E-COM is uncertain in its current form.

In addition, several companies are likely to compete with E-COM if it is successful. Tymnet has already begun a similar service, TYME-GRAM, which began operation before E-COM with 30 service centers.

The USPS, despite potential difficulties with E-COM, is looking beyond its current service to its successor, EMSS (Electronic Message Service System). EMSS would aim for next day service for 95% of all messages entered by 5.00 pm. Ninety service centers have been proposed for the initial offering.

FACSIMILE

In record services, each character in the message is translated into a binary code, usually the Baudot or ASCII codes. The encoded message is then transmitted to the receiving unit, where it is decoded, and the message is printed or stored in memory.

Figure 9-3.   How facsimile works. The page to be sent is scanned left to right, top to bottom. There are usually 64 to 200 scan lines per inch vertically and 64 to 200 dots (pixels) per inch horizontally.

   In facsimile, the page to be sent is scanned from left to right, top to bottom, as shown in Figure 9-3. The light/dark areas encountered during the scan are converted into electrical signals, which are transmitted to the receiving unit. The receiver then reproduces the original light/dark pattern on a new sheet of paper.

   A major advantage of facsimile is its ability to transmit logos, graphics, signatures, and other images, not just text. In some applications, this makes facsimile the only possible choice in electronic mail.

   The disadvantage of facsimile is its relatively long transmission time. A page of text will hold about 250 words. In a teletypewriter code that uses 10 bits per character, a page represents about 15 000 bits. At 2400 bits per second, the transmission time is about six seconds.

   In facsimile, however, a page requires a much longer transmission time, because efficient five- or ten-bit character codes are not used. All of the information picked up during the scan is transmitted. For most facsimile machines, transmission takes two to six minutes per page, and the image quality is only moderate. Even the newest digital facsimile devices, which are still quite expensive, typically require a 20- to 40-second transmission time per page after doing extensive compression. Facsimile transmission is normally done over ordinary direct dial telephone lines or leased lines. When long distance transmission is involved, the relatively long delivery times of facsimile translate into high costs.

   Facsimile was first demonstrated in 1843, but it was not until the 20th century that facsimile became economically viable. Even then, 'fax' was only used for special purposes, such as transmitting newspaper photographs or delivering weather maps. In 1966, Xerox introduced a low-cost 'Telecopier' originally engineered by Magnavox. This machine used modern solid state technology instead of vacuum tubes and was much easier and more pleasant to use than older facsimile machines.

   In 1968, the Carterphone decision forced AT&T to permit the low-cost attachment of facsimile and other non-Telco devices to the telephone network. Before then, AT&T had required the use of expensive connection devices. Even after Carterphone, AT&T installed low-cost attachment, but by the mid-1970s, facsimile was well launched, as shown in Table 9-3. The revenue figures shown in the table

TABLE 9-3
Growth in facsimile sales[4]

Year	Sales ($ millions)
1973	11.8
1974	16.4
1975	15.6
1976	16.9
1978	56.7
1979	107.5
1980	123.6

only represent terminal rentals, leases, and purchases. Users spend about as much on transmission charges as they do on terminal rentals.

Standards

Although many vendors did follow the Xerox/Magnavox specifications, quite a number did not, and among the early machines, compatibility problems were extensive.

Because of the importance of facsimile in communications, the CCITT has developed a set of international facsimile standards. So far, it has defined three separate standards, to handle machines in different performance ranges. It is likely to create more standards in the future, as technology evolves.

Its Group I standard was created for terminals that can transmit a page in six minutes over ordinary telephone lines. This Group I standard was roughly built around the original Xerox specification plus the specifications of 3M machines. Many 6-minute machines now installed on users' premises are not compatible with the Group I standard.

The Group I standard uses frequency modulation (FM). It transmits on either of two frequencies, one for black and one for white. Its normal resolution is 96 'pixels' (picture elements) per inch horizontally and 96 lines per inch vertically. This requires a transmission time of six minutes. There is also an option in the standard that allows a page to be transmitted in four minutes, at the lower resolution of 64 ppi by 64 lpi. Because four-minute transmission is optional in the standard, not all Group I machines offer it. In addition, readability of the 64 by 64 format is unacceptable for typed text.

For Group I machines, the two parties who wish to communicate call one another, make sure their settings are the same (e.g. four vs. six minute transmission), then make the transfer. This is very time consuming. Few Group I machines offer unattended sending and receiving or other service options.

Because Group I level machines started the facsimile revolution, they still dominate the installed base. At rentals starting from $70 per month and purchase prices starting from $1800, they are still the cheapest terminals. But their low transmission speeds translate into high transmission costs when long-distance lines are used, and they require extensive attention as well. Now that the costs of faster units have fallen very close to Group I terminal costs, Group I sales have plummetted, and sales of Group I machines should virtually disappear.

The next performance category is Group II. Group II machines use amplitude modulation and can transmit a page in three minutes over ordinary telephone lines at a resolution of 96 ppi by 96 lpi. There is an option in the standard for two-minute transmission at 64 ppi by 64 lpi.

A basic Group II terminal will lease for $80 per month and sell for $2000. This is only a little more than the cost of a Group I machine, and when savings in transmission costs and secretarial costs are weighed, Group II is usually much more attractive than Group I. Group II machines now dominate sales.

The base price for a Group II machine is somewhat misleading, however, because many users add extra cost options. Because Group I machines still dominate the installed base, for instance, many Group II machines can communicate with Group I machines.

Unattended operation options are also popular. Because transmission rates are lowest at night, many companies with very high traffic send much of their facsimile traffic overnight, in an unattended mode. Timers are set to transmit from the sending machines, and the receiving machines have unattended answering. Some machines can even poll 'satellite' terminals. Naturally, sheet feeders are needed in most cases. Because all 'hand shaking' is not done automatically on Group II machines, various preset options must be agreed to, for instance whether two- or three-minute operations will be used. Even when transmission is done during the day, unattended operation is still attractive, because an incoming call does not disrupt operations.

When the Group II standard was created, no provision was made for skipping rapidly over the vertical blank spaces between paragraphs. This vertical blank space is usually called 'white space' by facsimile vendors. Because white-space skipping can often result in one-minute transmission times, many vendors added it to their Group II machines. Each, unfortunately, developed a proprietary method. Because of these nonstandard white-space skipping features, there are still advantages in buying terminals from one vendor, although white-space skipping can always be turned off, allowing any Group II machine to talk to any other.

There is an even faster facsimile category, the Group III standard, which was created in 1980. Group III uses digital encoding, marking each picture element with a zero or a one depending on whether it is light or dark. It then transmits the information over telephone lines using 4800 bit per second modems and even optional 9600 bps modems. When line conditions are not right, many of these modems 'step down' automatically to lower speeds. This use of high-speed modems obviously creates very short transmission times.

In addition, the standard allows for compression before transmission. For horizontal compression (which is useful when there is a long horizontal run of

Figure 9-4.   The 9600 Group III Facsimile Console Transceiver from 3M can send an average business letter anywhere in the country in 20 seconds. The machine does not require a trained operator and features automatic dialing which allows unattended transmission during evening hours when telephone line charges are reduced.

dark or light), is specified in the standard. coding. There is also an option for two-dimensional (horizontal and vertical) compression.

Obviously, transmission time depends upon both the speed at which the modem can operate and the amount of compression possible given the nature of the text being sent. A typical time, however, is between 20 seconds per page and one minute per page. These high speeds are possible despite Group III's high resolution—normally 100 lpi vertically by 200 ppi horizontally and optionally 200 lpi by 200 ppi.

A nice feature of the Group III standard is its extensive hand-shaking capability. When two machines are connected, the sending device requests the conditions it desires—resolution, sending speed, type of encoding, and so on—and the two machines talk back and forth without operator intervention until

Figure 9-5.   3M's new EMT 9140 digital Group III disk top facsimile transceiver permits an operator without special training to send or receive exact copies of business and other documents to or from anywhere in the world in seconds via standard telephone lines.

the request has been accepted or an alternative is negotiated. On a 40-second call, it makes little sense to have the two operators spend several minutes doing this negotiation.

By slashing transmission times, Group III machines greatly reduce both operator labor and long-distance transmission costs. The terminals, of course, are more expensive than Group II terminals, a low-end Group III machine costing around $4000 or leasing for about $140 per month. Adding options such as Group II and Group I compatibility, a 9600 bps modem, and unattended answering features can boost the selling price to over $10 000 and the monthly lease to over $350. Firms with several main locations often place a fully configured Group III machine in each, placing less sophisticated Group III machines in secondary business locations.

Group III sales are still fairly modest, but as terminal costs fall and as users become more familiar with Group III machines, Group III should challenge the current market supremacy of Group II.

The CCITT plans to develop a standard for yet another class of machines, Group IV terminals. Group IV machines are expected to have higher resolution, probably 200 lpi and 400 ppi. They will probably be able to transmit at 56 000 bits per second and perhaps much faster. They will probably use even more sophisticated compression than Group III, and they will certainly be compatible with the X.25 protocol for packet switched networks. Error detection is also likely to be in the standard. The Group IV standard will bring facsimile fully into the realm of data communications.

Facsimile Networks

A real advantage of facsimile has been its ability to use ordinary telephone lines. This frees users from having to join a centralized network, as Telex users have always had to do. Any two departments needing to communicate can simply purchase compatible facsimile terminals, avoiding both corporate and common carrier authorities.

Despite these advantages, a number of common carriers have introduced networks to handle facsimile. Once a user attaches its terminal to a network, it can send messages to any other terminal on the network. Because most networks publish directories, sending messages to companies attached to the net is greatly simplified.

More importantly, a facsimile network compresses the transmissions from Group I and Group II machines, so long distance costs are reduced. A network can also allow incompatible terminals to communicate with one another.

Most facsimile networks use store and forward (message switched) transmission. The message is sent into the network, which delivers it when possible. Most networks offer several levels of priority, the highest usually guaranteeing a delivery attempt within ten to twenty minutes. If the receiving terminal is unavailable when the network makes a delivery attempt, the network calls back later to make another try.

In the United States, ITT (FAXPAC), Graphnet (FAX-GRAM), and Southern Pacific Communications (Speedfax) have already established facsimile networks. In West Germany, the PTT has established a similar service called Telefax, and in Canada, CNCP Telecommunications has established FacScan Electromail. Although these networks still play a small role in facsimile, they are advantageous for many users.

Delivery Services

When telegraphy first got started, messages were delivered to telegraph offices, where users either picked them up or had them delivered. A number of similar services now exist for facsimile. For instance, Graphnet's Class 3 FAX-GRAM service results in either receiver pick-up or messenger delivery. (Class 1 and Class 2 services deliver messages to terminals on the receiver's premises.)

Delivery services have been somewhat more prevalent for international delivery. The United States Postal Service, for instance, has an international delivery service called INTELPOST. Customers can bring messages to be sent to more than two dozen service centers around Washington D.C. and New York City. The INTELPOST system then facsimiles the message to any of more than four dozen service centers in the United Kingdom or any of two dozen or so service centers in Canada, Europe, and Australia. INTELPOST is actually the outgrowth of an earlier USPS experiment, Facsimile Mail Service, which began in 1971 and continued at varying levels for some time.

Western Union International (not to be confused with Western Union Telegraph Company) has a similar offering, International Facsimile Service. Users deliver messages to any of five IFS centers in the United States by Facsimile or physical delivery. The message is then facsimiled to a service center in Argentina, El Salvador, Japan, Switzerland, or Taipei. RCA Global Communications has a similar service, Q-Fax, linking four U.S. centers with sixteen overseas locations.

Image Processing

There is a growing feeling that facsimile is really only a precursor to a whole realm of information handling called *image processing*. Just as we can now store, retrieve, process, and distribute text and voice, we will be able to manipulate scanned images in very sophisticated ways.

Image processing should not be confused with graphics. In graphics, pictures are drawn using a few types of standardized elements, such as dots, lines, circles, shaded blocks, and colored blocks. Image processing, in contrast, scans the original and so can depict arbitrary visual information such as signatures and photographs.

A number of companies are developing image processing products. Burroughs and Xerox, for example, can store facsimile images on the file servers of their integrated office systems. The most advanced image processing system now on the market is IBM's Scanmaster I.

Scanmaster I marries an electronic copier/printer with facsimile. Scanmaster I is a slow electronic copier/printer that can be used for convenience copying or to print an incoming text stream. Its printing is limited to one font. Scanmaster I can also act as a Group III facsimile machine (with a Group II option).

The most important thing about Scanmaster I is its ability to be linked to IBM's DISOSS software package on IBM host mainframes. DISOSS was originally created to file, retrieve, and transfer text documents. It has been expanded to accept input from the Scanmaster I in Group III operating mode. It then delivers the image to one or many Scanmaster Is, or it stores the image. If the image is stored, it can be called up by people working with IBM's word processing products. Once called up, it can be delivered in ways specified by the WP terminal user to any Scanmaster I.

COMMUNICATING WORD PROCESSORS

Word processors have begun to revolutionize the creation of documents. But after a document has been created, it may have to be sent to another site, either within the company or outside of it. If the other site also has a word processor, it would be nice to be able to dial it up and transmit the document over ordinary telephone lines, so that it can be printed or even revised further at the remote site. Word processors that can do this have been around since 1973. They are called communicating word processors.

For a stand-alone word processor, the user buys a hardware 'communications module' plus software. The cost of this addition, which usually includes a modem or acoustic coupler, is typically around $300 to $1000. On stand-alone systems, the base system price is usually too low to encourage large investments in full featured communication, for example to support unattended operation.

On clustered systems, however, only one communication module is needed for the entire system. Since clustered systems often cost $100 000 or more, fairly extensive features are often purchased. A word processing operator, for instance, can simply specify a destination for the word processing file, and advanced systems will handle the details of the delivery.

Stand-alone and many clustered systems often use point to point communication, with each unit dialing the appropriate receiver whenever a message is sent. This is called peer communication. It is also referred to as a mesh network.

Other approaches involve the use of a centralized message controller. When one word processor wishes to send a document, it contacts the controller or waits until it is polled. Centralized controllers can provide extensive management functions and are often useful when the firm has a mixture of large and small word processing systems. But centralized controllers can drive up transmission costs if the firm is geographically dispersed, because most transmissions will take place over long-distance lines—even when two sites are near one another but far from the controller.

A middle ground is the use of several controllers, one in each major geographic area. Each controller handles transmissions within its area. For transmissions between areas, the responsible controllers communicate, usually in peer mode, to transfer messages among themselves. This is called a hierarchical approach.

A difficulty facing companies that want to use communicating word processors is that machines from different vendors cannot communicate with one another in a meaningful way. The problem is that different vendors have different internal formatting codes for underlining, tabulation, margins, and a host of other formatting needs. If a document with one vendor's formatting codes is sent to a machine from another vendor, it may be able to be transmitted successfully, but it usually produces garbage if the receiving unit tries to print or display it.

In addition, quite a number of managers and professionals are now writing their first drafts on-line, on personal computers or simple terminals attached to time-sharing systems. There are literally dozens of word processing packages in use on personal computers and large computers, and using these packages gives managers and professionals a *low cost* way to prepare text. Most managers and professionals do not want to do detailed editing work, preferring instead to edit drafts with pencils or pens, then transfer the marked up printout to a secretary's word processor for clean-up, heavy formatting, complex statistical work, and table typing. But the problem of incompatible codes again rears its head, and managers and professionals are often forced to do all clerical editing themselves, to require their secretaries to do editing on these relatively clumsy and limited personal computers or timesharing systems, or to print out the document for entry through fairly expensive optical character recognition (OCR) devices that often create bare text that must have new internal codes inserted.

A partial solution is to rip out all internal control codes and transmit the text as a 'flat' file, that is, a series of lines of text, each with a set number of ASCII characters. Tabulation, centering, and other formatting are handled by putting in the right number of blanks before transmission.

But ASCII is a very simple character set, without underlining or boldness. Another approach is to create a file formatted and ready to go to some popular type of printer. The text will then be neatly formatted and will have boldness, underlining, and perhaps such features as subscripts, superscripts, and the ability to handle Greek or other character sets. Of course, the two communicating word processors must both base their transmission on the same printer format, and their communication software must be able to transmit the embedded character codes.

But even the printer format solution proves to be unacceptable in practice, because the transmitted text can only be printed upon receipt—it cannot be edited. For example, most word processors use a combination of 'soft' and 'hard' carriage returns. Soft carriage returns are inserted during word wrapping and are subject to change as new text is inserted or other editing is done. Hard carriage returns, however, are inserted by the user or by the word processor to denote line breaks in tables and other parts of the document where line breaks are important and must not be changed during editing. But printer formatting uses all hard carriage returns. For this and other reasons, the text is usually not editable after transmission.

Manufacturers often add to the confusion by claiming that their systems can communicate with those from other vendors even when their machines can only emulate the other vendor's 'hand shaking' or can only communicate in some other weak and unsatisfactory sense. Another alternative is to use a 'black box' converter, such as Racal Vadic's 303 Protocol Converter, that can translate the format codes of one machine to another machine's format codes. Currently, these black box converters cost $5000 to $25 000.

But even the black box is not a full solution. Not all codes are translated, so the user is left with two options. First, after receipt the transmitted document can be manually 'repaired' by an operator. This is, of course, time consuming and expensive. Second, if you know in advance what the receiving unit can be, you can avoid using untranslatable formatting codes during composition and editing. This is called planned communication. Planned communication can eliminate or at least minimize translation difficulties, but it may not be acceptable to authors if formatting is affected, and it tends to throw away at least some of the sending machine's text processing capabilities—usually the advanced features that caused you to select that machine over others in the first place.

As black box technology matures, we can expect to see the emergence of communicating word processor networks that will handle translation. In Canada, CNCP Telecommunications established such a network, Infotex, in 1980, but black box technology is still fairly limited, and these networks will not provide magic solutions when they do appear.

The problem of embedded control codes needs to be solved at a general level. The proper way to do this would be to lay down international standards via the International Standards Organization (ISO) and the CCITT. In terms of the ISO Reference Model of Open Systems Interconnection, a standard at the sixth layer (the presentation layer) is needed. In the United States, the X3 Committee of the American National Standards Institute has been working on such standards. The ISO has recently organized a similar international effort, using the X3 Committee heavily but making the effort international.

In the short run, most users are likely to cope with the difficulties involving *general* communication among word processors by focusing instead on the more limited strategy of *planned* communication. As noted earlier, in planned communication you deliberately create the document to be sent in a way that will introduce no features found in the specific machine to which you plan to send it. Then, relatively simple software is needed for the conversion and transmission. Planned communication requires you to plan the specific type of machine to which you will send the document, even *before* you begin writing it. It also requires you to give up the advanced features used on your machine. And finally, it still requires conversion software. Planned communication is not a general solution, and the more kinds of machine a firm uses, the less satisfactory it is as a strategy. But under the right conditions, it is extremely effective.

Unless a company standardizes upon compatible word processors from one vendor, communication will be a difficult issue throughout the foreseeable future. It is important for the user to ask the following questions.

- Are the benefits of communication worth standardizing on a single vendor, since no vendor's system will be a good fit for the basic word processing needs of all operating units?
- What level of interworking do I need? In other words, is the use of flat files, printer formatted files, or planned communication sufficient?
- If editable transmission is desired, just how noneditable will the transmitted files really be? Can the damage be repaired by the receiving operator with only modest difficulty?
- What level of conversion are existing black box converters capable of for the systems our company will use? How much do they require at least partially planned communication?

These are extremely difficult and time-consuming questions to answer, and relatively few consultants know the mechanics of interworking well enough to be of great assistance. There are simply no easy or good answers available for most firms that want to use communicating word processors from several vendors.

ELECTRONIC MESSAGE SYSTEMS

Teletypewriter networks, facsimile, and communicating word processors are handled by secretaries. But suppose message terminals could be placed directly on managers' and professionals' desks, and suppose these terminals could offer simple but powerful tools for composing, sending, reading, filing, and retrieving mail. This is the idea behind *electronic message systems*, which are also known as *computer message systems*, *computer-based message systems*, and *computer mail*.

EMS Develops

Even the earliest time-sharing systems, such as MIT's 1965 Project MAC, offered primitive 'mailbox' programs, which allowed users to send messages to one another. When you sent a message, it went into a 'mailbox' file in the receiver's account. If the receiver was on-line, a bell would ring to say that a new message had arrived. If the receiver was not using the terminal, a message would be printed the next time they logged in, telling them that new mail had arrived.

Beginning in the late 1960s many service bureaux and private companies began to build long-distance computer networks to support remote terminals. These networks automatically transformed mailbox systems into long-distance communication media, but users all had to be served by the same 'host' machine.

In 1972, the ARPANET became operational. ARPANET was built to link dozens of hosts at research centers across the United States. At Bolt, Beranek, and Newman, Raymond Tomlinson modified an existing mailbox program, SNDMSG, to deliver messages *between* host computers as well as among users on a single host computer. The era of effective long-distance EMS had begun.

Most of the early systems only had two commands. READ printed, all messages in the user's in-box. COMPOSE, in turn, began a composition sequence, prompting the sender for the recipients' names, a brief title, and the text of the message.

When users began to receive five or ten messages a day, however, users began to demand more tools to handle their mail. The first advanced system, RD, was actually written by a user—Larry Roberts, who later founded Telenet. Some time later, John Vittal built MSG, which soon became the most widely-used mail system on the ARPANET.

After 1977, the momentum shifted to the commercial world, as service bureaux 'came out of the closet' and began to promote EMS publicly. These new designs were more advanced then their mailbox predecessors, and most had the simple elegance and power characteristic of ARPANET systems. Actually this similarity to ARPANET message systems was hardly suprising, since a number of the initial commercial systems, including Telenet's Telemail and the Computer Corporation of America's COMET, were direct outgrowths of ARPANET experience. Some designs, however, such as TYMNET's OnTyme, were totally fresh developments.

Today, the market offers more than two dozen commercial electronic message systems on networks, plus a large number of software packages to run on the user's own machines. The early stages of EMS are over. The commercial era has begun.

A Scenario

When the user turns on his or her terminal in the morning, a log-on message will be printed if new mail has arrived. When the user enters the mail system, new messages are summarized: for each message, the receiving date and time, length, sender, and brief title are displayed.

Most users step through their messages one at a time, in order. They begin by giving the NEXT command, which causes the first message to appear. After reading or scanning it, the user normally does one of the following:

deletes the message,
types a brief reply,
forwards the message to another person, or
prints the message on a nearby printer for more leisurely reading.

The person then disposes of the next message in a similar way, then the next, and so on, until the morning's mail is finished. The process is very rapid, because messages are handled and replies sent immediately, without secretarial intervention.

All incoming and outgoing messages are filed automatically by sender, receivers, title, date, and any special fields. The user can also file them by project or broad topic area. Filed messages can be reviewed later by any characteristic or combination of characteristics, sometimes even by words or phrases in the body of the text.

The use of EMS is often distorted by the limited file space available on most computers. Users must either delete most of their old mail periodically (some new mail, of course, is deleted immediately after reading it) or archive their old mail, i.e. dump it onto magnetic tape, paper, or some other low-cost medium. A good system archives old mail semi-automatically but will leave scanning information (sender, title, etc.) on-line. This way, a user can scan through old mail over a long period of time. If an on-line message is needed, it can be recovered immediately. Otherwise, it is recovered from the archive.

Limited file space is also a problem for long messages. After completing a position paper, a person might want to send it to a dozen or more colleagues. But if a full copy is sent to each, their computers' file spaces may be completely overwhelmed. For long messages, good systems send the user a brief message (like an envelope) that gives the title and a brief abstract. Only one actual copy of the message is kept on each machine. When the READ command is given, the full text is pulled in automatically.

When the user composes an outgoing message, the EMS prompts for basic fields, such as main recipients, secondary recipients, and title. It then allows the user to compose the actual text. On good systems, word processing tools are provided, including a spelling checking program. Of course the text may also come from a pre-existing document. After the composition is completed, the user may be allowed to specify other special fields, such as delivery priority.

Some systems allow the user to leave the terminal on throughout the day. When a new message arrives, the bell usually chimes, and a one-line summary is printed, showing the sender, title, length, and priority. The user may reply immediately to an important message or wait until a more convenient time to handle the accumulating mail.

This scenario certainly does not describe all of the capabilities present in EMS, but it has focused on a few trouble spots in current designs, including archiving and the handling of long messages.

The scenario focuses on message reading and disposition tools rather than composition tools. This is because EMS is used predominantly for reading and disposition (filing, deletion, etc.) tasks rather than composition, as shown in Table 9-4. This makes EMS extremely different from other forms of electronic mail, in which the message is simply printed on receipt. Only communicating word processors allow any after-delivery handling, and even for them it is usually modest.

TABLE 9-4
Use of HERMES commands[5]

Command category	Percent of commands
Reading	46
Discarding or filing	18
Composing and editing	17
Ending a session	18
	99%

Note: Total does not add to 100% because of rounding errors.

The heavy use of reading and disposition tools in EMS mirrors the realities of normal written communication in an organization. The average letter or memo probably goes to three or four people, and their combined labor after receipt usually exceeds the amount of work required of the sender. Much of the sender's time, moreover, may involve searching through past messages to recall one or more items for reference.

In most organizations, EMS becomes an informal communications medium. Managers and professionals rarely try to polish their prose and, unless the system has a very simple word processor or spelling checker, they often ignore minor typographical errors. Many users have said that using EMS is like sending hand-written notes, but to a desk that may be miles away. There is even some soft evidence that if EMS substitutes for any existing medium, it substitutes primarily for the informal telephone call.

User Reactions

The normal reaction to a well-implemented electronic message system is very positive, as indicated by the following comments:

> I used to get six inches of paper in my in-box every day. Now I get less than half an inch, and the things that come in by computer are easier to handle. *I have a lot more time to spend with my managers, a lot more time to do my real job.*
>
> Bob Schiewe, Vice President,
> Continental Bank

> It gives us *a real competitive advantage.* I have people in Europe and the Far East, and I can communicate with them as easily as I can with people here in Chicago.
>
> Bob Champion, Vice President,
> Continental Bank

The enthusiasm demonstrated by these quotations is backed by survey data. Table 9-5 shows reactions among EMS users in a large Army organization, DARCOM. Among the managers and professionals who used EMS in the conventional way—handling their own mail directly through desk-top terminals—71% gave the message system a strongly positive rating, and 94% gave it at least a positive rating. The other 6% were neutral toward the system. This is a very positive reaction, especially since the particular EMS was extremely complex and rather difficult to use.

Not all managers used the system directly. Quite a few delegated terminal work to their secretaries. Even among these 'indirect' users, ratings were very positive, with 40% giving the system the highest possible rating and 78% giving at least a positive rating. The other 22% gave the system a neutral rating; again, there were no negative ratings.

The indirect users, then, did not dislike the system. They simply preferred to delegate the terminal work for a variety of reasons. When asked, in the survey, why they did not work at a terminal directly, respondents were split between those citing lack of time and those actually considering terminal work inappropriate for their position.

Although even secretaries gave the system a 46% very positive rating, they were clearly the least taken by the system. Thirty-eight percent did not even give a positive rating, and a few of the secretaries actually gave negative ratings—the only negative ratings among the respondents. When questioned, secretaries often complained about the system's clumsiness in handling delegators. If they served three or four delegators, they had to log in separately into the individual accounts. This was a frustrating experience. Perhaps the most interesting thing about the secretarial ratings was the low percentage of simple 'positive' ratings—only 16%. Secretaries either really liked the system or did not take to it very much at all.

The DARCOM survey documented what anecdotal evidence had long said—that when a message system is introduced properly, it is widely and positively received. Although current EMS designs still have many flaws, user resistance is not a problem in well-implemented systems. In fact, user demand

TABLE 9-5
Reactions of EMS users at DARCOM[5]

	Direct users			Delegators
Reaction	Managers	Professionals	Secretaries	Managers
Strongly positive	59%	78%	46%	40%
Positive	93%	95%	62%	80%

Note: User reactions were based on a 5-point scale, with '5' being strongly positive, '4' being positive, '3' being neutral, '2' being negative, and '1' being strongly negative.

quickly drives the system's growth, often faster than the implementer would like. Quite simply, user reactions can be summarized with three words. They like it.

Cost

Cost is critical in the implementation of any computer system. If costs are prohibitive, no system will be implemented, no matter how well liked. In the past, vendors have attempted to discuss EMS costs in terms of simple benchmark tests in which the person logs in, reads a message, sends a message, then logs off.

Such tests are unrealistic. In most message systems, the average log on does not produce an outgoing message,[6,7] and there are many more reading commands than composition and sending commands given. People do not merely log in, read, send, then log off. They tend to spend time on the system looking through their mail.

To get a more realistic view of costs, we surveyed total costs for a number of systems, then divided by the number of messages received to get a more realistic picture of the cost per message.[8] In that same study, we then projected costs to the future. Table 9-6 gives the results.

In 1977, PLANET cost about $1.34 per message. But PLANET was then operating on an obsolete DEC PDP-10 'KA' computer, and users were employing expensive long-distance circuits to reach the computer. If a local computer were used for everything but message transmission, at which point long-distance lines would be necessary, and if the PDP-10 'KA' were replaced by a 1977 DEC System 10, then PLANET would have cost only $0.35 per message. Since non-obsolete local computers would certainly be used in any large-scale corporate message system, we set $0.35 as our 'state of the art' 1977 estimate. Using relatively conservative assumptions that would tend to understate actual cost declines, we projected 1985 costs at $0.17.

Two things suggest that this cost projection actually may be too high. First, the average connect time in our data was 5.1 minutes per message sent. In one contemporary commercial system, it is only 2.5 minutes. Cost is directly proportional

TABLE 9-6
A cost projection for EMS

Category	1977 State of the art	1981 Projection	1985 Projection
Computer center hardware	$0.15	$0.06	$0.03
Computer center labor	0.15	0.06	0.03
Transmission	0.05	0.02	0.01
Total	$0.35	$0.14	$0.07

Note: Costs are based on constant 1977 dollars and exclude the cost of terminals.

to connect time. Second, computers have fallen more rapidly in price than our projections indicated. One commercial EMS serves a thousand users with a $200 000 computer. This represents a *capital* investment of only $200 per user.

These costs, unfortunately, have all excluded one thing—the cost of the terminal. Most terminals today cost at least $750. At a healthy five messages received per day, this represents $0.38 per message. In other words, terminal costs can swamp the very low computer and transmission costs of EMS.

If the terminal is to be used for other purposes beyond EMS, then EMS can still be less expensive than postage. But if EMS must be charged the whole cost of the terminal, much cheaper terminals are needed. Manufacturers have been loath to build really low-cost terminals, but the technology certainly exists. Matra has introduced a terminal with autodialing capability for less than $700 (this product is sold in the United States as the Scanset by TYMNET), and much cheaper dumb terminal designs are possible.

Even without heroic declines in terminal costs, however, EMS is likely to be less expensive than postage before the end of the 1980s. This is the central fact that the detail must not be allowed to bury. Before the 1980s are over, cost alone should make EMS the mainline communication medium in many organizations.

How to Win

Although EMS has a bright future, many EMS systems have failed miserably, sometimes within a few weeks of their introductions.[9] Two factors seem to be at work in systems that have failed.

The first is a preoccupation with the scenario given earlier, in which the user works *directly* at the terminal, handling his or her mail without a secretary. This is an appealing scenario, and it fits many users, but it is only part of the picture.

At DARCOM, for instance, managers were divided into direct users, who fit the scenario, and indirect users or delegators, who let secretaries handle their terminal work. Even among the direct users, there was considerable variation in use. Some managers used virtually every feature of the system and spent a great deal of time on-line. Others rarely or never used even such simple functions as editing, filing messages, or retrieving old messages. Table 9-7 shows the percentage of heavy users (who at least file messages sometimes), light users, and delegators among the users surveyed at DARCOM.

The particular EMS used at DARCOM was well suited to only one of the three groups, the heavy users. It was a powerful but complex system that tended to disorient inexperienced users. With a simpler system, in fact, it seems likely that many delegators would have become light users.

System designers tend to respond to the skewed use shown in Table 9-7 by calling for more selling and better user education. But this is naive. Every consumer product has heavy users, light users, and nonusers. Instead of railing against 'lazy' or 'uneducated' consumers, manufacturers in less immature industries simply take stratified use as a given. While they do try to move users 'up the ladder' they take skewed use as an inevitable pattern.

TABLE 9-7
Stratification of EMS use at DARCOM[5]

Category	Percentage of managers	Percentage of professionals	Percentage of managers and professionals	Percentage of secretaries
Heavy direct users	18	42	26	22
Light direct users	14	37	23	70
Delegators	68	21	50	8'
Total	100	100	99	100
Number (not percentage)	85	52	137	63

Note: Light direct users are those that rarely or never file messages.

Where possible, they design product *lines* instead of one product. Each offering in the line is geared to a different level of use. For EMS, this product line approach seems very attractive because it can be implemented fairly easily.

For direct users, the basic product would be designed for light users, who are easily turned off by system complexity. A sample set of commands for light users is shown in Table 9-8. Most likely, added functions would be enabled incrementally, providing a growth path from light to heavier use.

For indirect users, a secretarial subsystem is needed. A typical secretary will serve a number of delegators. When the secretary logs in in the morning, scans of new messages for *all* delegators under his or her care would be shown. A single command would print all incoming messages on a printer for hand delivery. For outgoing mail, the secretary would point to a name on the delegator list when sending a message for that person. The message would go out in the delegator's name with the name of the secretary attached as typist.

The secretarial stations would have other roles as well. Suppose the *direct* user wants to send a message to a mailing list, only half of whose members are tied to the system even indirectly. The mail for nonconnected recipients would then be printed at the secretary's terminal for stuffing into an envelope and mailing via interoffice mail or the U.S. postal service.

If a direct user goes on a trip or fails to read a message within a preset period of time—say two days for nonpriority messages—the responsible secretary would then be sent a copy of the message for handling.

Furthermore, many direct users want to work in tandem with their secretaries for much of their work. For example, they may want the secretary to scan through incoming mail before reading it themselves. They also may want to dictate long messages for the secretary to type.

In terms of hardware, the secretary's terminal probably would be fairly intelligent and would have a printer. It would, in fact, probably be a word processor. For light users, simple $200 to $500 terminals would probably connect

TABLE 9-8
Commands for light users

Level 1 Design

All incoming messages are printed at a secretarial terminal. All outgoing messages are typed by a secretary or dictated to a word processing center.

Level 2 Design

SUMMARIZE: To print one line summaries of all new mail.

READ: To print all new mail on a printer or printer terminal.

COMPOSE: To begin a composition sequence in which the user is prompted for the primary recipients, secondary recipients, title, and text of the message.

QUIT: To exit from the system.

Level 3 Design

Level 3 is an open-ended design, but most users would initially be given a small subset of commands. The following are likely to be in the initial command set.

READ: To read one message or a group of messages.

NEXT: To read the next message (useful when reading through the morning's accumulated mail).

LIST: To list one or more messages on a printer.

SUMMARIZE: To show one-line summaries of a message or group of messages.

REPLY: To reply to the message just read; the system handles the details of addressing, and the user merely types the text.

FORWARD: To forward a message to another person, usually with the option of adding a comment.

COMPOSE: As in Level 2, but with options at the end of the composition sequence to control delivery conditions.

WHO: Every user must be given a unique name for the system; if you come across an identifier you do not recognize, this command will give you the person's full name and organizational affiliation.

WHERE: To obtain the person's unique system identifier name, given their common name.

EDIT: To edit a document using insert, replace, delete, move, and copy commands.

FILE: To file messages in special topical file folders (messages are automatically filed by date, sender, recipients, title word, and other standard information on receipt).

DISCARD: To discard one or more messages (renumbering the messages in the file is optional).

HELP: To give specific advice when the user is uncertain of what to do.

PROFILE: To tailor the user's interaction with the message system, including the enabling of these or more advanced commands.

QUIT: To leave the message system.

to it by cable, sharing its intelligence. More powerful terminals for heavier users might also be attached, using the secretarial station as a switch to the outside world. Figure 9-6 illustrates this arrangement.

Stratified service and a secretarial system will address the first problem facing EMS—stratified use. If there is also a printer in the corporate mail room plus an EMS terminal for dictation in the company's word processing center, then *everyone* in the corporation is immediately connected to the system. Yet each user receives only the service desired.

This approach also addresses the second common fatal problem in EMS, namely expensive terminals. With a terminal on every direct user's desk, it is not much of a burden to query the system at least once a day for new messages (particularly if there is a 'message waiting' light on the keyboard).

But because terminals are so expensive, their number is usually limited. Users must trudge to a terminal, usually to find that there is no new mail. Soon, traffic falls because the system is difficult to use, and users log in only once a week or less. In one system,[9] a manager sent a meeting notice to 13 people two weeks after the system was implemented. Only three picked up the message.

The system shown in Figure 9-6 provides a cushion for non-use. Every message gets through. Even if a direct user forgets to read the mail, it is brought to the secretary's attention in a day or so. Because messages do get through, the system is used more, and the cushion gradually becomes less important.

Furthermore, costs are slashed greatly. Delegators do not even need a terminal. Light direct users, in turn, can use very low cost dumb terminals, sharing the secretarial station's intelligence, since each terminal would be used only ten to twenty minutes each day. Only heavy users would need a full terminal, and for their extensive use, the cost per message would still be low. In other words, EMS can be built fairly inexpensively even today, and it can grow gradually as EMS sophistication grows. It can also grow into a general support system for managers and professionals.

Figure 9-6. Secretary handles all messages for delegators. Light users' terminals employ the secretarial station's intelligence. Heavy users have intelligent terminals or personal computers. The secretary handles some work for light and heavy users.

NEW OPTIONS

Public record services, facsimile, and communicating word processors dominate electronic mail today. But several new technologies besides EMS are emerging to challenge the leaders. Some of them are, right now, the best solutions for some or all of the electronic mail needs in certain companies.

Voice Message Systems

Managers spend about half their day talking face to face, and another 5% of their day talking on the telephone.[11] Most managers, in fact, seem to prefer oral communication to text communication when both are possible. Even such professionals as laboratory chemists and programmers spend a third of their days talking face to face and on the telephone.[11]

Many office workers today have telephone answering systems to take their messages when they are out. But these answering systems are often disturbing to the caller, who was expecting to talk to someone, not leave a message. Most systems leave only a few seconds to compose a message, and many callers feel awkward speaking impromptu messages that are often filled with long pauses. Yet even with these flaws, the ability of answering systems to take messages at any time has spurred their growth in many firms. Continental Bank in Chicago, for instance, gave answering systems to all but its lowest level managers.

Now, a number of companies, including IBM, Wang, and ECS, are offering more sophisticated *voice message systems*, which offer a number of advances. First, they are usually centralized systems, and as soon as they are installed, everyone in the building complex usually has the service available to them immediately. The VMS quickly becomes a mainline communication system.

Second, several VMSs automatically delete any pauses in a person's message. So if a sender reaches a part of the message in which he or she is uncertain of what to say or how to say it, he or she can simply pause before going on.

Third, voice message systems give the user fairly extensive control over the conditions for creating, sending, and receiving messages. VMSs allow the buttons on push button telephones to be used to control the communication.

During composition, for example, the sender can usually review parts of what has been sent, sometimes even erasing it. When the recipient calls in for new messages, in turn, he or she can skip over uninteresting messages, review all or part of the message just heard, or initiate an immediate reply, letting the system supply the extension number of the original sender for the reply message.

Probably the most important features of voice message systems involve their ability to control delivery conditions. For instance, it is possible to broadcast a message, say to everyone in a department. This is often a good way to call meetings or get everyone 'in the know' on an important development. Message delivery can also be delayed: to take advantage of overnight telephone rates for messages going to another VMS across the country; to allow a message to be composed in advance, letting the sender scratch the transmission off his or her 'to do' list; or to remind the sender or someone else of a deadline. And of course the VMS can be used to dictate letters to a secretary or to the word processing center.

VMS is still very new, and while vendors and implementers have reported great success, empirical research on actual users has not yet been reported. But the service appears to be attractive and will almost certainly catch on with users.

What makes VMS especially attractive to user organizations is its low cost, generally quoted at only $100 to $500 per user. Because the biggest factor in cost is the amount of memory space to be made available to store messages, buyers should compare the file space per user (as well as other factors, of course) when comparing systems.

This low cost is available because ordinary push button telephones can be used. But ordinary telephones lack one very useful feature—a 'new message' light to advise the user when messages are waiting. Optional waiting light attachments are available on some systems. These are probably a good investment, because if even a small fraction of the user base chronically forgets to check their voice mail boxes frequently, the usefulness of the system will be limited. If a *significant* fraction do not check their mail (this is particularly likely early in a system's life), the system can actually fail.

Intelligent Terminals and Personal Computers

One of the advantages of facsimile is that any two users can send messages to one another, over ordinary telephone lines, without becoming involved in a larger network. But the two users can also communicate as easily by purchasing intelligent terminals or personal computers, plus the software and hardware needed for communication. Communicating word processors already do this, and there is speculation that many people will be communicating frequently via intelligent terminals and personal computers in the future.

MICROCOM's Microcourier, for example, is a mail package already available for Apple II computers. A potential user must buy the software package, a modem, and a controller for the modem. And, of course, he or she must find other Apple II users who have done the same. One interesting feature of Microcourier is its ability to send graphics in its messages, taking advantage of the Apple II's inherent graphics capabilities. SSM's Transend 3, also an Apple II-based product, is another of the emerging mail systems for personals. Software Connections' Mail Monitor can connect Apple IIs and Corvus Systems Concept computers. The Source has taken another approach to personal computer mail, providing mailboxes that users can access. The users prepare mail before connection and read it after the connection, thus minimizing connect time.

Although the use of personal computers and intelligent terminals for electronic mail is an appealing idea, the poor standardization among these machines and the flood of incompatible mail packages that can be expected to appear make the future of personals and intelligent terminals uncertain. The emergence of standards for software, however, even if only for CP/M, Apple II, or MS-DOS operating systems, could crystallize the market.

Videotex

During the mid 1970s, the British Post Office (now British Telecom) developed a service originally called Viewdata. The name of this service was subsequently changed to Prestel, because it was discovered, much to British Telecom's embarrassment, that the name 'Viewdata', being made of two common words, could not be trademarked in the United Kingdom. To add to the confusion, the technology is generally being marketed outside the U.K. as Viewdata.

The idea behind Prestel was to add sufficient electronics to otherwise ordinary television sets to convert them into information retrieval display devices. The user would also have a simple keypad for input. Each frame of information would present the user with two or more choices. By pressing appropriate keys, the user could go to another frame, confirm that he or she wanted to purchase a product offered for sale, or take other actions. Ordinary telephone lines would link the user to the relatively simple computer that would manage the information base.

In 1977, Prestel devices began being placed in homes, and other countries began to develop similar systems, most notably France's Antiope, Canada's Telidon, and Japan's Captain. Soon the generic name Videotex emerged to denote all systems that (1) use low-cost terminals and (2) use two-way transmission, whether over the telephone lines, cable, or some other medium.

Although there has been a great deal of Videotex activity among vendors, the market acceptance of Videotex is still uncertain. The service is still too new to be evaluated, and its current pricing is based upon anticipated levels of service and could change substantially as experience increases.

Videotex has been viewed as a way to deliver electronic mail, and this may be an important role for it in the long term. But its general outlook is uncertain, and messaging would require more sophisticated input devices, the acceptance of which is yet another question. More expensive computers would also be needed for true messaging. All in all, it will probably be the late 1980s before the long-term potential for Videotex in electronic mail can be evaluated.

Electronic Copier/Printers

To make a reproduction on an office copier, you place the original face down on the glass platter. The original is illuminated from below by a strong light source, which is often a laser on more expensive copiers. The reflected light hits a photosensitive drum, which receives a pattern of charges over its surface according to the intensity of reflected light that hits each region. The paper on which the copy is to be made is passed over the drum, and the charge pattern is transferred to the paper. Finally, charge-sensitive ink darkens the appropriate areas, and the paper is ejected.

There is a relatively straightforward, although far from simple, way to turn a laser copier into a powerful printer for electronic mail. The laser can be pointed right at the photosensitive drum, drawing whatever pattern is desired. The laser can actually produce a better picture by pointing directly at the drum, because the optics of reflected light are never perfect.

The logic circuits that drive the *electronic copier/printer* can handle text, facsimile, and even high-density graphics—even mixing various input modes on a single page. Of course existing products offer only some of these capabilities.

The electronic copier/printer is not an electronic mail category by itself. Instead, it is a powerful office device that can potentially print the output from nearly all kinds of electronic mail. Some existing electronic copier/printers are already cheap enough to use in general office areas. As prices continue to fall and capabilities grow, electronic copier/printers will almost certainly be a key linkpin in the integration of electronic mail.

INTEGRATION

If you were the only person in the world with a telephone, it would not be a very useful device. In electronic mail, too, the value of a terminal depends on the number of other terminals you can reach.

Within certain types of electronic mail, most notably the public record services and facsimile, standards have brought a high level of interconnection. Within other categories, including word processing, EMS, intelligent terminals, and personal computers, however, people who need to communicate with one another usually have to stay with a single vendor.

In the future, there should be good standardization within each electronic mail technology, but even this will not be enough. The real challenge will be to create broad standards for all electronic mail, so that, within certain boundaries, different types of terminals will be able to exchange messages, and so that individual messages may contain a mixture of text, images, voice, and even video.

Integration across categories has already begun in two ways. The first is pragmatic interconnection, in which vendors offer products and services that link one or more existing forms of electronic mail. The second is a large ongoing effort in many national and international standards bodies to build a general framework for electronic mail standards. This comprehensive framework should have most of its elements in place by 1990, and well before that will offer useful substandards for vendors to adopt.

Pragmatic Interconnection

As noted above, Telex, Teletex, and facsimile already have excellent standards, and the easiest way of adding simple interconnection to an electronic mail system is to give it links to the Telex, Teletex, and facsimile worlds.

In the text domain, many communicating word processors can already connect directly to Telex and Teletex. A growing number of terminals, furthermore, can communicate via computer protocols such as TTY and 3270.

For facsimile, a number of devices on the market can now convert text into the facsimile standard. This allows a text terminal to transmit messages to either text terminals or facsimile terminals with the flip of a switch. It also allows a facsimile terminal to accept input from various text systems.

During the next few years, we should see the emergence of a number of 'Panmail' networks that can accept input from many kinds of electronic mail terminals or services and deliver these messages to many others.

A number of companies have already begun to build the first stages of such networks. Western Union Telegraph Company has long connected Telex, TWX, Infocom, and other record services, and its new Access service carries it outside the traditional public record service domain. CNCP Telecommunications, Tymnet, GTE Telenet, Graphnet, and a number of other public networks are also evolving toward the panmail concept.

For the near future, input to a panmail network will be in the form of text, and terminals will include communicating word processors, computer terminals attached to the telephone system or some computer network, and Telex, TWX, or Teletex terminals (all panmail networks will have links to public record services).

Output will come through all of the text terminals just mentioned, and it will also come via facsmile terminals and electronic copier/printers. Of course the panmail network will have to have extensive protocol conversion capabilities.

Initially, facsimile input will only be accepted if the output terminal is also a fax unit. While the conversion of text to facsimile is a relatively simple process, the conversion of facsimile to text is more difficult. Although OCR (optical character recognition) is a rapidly maturing technology, facsimile resolution is often too low to allow high reliability in translation. Without very high levels of reliability, few commercial electronic mail services are likely to offer fax to text conversion.

Facsimile to text conversion will certainly come during the next few years, however. It will come first for the high resolution Group III and Group IV machines, then perhaps for the lower resolution Group II machines.

Protocol conversion and delivery will not be the only services offered by panmail networks. In some cases, they should be able to reduce costs. They will also provide store and forward delivery. But their biggest advantage may be their ability to offer a directory service analogous to the white pages of the telephone system. If you need to send mail to someone, you will pick up your directory. If they are also attached to your panmail networks, you can simply send them a message regardless of the kind of terminal they have. Unfortunately you will probably need several directories, because there will be several panmail networks, and because the Telex/Teletex vendors directories may not be included in the directories of panmail networks to which they are linked.

The black box technology needed to link incompatible systems via panmail networks should gradually become available to individual corporations. These panmail black boxes will be much more sophisticated than the WP-to-WP and text-to-fax converters now on the market. Given the high cost of developing conversion software (often $50 000 per pair of machines to be connected), black boxes spun out of panmail networks are likely to be reasonably expensive.

While the panmail networks will provide the fullest forms of interconnection, many vendors are including integration in their own product lines on a more modest scale. Take the Xerox 8000 Network System product line, for example. Its Communications Server can provide links to Telex, TWX, and to any terminal on a direct dial line. The system also has a native electronic message service, and its word processing products can communicate via the system's Ethernet link. Simple text files, moreover, can be exchanged among the System's 8010 and 8012 (Star) information processing systems, its 860 IPS (its word processor), its electronic typewriter, and its file server.

Xerox also has facsimile devices that can send information into Ethernet for storage in image form on the System's File Server. Through products built by Xerox's Kurzweil subsidiary, OCR can even be used to convert the facsimile transmission into Text. Finally, the System's Print Server is an electronic copier/printer that can print text output and will soon be able to print a facsimile message. Other vendors, especially Burroughs and IBM, are also beginning to integrate facsimile with text tools.

Even with the progress that will be made among the panmail networks and equipment vendors, standards will remain a problem. EMS and communicating word processors do not even have effective hand shaking standards yet, and standards to allow formatted text to be exchanged are even further away. If interconnection is to continue to evolve, a more general standards framework is needed.

De Facto Standards

The job of creating panmail and black box interworking would be greatly simplified if one vendor developed a proprietary standard that would become a de facto standard widely used in the industry. Such a development now seems possible, thanks to IBM announcements in 1981 and 1982.

IBM announced three major standards.[11] The first was IBM's Document Interchange Architecture, DIA, which specifies how text files are to be moved among processors in a flexible and intelligent way. IBM's subsequent announcement of Scanmaster I (discussed earlier in the chapter) indicates that image communication will also be part of DIA. In fact, the Scanmaster I protocol was essentially similar to DIA even in its earliest form.

IBM also announced its Document Content Architecture to specify formatting codes in text files. If DCA becomes a popular standard, it should be a potent factor in allowing easier interworking in all text areas.

Third, IBM introduced its Graphic Codepoint Definitions (GCD) standard which specifies the meaning of every 8-bit code symbol in the text.

The three standards form a family of standards within the seventh layer of

IBM's Systems Network Architecture. The GCD is embedded within the DCA, which is embedded in turn within the DIA.

It seems unlikely that all vendors will accept IBM's DIA and DCA, so, in the long run, true interworking must depend on the creation of legitimate international standards.

Standards

The international standards agencies have been engaging in an intense, long-term effort to develop electronic mail and other text standards since the mid-1970s. The International Standards Organization (ISO) and the Consultative Committee on International Telegraphy and Telephony (CCITT) have spearheaded this effort and have worked closely with each other. The national members of these organizations, such as the American National Standards Institute (ANSI) in the U.S., have actively contributed to these efforts, as have a number of independent bodies such as the International Federation for Information Processing (IFIP).

In 1980, these organizations produced a general framework for standards setting. ISO called it the Reference Model of Open Systems Interconnection (OSI). The new framework has a series of seven layers, each performing different and independent functions. Layering has freed the (high-level) mail standards builders from worrying about low-level data communication issues, allowing them to concentrate on more substantive issues at the fifth (session), sixth (presentation), and seventh (application) layers of the model.

The Teletex standard, for instance, is built in the fifth and sixth layers of the model. For actual transmission, Teletex can use any existing standards for the lower four layers. It can communicate over public packet switched networks via the X.25 and X.75 standards, for example, or it can communicate over direct dial telephone lines.

Groups desiring to build an application standard on top of Teletex, furthermore, can worry only about the seventh layer, using the Teletex standard and various existing lower level standards for the bottom six layers to handle the message communication needed for their standards.

The Teletex standard was the first fruit of OSI, coming in 1980, the same year model was released. Since OSI had long been under construction, its outlines were clear before its release, so the Teletex effort could proceed in parallel.

Because the International Telecommunications Union (ITU), which is CCITT's parent organization, is a treaty organization, its 'recommendations' are relatively effective standards. So the ITU's Plenary Assemblies become major standards certification events. These Plenary Assemblies come every four years. At the time of writing, the next is due in 1984.

For the 1984 Plenary, part of the CCITT's Working Group VII is concentrating on Question 5, Message Handling Facilities. This will be a seventh-layer standard. In contrast to Teletex, which is still a terminal-to-terminal system, the

MHF will allow messages to be sent to names of people and even computer programs. The standard will specify how such messages are to be delivered and a range of services that will be either mandatory or optional during delivery.

Because the MHF will be a seventh-layer standard, it is free to use a wide variety of lower-level standards. Although often viewed as an extension to Teletex, it will be able to use many other fifth- and sixth-level standards, for example the anticipated Group IV facsimile standard. MHF will even be able to handle voice and video when those standards emerge, and it will eventually be able to handle multimedia messages that have a mixture of text, images, voice, and video.

Interestingly, Teletex will *not* fit well into the MHF. Teletex, being an early development, contains some constraints that the MHF designers decided not to live with. As a result, service providers of message handling facilities will have to provide an extra service to convert Teletex messages into full MHF format. Once translated, the Teletex message will be handled within MHF as any other message. At the other end, the message will be retranslated into Teletex format for delivery to Teletex machines.

Standards do not emerge full blown when they do appear. A comprehensive core must be produced first, but some key features are often left for later development. Encryption, for example, will probably be added to Teletex in the future. The message handling facility standard, in turn, may be released without a standardized directory capability.

The most important omission from Teletex today, and an omission that may continue when the MHF standard is adopted, is a lack of standards for text structure. Although Teletex has a large international repertoire of characters, its presentation layer has few other features beyond the notion of pages, and this last feature actually runs counter to trends in word processing.

As noted earlier in the chapter, the biggest impediment to interconnection among communicating word processors is the lack of standards for text formatting. While Teletex offers a world-wide delivery standard, its text is not editable after delivery. This is unacceptable for any but the simplest applications.

The ISO has released a draft standard on text formatting, but this is only a first step, and unless the CCITT adopts it as a standard, the ISO is not likely to be able to impose even this limited standard on vendors. In general, the prospects for the acceptance of a full international standard for text formatting before 1988 can only be rated as fair at the time of this writing.

The MHF standard should, however, be able to standardize the names of fields within a message. Because users often search through old messages by author, date, or title word, these and other fields must be parsable, and this will require a very good standard. Parsability is also used in many other aspects of EMS, for example, generating the header fields when a 'reply' command is issued.

Within the United States, the National Bureau of Standards has already released a series of FIPS (Federal Information Processing Standards) for computer-based message systems, that is, EMS. These standards are based upon NBS's anticipation of what the MHF standard will be. A number of EMS vendors have already endorsed the NBS standards, and this indicates that MHF and other advanced standards will find good acceptance among vendors.

CONCLUSION

For the next few years, pragmatic approaches such as protocol converters and panmail networks should continue to dominate efforts to link various forms of electronic mail. But before the end of this decade, a fairly comprehensive set of standards should be in place, and there should finally be a service that we can call, simply, electronic mail.

REFERENCES

1. The Yankee Group. Personal communication with Mr. Howard Anderson.
2. Study performed by Mackintosh International and Communications Studies and Planning, Ltd. Reported in Connel, Steven, and Galbraith, Ian A.: *Electronic Mail: A Revolution in Business Communications*, Knowledge Industry Publications, White Plains, NY, 1980, 1982.
3. Kirchnar, Jaka: No Market Research Done Before Offering E-COM, USPS Official Admits. *Computerworld, p.* 8, February 26, 1979.
4. Electronic Industries Association, *Electronic Market Book*, 1981.
5. Panko, Raymond R., and Panko, Rosemarie U.: A Survey of EMS Users at DARCOM. *Computer Networks*, pp. 19–23, March 1981.
6. Statistics on HERMES data supplied by Bolt, Beranek, and Newman.
7. Bamford, Harold E.: Computer Conferencing: the Exchange of Experience. *Telecommunications Policy*, pp. 215–220, September 1980.
8. Panko, Raymond R.: The Cost of EMS. *Computer Networks*, pp. 35–46, March 1981.
9. Tucker, Jeffrey H.: Implementing Office Automation: Principles and an Electronic Mail Example. *Proceedings of the SIGOA Conference on Office Information Systems, Association of Computing Machinery*, pp. 93–100, June 21–23, 1982.
10. Panko, Raymond R., and Sprague, Ralph H., Jr.: Toward a New Framework for Office Support. *Proceedings of the SIGOA Conference on Office Information Systems, Association of Computing Machinery*, pp. 82–92, June 21–23, 1982.
11. Schick, T., and Brockish, R. F.: The Document Interchange Architecture: A Member of a Family of Architectures in the SNA Environment. *IBM Systems Journal*, **21**, No. 2, pp. 220–246, 1982.

Section IV: Productivity

Advances in Office Automation, Vol 1
Edited by Karen Takle Quinn
© 1985 Wiley Heyden Ltd.

Chapter 10

ISSUES IN PRODUCTIVITY MEASUREMENT

Ed. R. Berryman

Exxon Corporation

INTRODUCTION

The Challenge

The task of measuring the effects of automated equipment on the productive output of office staff is a continuing challenge that has remained largely unanswered. Office work assignments being what they are—often varied in content, limited in tangible output, and only broadly specified—complicate the process of translating actual work results into a system of numerics that can be evaluated. Consider the impediments to data collection—restrictions on access to some office workers, limits on available time, and the cost of diverting staff from their assigned responsibilities to supply measurement data. Add to this the problem of defining a single work metric that is meaningful across a variety of office environments, and the scope of this challenge becomes clear.

Issue: How can we make measurements in an environment that is typically unstructured, dynamic, and unpredictable?

While the impact of word processing on the productivity of support staff has been evaluated extensively in the past, there has been little definitive work to date in the area of professional productivity. The reason is simple: few techniques have the ability to both discern and quantify those aspects of the professional's job which account for its productivity. By very definition the professional's role is loosely defined. Tasks are often difficult to describe, and even harder to predict. The very essence of a professional assignment implies the use of judgment and decision-making skills that seem to defy direct quantification.

Issue: How can we measure a quantity like productivity when it appears to be largely intangible, elusive, and ill-defined?

The Response

The response to the challenges of productivity measurement in an office environment begins with a usable definition of productivity. This definition must be both broad enough to be *meaningful* within a variety of work contexts and, at the same time, adequately defined so as to be *measurable*.

Adequate breadth of definition yields results that are meaningful. We find that productivity measures that are meaningful to one set of occupations are often irrelevant to another. Managers, professionals, and support staff in the same organization typically share a common business objective, but make their contribution through different means. In a similar way, administrative, engineering, and research disciplines each have characteristics that make them difficult to analyze and compare. Our approach to productivity must be sufficiently broad to apply to a wide number of office situations.

Adequate depth of definition yields results that are measurable. Office tasks are notoriously difficult to capture and categorize. Just as office environments differ from business to business, there exist subtle terminology and procedural distinctions that affect the way office workers describe their efforts, even within the same function. These localisms compound the difficulty in measuring and projecting the productivity impacts of office automation. Consequently, our choice of approach must be sufficiently precise to permit consistent quantification of office activities.

The purpose of our efforts has been to focus on the complete spectrum of office work, encompassing the duties of the manager, nonmanagement professional, and member of the office support staff. The underlying philosophy is to capture productivity where it occurs, regardless of the job class or organizational level of the contributors. In this sense our approach differs from other techniques that have been chosen to focus on a particular occupation or work group. Our efforts are made possible by a study framework, procedures, and tools specifically tailored to the job of measuring productivity in office situations. As an added benefit, these study components have been constructed to be applicable to a wide range of office populations and business environments.

In the course of this chapter we will describe a number of key issues impacting productivity measurement in office environments. Rather than represent these views as an entirely novel or exhaustive treatment of the subject, it is more appropriate to say that it reflects our best experience in the area to date. Continued refinement of the underlying principles, aided by parallel developments by others, will undoubtedly furnish added insight in the future.

For clarity, the discussion presented here is structured into a series of topics. These topics are sequenced to follow the normal progression of a study focusing on office productivity measurement. These topics are:

- Objectives.
- Framework for office analysis.

- Study procedures.
- Measurement tools.
- Results.
- Conclusions.

OBJECTIVES

The Focus

With all the excitement over the promise that advances in office automation bring—new tools for collecting, analyzing, and managing information—it is easy to become entranced by the technology while losing sight of the factors that matter most to the business: those that impact on the firm's bottom line. And while the introduction of the latest technologies can enhance the company's image and provide a positive lift to employee morale, only those developments that can be converted into improved revenues or streamlined costs will be profitable in the long run.

But there should be no denying the importance of these new tools and techniques to the future health of the typical business enterprise. The key dilemma is how to incorporate office automation into an ongoing concern while deriving the implied benefits. The successful introduction of office automation is, in turn, much more than a technical strategy, a systems development program, and a set of pilot tests. Any effort that is to meet and sustain the firm's objectives for bottom line performance will be well-planned. Further, it will be based on a continuing program of measurement (and control) that is tuned to the specialized needs of the organization.

Key Issues

When developing plans for office automation, being prepared to deal with the following issues becomes critically important:

- What are the operational requirements of my organization?
- How do these requirements translate into needs that can be profitably satisfied through office automation?
- What is the probable payoff of a program involving the introduction of office technology?
- What is the likely reaction of my staff? How long will it take? Where should we begin?

And just as these planning issues rank foremost in the minds of managers embarking on new ventures in office automation, related concerns surface as system implementation proceeds. Typical implementation issues include:

- How effectively have our office systems installations met their goals?
- What fine tuning of equipment and procedures is necessary?
- How far can we carry the present plan?
- What are the bottom line effects on the firm?

At later stages in the development process the issues become increasingly specific, demanding measurement information that fits the framework of earlier discussions and, at the same time, is increasingly more precise. Since actual implementation makes the total development more visible within the firm, these latter issues are likely to involve a wider range of interests, originating from groups with differing viewpoints and agendas.

Problem Dimensions

What is needed is a versatile and consistent way of meeting these recurring needs for predictive, descriptive, and analytical information. Experience indicates that regardless of the apparent simplicity of the office situation under examination, the demands for reliable and consistent information will represent a sizeable investment of time and effort. Planning is one effective way of meeting these information requirements naturally within the context of the overall work program.

Another axiom addresses the planning process itself. When adopting a technique for this sort of data collection and analysis, choose one well-suited to the situation under study. In this chapter we describe the characteristics of one such approach that has been developed expressly for use in the analysis of office environments. The technique is built from a common methodology for systems analysis. The key components of this approach are its framework, study procedures, and measurement tools as illustrated in Figure 10-1.

The *framework* serves as the foundation of the approach, defining the principal study components and their structure. *Procedures* describe how study information is to be collected, analyzed, and presented. Finally, the *tools* are the actual mechanisms of data collection and analysis. They supply information about the dynamics of the office situation under study, taking into account key interactions

Figure 10-1.   Methodology for systems analysis.

and time dependencies. Tools also act as the facilitators of analysis. When properly constructed and applied, they add to the efficiency and effectiveness of the study technique. Together, the framework, study procedures, and measurement tools are the building blocks of office analysis.

Some Definitions

Note that throughout this chapter we will use the word 'office' to describe any number of work situations that are characterized by a high degree of individual task diversity. As we will argue, the actual place where office work is performed and the identity of the individual workers are not constraining factors. Work performed in the mailroom, in the laboratory, and on the executive jet can qualify as office tasks, as can work performed by a company attorney, engineer, or administrative secretary.

This notion stems from the observation that managers, nonmanagerial professionals, and support personnel engage in activities that are generically similar. Meetings, telephone conversations, even decision-making and typing are examples of pursuits shared by personnel at many organizational levels. And while it is true that organizational level will define the scope of responsibilities and the amount of time spent in each activity, the notion of a generic set of job-independent office activities seems natural.

During the rest of this chapter we will describe one approach for analyzing office situations that has been constructed to address many of the issues just presented. We refer to our technique and its underlying principles as Office Systems Analysis.

Office Systems Analysis

Simply stated, Office Systems Analysis (OSA) is a methodology and tool set designed to assist in the exploration of the *human side* of the work environment. As such, this technique focuses first on *what people do* in the context of their occupation, *what tools they employ*, and *with what result*. The objective is simply this:

> to improve the overall effectiveness, efficiency, and satisfaction that
> office workers derive from their efforts through a better understanding
> of their work environment and how they function in it.

This workplace is made up of the totality of human, organizational, and procedural factors that influence the office process. Our contention is that only by investigating (and coming to understand) the full spectrum of office variables can the true relationship between the environment and its key components—people, procedures, and equipment—be derived. Once armed with this knowledge, management can begin to deal confidently with the key issues of efficiency, effectiveness, and satisfaction and their effect on the corporate bottom line.

FRAMEWORK FOR OFFICE ANALYSIS

A pivotal issue in office analysis is the accepted view of the office environment. In office studies today, there are two such frameworks in common use. The first contains '*process-centered*' views, while the second can be described as '*product-centered*'. While not totally incompatible, these two approaches to office analysis do stress different objectives.

Process Orientation

The process orientation gains its title from its characterization of the office as a '*process*', not merely a place. This approach emphasizes that office work can, and does, occur in a variety of physical environments in addition to the place traditionally defined as 'the office'. According to the process definition, office work performed while in transit, at the plant, or at home qualifies as part of the total work experience and should be accounted for. The process orientation also is noteworthy for its role in addressing the particularly *dynamic* quality of the office environment. Not only can work assignments change over the course of time, as some assignments are completed and others begun, but conditions can change minute-by-minute, affecting both work content and priorities. Process techniques are particularly well-suited to the dynamic nature of office work.

Referring to the office process model of Figure 10-2, we see the office environment represented in block diagram form. The office complex, as represented here, is likened to a manufacturing plant that employs people, procedures, and tools to convert raw inputs into refined products according to a prescribed process. The inputs to the office complex are the *prerequisites* of office work. They include work requirements, information, and finances sufficient to support the work program. Other prerequisites may be present in specific circumstances.

The *process* that categorizes the office complex may take on many forms. In

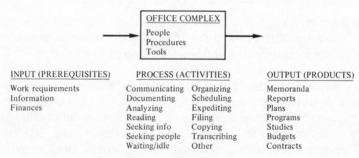

Figure 10-2.   Office process model.

this case, as throughout this chapter, we have chosen a variation on the method of describing office activities first advanced by Booz, Allen, and Hamilton, Inc. Although certainly not the only such alternative, we have found this lexicon to work remarkably well in a variety of work situations. This potential for broad cross-organizational applications has a variety of benefits which will be described in more detail later.

The outputs of the office complex are its *products* which consist of any number of specific objects and events. Different organizations use different nomenclatures and attach varying levels of importance to each. Because of the apparent impossibility of listing them all, a representative number of products are included in Figure 10-2 as examples. Together, the prerequisites, activities, and products are the variables in our office process model. The interrelationships among variables define how the office functions.

Transfer Function Concept

It is useful to begin by visualizing the general association among office variables in terms of an overall *transfer function*. This function is a representation of the office complex that describes how the office prerequisites are converted into products. In more familiar terms, the transfer function represents the process by which people, procedures, and tools interact to generate work products, based on the established prerequisites. Any workable representation of this transfer function would be expressed in terms of our list of office activities. In addition, a knowledge of how each of these activities contributes to the formation of final products would be essential to our description of such a quantity.

Below is one possible representation of a generalized transfer function, where OUTPUT is shown to be the product of the office INPUT and the TRANSFER FUNCTION itself:

$$\text{OUTPUT} = \text{TRANSFER FUNCTION} \times \text{INPUT}$$

where

INPUT = composite of office prerequisites
OUTPUT = composite of office products
TRANSFER FUNCTION = composite of office activities.

The transfer function is a useful conceptual device. Theoretically speaking, it uniquely describes the output of the office complex for all ranges of input. Knowledge of the transfer function could be used to predict the impact of future input changes on the products produced. While we do not suggest that a transfer function be calculated mathematically, we do maintain that an equivalent understanding of the office complex can be a powerful tool for:

- Predicting the effects of changing input conditions on office output
- Analyzing requirements for office procedures and equipment
- Assessing productivity and quantifying results.

Most importantly, the components of the transfer function—the office variables and their interrelationships—are fundamental to our understanding of the office process.

Product Orientation

An alternative to focusing on the office process is an examination of the office products. Unlike the transfer function concept, which is inherently a top-down view of the office, product-centered approaches tend to be built bottom-up from analysis of many output components. Product studies track the numbers of presentations, reports, memoranda, and the like, attempting to construct an office profile from output elements.

While often more exacting than process-centered approaches, product-oriented techniques are rarely as comprehensive. They frequently fail to account for the interrelationships among products and do not reflect time dependencies. Since a significant portion of all office work may not yield tangible output, product techniques may omit key factors from consideration. And because they must deal with specific products that may be unique to a particular department, firm, or industry, product-oriented designs need to be tailored to each new study environment. Tailoring, in turn, makes cross-organizational comparisons difficult and adds to the cost of implementation. Additional drawbacks include the highly detailed data requirements and the resultant demands on analyst and professional time.

Still, product-oriented approaches offer an apparent level of precision that is difficult to achieve through alternative means. These techniques do have a place in highly-focused studies and are useful in cases where objectivity and precision are the major considerations. Figure 10-3 compares the major characteristics of the process and product approaches.

Choosing a Study Framework

The road to a truly useful office systems methodology seems to include, first, the realization that any practical measurement of an office environment will contain some level of ambiguity. Office functions take place in an environment that tends to be cognitive rather than mechanistic, dynamic as opposed to static. In addition, there are countless other factors, many cited previously, that com-

CHARACTERISTICS	PROCESS ORIENTATION	PRODUCT ORIENTATION
Focus	People/tasks	Output
Variables	{ Activities performed	{ Costs
	{ Tools employed	{ Benefits
Scope	Comprehensive	Segmented
Viewpoint	Top-down	Bottom-up
Generality	Generic	Specific
Quantification	Categorical	Precise
Application area	Classification	Calibration

Figure 10-3.   Orientations for Office Systems Analysis.

plicate any attempt to measure the office environment with both comprehensiveness and precision.

Once we have agreed to accept results that fall short of absolute mathematical precision, we find process-centered techniques attractive for categorizing office activity. Process-oriented designs have the added virtue that they can be made largely situation independent. This offers promise of a growing body of information about the office worker, based on the use of uniform study conventions across many environments.

On the other hand, the task of acquiring explicit measures, such as information about professional effort levels and productivity impacts, is considerably more complex. Here is where product-centered approaches aid in calibrating subjective estimates and validating measurement results.

In designing the OSA Methodology, we have employed a strategy that draws on attributes of both process- and product-centered techniques. The orientation is largely process-centered, while the implementation makes use of product-centered data collection mechanics to add focus to the results. We consider the OSA technique appropriate for analyzing the office complex and for measuring the costs and benefits of managerial, professional, and support staff activities.

STUDY PROCEDURES

Key to success of any method of systems analysis is the choice of study procedure. The selected alternative must be consistent with the nature of the office environments under study, and capable of supporting the required data collection and analysis. We begin our task with several design criteria. To be considered successful the final form of our study procedure must meet these objectives:

- Source of measurable information in quantities sufficient to support meaningful conclusions.
- Arranged for straightforward implementation.
- Relevant to productivity assessment.
- Sufficiently general as to allow use in multiple environments.
- Adequately supported through self-instruction, reference documentation, and automated tools to facilitate its use.

In striving to meet these criteria we present four classes of study procedure. Our classification for each of these, together with an example of a common approach for each case, is described below.

External Monitoring

External monitoring relies on the use of trained observers to gather information about office activity through direct oversight of the study participants. Typical examples are found in psychological testing of human behavior. Some testing approaches rely on one-way mirrors, others use cameras or human proctors to monitor experimental activity.

An obvious advantage of such a technique is that it is possible to obtain a continuous accounting of the office situation under study with little or no additional effort by those being observed. Use of trained observers helps uncover significant patterns in activity that may not be apparent even to the study subjects themselves.

The drawbacks of external monitoring in an office environment include a general aversion to such an intrusive method of data gathering, the large investment of observer time, and the difficulty in classifying office tasks exclusively through third-party observation. Add to these limitations the impact of observer-introduced biases and the distorting effects of such an intrusive technique on study group behavior, and you have an approach that is limited to a select number of actual office situations.

Nevertheless, external monitoring may be helpful where it serves as a secondary data collection mechanism. For example, traveling observers may be used. These individuals act primarily as a source of information to the study participants, while concurrently observing study group behavior. The external monitoring technique also may be useful in monitoring critical resources such as copiers or printers to obtain information on their patterns of use. In each case there is a crucial trade-off between overt monitoring, which may distort actual behaviors, and covert monitoring which, when acknowledged, may undermine employee trust.

One effective compromise is an overt monitoring program that extends over several months to allow time for aberrations in normal behavior to subside. Other techniques use computer, time clock, or calendar information as a source of supplementary input.

Self Monitoring

Self monitoring is in itself something of a compromise. It removes a number of the common objections to external monitoring since study participants serve as reporters of their own activities. Like external monitoring, the experimental plan may include continuous data collection during a specified period of time, or sampled inputs. In either case it is expedient for participants to have background on the objectives and methods of data collection, as well as access to a data recording device. Many studies make use of an activity log containing brief instructions and a shorthand notation to facilitate data entry.

Besides reducing the intrusiveness of the external monitoring approach, self monitoring provides a potential source of insight into work activities that is often difficult for a third-party observer to obtain. With self monitoring, too, since many observer/respondents can be recording data about themselves simultaneously, results can be obtained more quickly with a smaller analytical staff.

Because self monitoring requires active study group participation, another byproduct may be increased enthusiasm and an added sense of commitment to the study objectives. This is support that can be important in later stages. One important caveat, however, is not to allow these future expectations to escape the business realities. No matter what the study results indicate, participants should understand beforehand that the decision to commit corporate resources for office automation, like any other investment, will depend on the business incentives to do so in the light of other opportunities and constraints. Oversold solutions and unreasonable user expectations are among the greatest causes of office systems failure.

When we look at the self monitoring approach we see that employing multiple observers does risk several shortcomings. Chief among them are the varied biases that these observers introduce into the experiment. These biases can be traced to differences in the observers' understanding of their task, varying levels of con-scientiousness in data recording, and subtle pressures to supply results that will be considered acceptable. Past studies employing this approach, as is true in all of the self-measurement techniques described here, suffer to some extent from these experimental realities.

An additional limitation of self monitoring is the importance of the data collection interval. Observations collected during too-brief a time interval may omit key activities or over-emphasize those that take place infrequently, depending upon the sampling period. A trend toward longer measurement intervals helps reduce this problem as does the use of several sampling periods that are randomly scheduled. Of course both remedies imply greater data collection costs and an increased investment of respondent time.

External Appraisal

External appraisal, as the name implies, involves a third party data collector. Unlike the observer in external monitoring, the third party in external appraisal is, well, an appraiser. Rather than seeking a comprehensive accounting of the respondent's activities, the appraiser looks for specific characteristics and trends. A typical example of such a technique is a one-on-one interview between a member of the analytical staff and the study group.

Like external monitoring, this approach involves a type of overt contact between the study group and the analytical staff. Like external monitoring there is a significant opportunity to gain additional insights through third-party observations during the course of the interaction. Since appraisal is used in place of monitoring, it is typical not to obtain information that is as specific as either of the monitoring techniques.

The key to external appraisal is its focus. It places greatest emphasis on trends and opinions rather than specifics. The reasoning is that while detailed data may be important in some circumstances, it is less important than the broader insights that appraisal provides. Unlike external monitoring, which offers no direct recourse for resolving ambiguities, external appraisal supports a level of interaction between the respondent and study analyst necessary to handle such eventualities. And unlike self monitoring, there is a trained appraiser involved to guide the information exchange sessions.

When handled appropriately, external appraisal can be a valuable source of information on perceptions and attitudes that are often missed with monitoring methods. It is frequently the case that these 'impressions' tell more about likely acceptance or rejection of office automation than do observed work behaviors.

Drawbacks of the technique include the required investment of study analyst and respondent time, as well as the impact of appraiser and respondent personalities on information supplied and ultimately recorded. Another characteristic of all appraisal techniques is the lack of true precision in the final results.

Self Appraisal

Self appraisal commonly avoids use of comprehensive record-keeping methods in order to minimize the impact on respondent time. Instead, a standard, single-pass data collection device, like a questionnaire, is used to collect information from study participants.

To their credit, self appraisal methods offer the opportunity for gathering information on observations and trends that can be missed in monitoring methods. They are also a ready source of attitudes and opinions, not unlike external appraisal. Most importantly, once the appraisal materials are constructed, the data collection proceeds quickly with only modest respondent effort. This is a marked advantage over self monitoring and external appraisal, both of which can require substantial investments of study group time. With appraisal, study analyst time is conserved as well, saving resources over both external techniques mentioned earlier. And like self monitoring, the data collection methods available for use in self appraisal can facilitate the analysis of results through a proper structuring of responses, but more about this later.

Shortcomings of the self analysis method include the lack of data precision and limited opportunities for qualitative feedback from the study group. This limitation is shared by both appraisal techniques. Also required is a greater investment

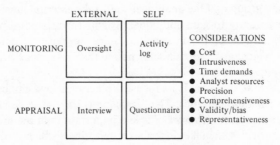

Figure 10-4.   Study procedures.

of respondent time than is demanded by the external approaches. Figure 10-4 illustrates graphically how these procedures interrelate.

Choice of Procedure

Which procedure is best for office analysis? The answer depends in part on the objectives of the analysis. Requirements for high levels of precision will obviously favor the monitoring techniques mentioned; needs for more information on trends and opinions, alternatively, will point toward the appraisal methods. Environmental and business constraints will also play a part in the choice of method. Concerns about disruption of normal office operations may limit the choice to an external method, while cost considerations may favor an appraisal technique. The answer is by no means a simple one. A growing number of studies, including Office Systems Analysis, rely on one procedural approach for the bulk of data gathering, with other methods used selectively to further support the analysis. The next section describes how such an integration of procedures is applied in practice.

MEASUREMENT TOOLS

Design tradeoffs resurface frequently in the development of any measurement tool. Data quality versus quantity, rigor versus brevity, explicitness versus conciseness, and structure versus flexibility are representative of the dimensions of this balancing act. How each tradeoff is decided ultimately will affect the data collection process. There are, unfortunately, few definitive rules for making such choices.

In dealing with the design choices that faced us, we found three factors to be of uncommon importance:

- structural issues
- data quality issues
- data quantity issues.

For the purposes of this discussion, our focus will be on one common type of self appraisal tool, the questionnaire. It should be noted that the same observations extend to other study tools. These will not be discussed explicitly, but should be considered in the context of the following observations.

Structural Issues

Structure is a property of any data collection vehicle. Like its 'content', a questionnaire's structural properties can markedly influence the quality and quantity of survey information collected. At one extreme of questionnaire design are the *unstructured* approaches which deliberately impose few limitations on questionnaire responses. At the opposite extreme are the *structured* designs which dictate both the form and scope of questionnaire completion.

Among the unstructured approaches to questionnaire design are essays and suggestion-box designs. These techniques are most effective in ill-defined situations and in cases where there is little record of past information. They are effective also in situations where *opinion* is as important as the *facts*. Being, by nature, non-explicit, unstructured approaches leave much to chance, relying heavily on the respondent's diligence and insight to uncover the salient issues. These questionnaires require the respondent, in a sense, to supply both the right questions and their answers. As a consequence, the results obtained often suffer from a form of *situational myopia*, where inherent biases distort individual perceptions. We know from our own experience that our objectivity is impaired every time we engage in self analysis. The study population is likely to suffer from these same limitations.

Further, unstructured methods of data collection, since they provide little actual guidance, often yield results that a difficult to categorize. Each respondent has a different view of the world that is expressed in personal terms. It becomes the job of a study analyst to correlate common issues among respondents and to fill in any informational gaps. As a result, unstructured approaches almost always require multiple rounds of data collection for clarification and resolution of open issues.

Highly structured techniques, on the other hand, begin by constraining responses to a defined subset of all possibilities. True-false and multiple choice are representative of these designs. These techniques are useful for exploring particular points of interest and registering opinion on explicit topics.

While structured inputs require less interpretation than the less-structured designs, there is greater danger that key issues will be omitted from analysis. Another danger is that all respondents may not interpret even structured questions uniformly and these answers may not be strictly comparable. Fortunately, sampling techniques and statistical analysis can help offset these drawbacks.

With these considerations in mind, the choice of questionnaire structure will depend on the type of situation under study and the nature of the desired results. In any case, there are key tradeoffs that must be made at the outset. This structure decision profoundly affects the form and substance of the data collected.

Data Quality Issues

Quality/quantity tradeoffs are common in questionnaire design. In this context quality describes the extent to which the data collected meets the established study objectives. The better the match between objectives and data, the higher the quality.

It is important to note that study objectives may cover a wide range of goals. In some situations the intent may be to acquire definitive information largely independent of respondent biases. Governmental Tax Agencies strive for this sense of objectivity. On other occasions the intent may be to measure these respondent biases themselves. Recording individual perceptions of well-defined phenomena is common in psychological testing where many studies focus on the observer's behavior, rather than the situation observed. In either case it is important to first define *what* is to be measured, then to use the data collection and analysis techniques best suited to the task.

Data Quantity Issues

The notion of data quantity is obvious. Unfortunately, deciding *a priori* how much information is necessary to meet study requirements is not so apparent. Like a mathematical modeling problem, greater situational complexity increases data requirements, and so do time dependencies and factors beyond the environment under examination. Study environments that are internally complex, highly dynamic, and closely tied to external influences will demand larger quantities of data to describe them. In many respects today's office environments exhibit these tendencies.

Quantity requirements are affected also by the number of dimensions being measured, the degree of precision demanded in the final result, and the number of situational unknowns. Multidimensional experiments with exacting requirements, and facing a large number of unknowns, are common in areas as diverse as space exploration and pharmaceutical testing. The extraordinary data requirements in both areas are by now well known.

Finally, quantity considerations come into play from a statistical standpoint. In order to increase confidence in study results it is frequently necessary to include restatements of key issues to help verify interpretations and to ensure consistency. All this adds to the number of data items required.

The tradeoffs between the quality and quantity of information collected are clear. The data collection method chosen must provide sufficiently substantive communication between the study analyst and the respondent to ensure quality responses. At the same time adequate data quantities are needed to describe the study environment completely. Both quality and quantity objectives must be met simultaneously, to the extent possible, while maintaining the willing participation of the study respondents.

RESULTS

The OSA Methodology views the office as a process rather than merely a place. We observe that, although work activities are often conducted within the office (the place), tasks essential to company operations often occur elsewhere as well. All activities necessary for the achievement of organizational objectives are considered to be part of the office process originally depicted in Figure 10-2.

Armed with Booz, Allen, and Hamilton's taxonomy for categorizing office activities, we have built the OSA Methodology upon an extension of our funda-

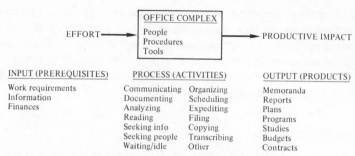

Figure 10-5.   Office process model.

mental framework for the office process. Added to those office activities, which describe the office process, are measures of effort and productivity. The *effort* required to perform each office activity serves as the process input. The *productive impact* of each activity represents the process output. By examining each office task in terms of the effort exerted and productivity achieved, we can begin to categorize office work into performance categories. Figure 10-5 illustrates our earlier view of the office process with effort and productive impact components shown explicitly.

Performance Matrix

Office tasks are plotted, based on their effort, productive impact, and relevancy dimensions, using the performance matrix similar to the sample shown in Figure 10-6. Effort is graphed on the horizontal axis from low-to-high and productive impact is graphed on the vertical axis. The intensity of the data points represents three levels of relevance to the study population. High relevance activities are those that generally involve a significant investment of personal time or attention.

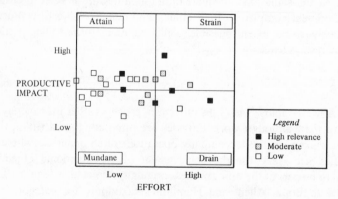

Figure 10-6.   Performance matrix.

Moderate and low relevance pursuits are those that are of successively lower importance to the population under study. By noting where particular activities fall within the matrix, together with their relevancy, we are able to determine what type of action is appropriate in each case.

Activities characterized by low effort and low productive impact fall in the lower left-hand corner. These activities are labeled as '*mundane*', adopting a term commonly used to describe them. Tasks of this genre are candidates for delegation to office staff who are appropriately skilled to perform them most efficiently.

At the opposite extreme are activities that fall in the upper right-hand corner of the performance matrix. These represent a '*strain*' on corporate resources. The productive impact is high in these instances, but at the cost of significant effort. Automation provides the best solution by offering to improve performance by lessening the effort invested.

Activities that are low in productive impact and high in effort represent a real '*drain*' on corporate resources and fall at the lower right. These are the ones that must be dealt with most vigorously. The choice is whether to delegate these activities or to automate them in an effort to improve office worker productivity.

Finally, in the upper left-hand corner are those low effort, high productive impact activities that we wish to emulate. These have all the appropriate ingredients for high performance. The goal of our automated office program, then, is to migrate activities toward the '*attain*' segment of the performance matrix through a balanced program of task delegation and automation. For example, high-effort tasks can be enhanced through effort-saving automation. In this way activities that represent a *strain* on company personnel or a *drain* on resources can be improved. For low productivity pursuits, task delegation may be a more appropriate policy. Using proper delegation strategies, those activities identified as *mundane* or as a *drain* on resources can be reassigned.

By looking at office activities in this way it is possible to identify problem areas quickly. Activities not in the quadrant marked '*attain*' are candidates for possible action. Second, action priorities can be established since relative positioning on the performance matrix is important—the further particular observations are from the target area, the more significant the action necessary to effect a change. Third, acknowledging the limits to precision, it is possible to compare activities based on matrix positioning. Comparisons can be made among several different activities at a single point in time or for a single activity at different times. We have even used the performance matrix to compare the characteristics of different office populations, each time with consistent results. This cross-organizational quality of the OSA approach is a key benefit that permits us to build an expanding base of knowledge about the office environment.

Study Guide

The Methodology for Office Systems Analysis (OSA) is one part of a total framework for productivity measurement. When used within the context of a well-administered program of analysis, OSA can provide valuable insight into the human side of the office environment. Designed to handle a wide range of office situations, organizational levels, and degrees of technological sophistication, OSA is a useful technique for problem definition, project scoping, exploration, and post-implementation appraisals. The components of OSA include study briefings, a questionnaire, reference package, optional activity log, and follow-up interviews. All have been designed to (1) work together, while capitalizing on the strengths of each component, (2) conserve the time invested by study participants and analysts in handling data, and (3) maximize the quantifiable results, without sacrificing valuable qualitative input.

As currently employed, Office Systems Analysis is applied in three phases. Phase I is a Base Case Measurement that furnishes initial insight into the office environment. At this stage a 'profile' is created describing the scope of work activities under way, the effort invested, and the resulting impact on productivity.

The tools of the OSA Methodology are key to its operation. These are described in the following:

OSA Reference Package

A presentation of study objectives, terminology, and descriptions of automated office system alternatives. Designed to provide a common set of terms to enhance study group dialog, increase understanding of study materials, and create awareness of office system alternatives.

OSA Questionnaire

A multipart data collection tool designed to explore activities key to professional productivity. The Questionnaire is designed to optimize data input over a wide range of business environments, while limiting the intrusive effects commonly associated with such tools.

Activity Record

A data collection tool used optionally by each study participant as the basis for development of Questionnaire responses.

Interviews

One-on-one discussions of key issues between a member of the study team and individual participants with the objective of gaining additional insight into the study environment by assessing certain qualitative issues.

Study Group Orientations and Management Briefings

Sessions used to familiarize study participants and the responsible management with the study process, tools, and objectives.

Phase II presents an opportunity to introduce change in the form of new processes, organizations, or resources. Often, Phase II brings with it the addition of new office equipment, together with the procedures designed to support it. Other changes, like a modification in staffing arrangements, alteration in work flow, or organizational realignment, would constitute further developments we might choose to evaluate with this technique in other circumstances.

Phase III is a post-implementation audit. In effect, this latter stage repeats the data collection and analysis carried out during Phase I. By comparing the results of Phases I and III, OSA can provide a measure of change due to actions taken in the interim. Naturally, the impacts of these actions on office worker productivity are of central interest.

With Office Systems Analysis, it is possible to trace the evolution of a single organization over a period of years, using the Phase III results of one analysis as the base case for the next. Since a process-oriented set of work classifications is used to record professional activity, the study results and the technique used to produce them remain consistent in the face of organizational restructuring and personnel changes. For these same reasons comparison among diverse organizations is possible as well. Business, engineering, and research groups have all been parties to the OSA form of analysis. A third consequence of the approach is the potential for a growing base of data from which to investigate professional activity broadly and to assess the factors that affect performance.

As Office Systems Analysis is designed to focus on the human side of the productivity measurement issue, other techniques are more appropriate for evaluating the related dimensions of equipment and cost/benefit analysis. These subjects become successively easier to investigate once armed with a sound understanding of the office complex and its people, procedures, and tools.

CONCLUSIONS

This Chapter Revisited

This chapter began with an introduction to the subject of productivity measurement in the office environment. It went on to describe the issues and objectives that are integral to activity in this area. Considerable attention was directed toward laying the groundwork for an appropriate productivity measurement methodology. In support of this goal, we examined two frameworks for office analysis in common use—process-oriented and product-oriented techniques —and their implications.

Later, we described alternative study procedures and measurement tools relevant to office analysis. In this connection, Office Systems Analysis was highlighted, together with its principal components, as one method used for studying office situations. Finally, we reviewed how the results of such a study technique might be used in practice.

The Final Analysis

As the concluding subject in our examination of *Issues in Productivity Measurement*, we review the Office Systems Analysis approach in terms of its originally established design criteria. These criteria were first discussed in the section entitled '*Study Procedures*'. Our intention is not only to judge conformance of the methodology with the original objectives, but to highlight key considerations that impact its use.

Our original design criteria are repeated below for reference:

● Source of measurable information in quantities sufficient to support meaningful conclusions

Office Systems Analysis is based upon a combination of study procedures and measurement tools designed specifically for the task of information gathering in office environments. The OSA Questionnaire highlights key areas worthy of further investigation, while demanding only a modest investment of study group time and effort. An Activity Record is provided for the optional use of study participants to permit data validation, where appropriate. Finally, interviews with selected study group members help to confirm earlier responses, eliminate discrepancies, and supplement questionnaire results with useful qualitative background. These procedures and tools function collectively to meet the information requirements necessary for office analysis.

● Arranged for straightforward implementation

The use of an organized approach to the study process is key to both respondents and study analysts. The Framework for Office Analysis defines the principal study components and their structure. Procedures describe how study information is collected, analyzed, and presented, and tools support the efficiency and effectiveness of the study process.

● Relevant to productivity assessment

Office Systems Analysis is based on a common set of activity definitions that describe the office environment. These classifications have been used successfully in previous studies as a means of categorizing work effort. Respondents in a variety of business situations appear to have little difficulty relating these definitions to their own disciplines.

● Sufficiently general as to allow use in multiple environments

By focusing on office activities rather than office products or output, Office Systems Analysis preserves its situational independence.

Some alternative methods of analysis rely on detailed examination of particular work products, like reports, plans, and letters. This product orientation commonly requires a data collection technique 'tailored' to the situation and, consequently, operates at a high level of detail.

By contrast, Office Systems Analysis sacrifices some of this precision to attain a broader view of the study group. In so doing we gain occupation-independent information that describes the activities performed and the interrelationships among them. At the same time we have at our disposal a study technique with potential for application in a variety of office situations.

● Adequately supported through self-instruction, reference documentation, and automated tools to facilitate its use

The Office Systems Analysis strategy is to employ a full range of instructional materials to assist in data collection and analysis. At the present time the *OSA Reference Package* serves as the key information resource. It provides background on the study context, tools, and terminology.

Instructions and definitions within the Questionnaire itself provide guidance on response recording. The Activity Record, distributed with the Questionnaire, is another aid to the respondent. Finally, a set of automated tools to assist in data collection, analysis, and reporting exists to aid the study analyst.

Some Caveats

Like any questionnaire-based data collection technique, the approach described here relies heavily on the subjective assessments of the study population. The Questionnaire is driven by individual perceptions expressed in subjectively assigned terms. As a consequence, it shares the limitations inherent in all such designs. These shortcomings might be unacceptable in a highly-controlled production line experiment where production parameters are well-known and comparatively predictable over time. But in the dynamic environment of the office the rules are much different. Here, human judgment is a key input, information (of all forms) is a principal substance, and decisions make up a significant share of the output. These parameters defy simple quantification. When enumeration succeeds, it is often at considerable expense with no guarantee that the conditions measured will in fact remain.

The self appraisal approach sacrifices some objectivity for the opportunity of exploring the interacting elements that comprise the office environment. The technique relies on the size and composition of the sample population to help ensure the comprehensiveness of the results, while at the same time limiting the impact of errant and unrepresentative responses. Design factors help provide consistency among responses from a single individual, while reference documentation and questionnaire instruction help preserve comparability throughout the study group. Interviews and Activity Records serve as auxiliary information sources.

The Bottom Line

Harvey Poppel, Senior Vice President, Booz, Allen, and Hamilton, Inc., points out that 'case study results indicate that no cookbook exists for taking or measuring the benefits of automation. Knowledge is eclectic, and the potential gains, while cumulatively large, will come in small pieces. If not planned and measured, they could leak away'. He goes on to point out that 'the winners . . . will be those corporations and government offices whose senior executives identify a productivity program and begin now to organize for and plan the introduction of automated office tools'.

We believe that with Office Systems Analysis, and similarly focused techniques, management can begin to explore the world of the office worker with confidence and efficiency. By refining the framework, study procedures, and measurement tools, its users will be better able to measure the key factors that comprise the office environment and evaluate their impact on office worker productivity—and ultimately the firm's bottom line.

SUMMARY

Introduction

- The challenge
  - *Issue: How can we make measurements in an environment that is typically unstructured, dynamic, and unpredictable?*
  - *Issue: How can we measure a quantity like productivity when it appears to be largely intangible, elusive, and ill-defined?*
- The response
  - Adequate breadth of definition yields results that are meaningful
  - Adequate depth of definition yields results that are measureable.

Objectives

- The focus: bottom line performance
- Key issues
  - Planning
  - Implementation

- Problem dimensions
  - Framework of Office Analysis
  - Office study procedures
  - Measurement tools
- Office Systems Analysis
  - What people do in the context of their occupation
  - What tools they employ
  - With what result.

Framework for Office Analysis

- Process orientation
- Transfer function concept
- Product orientation.

Study Procedures

- External monitoring
- Self monitoring
- External appraisal
- Self appraisal.

Measurement Tools

- Structural issues
- Data quality issues
- Data quantity issues.

Results

- Performance matrix
- Study guide
  - OSA reference package
  - OSA Questionnaire
  - Activity Record
  - Interviews
  - Study group orientations and management briefings.

Conclusions

- Source of measurable information in quantities sufficient to support meaningful conclusions
- Arranged for straightforward implementation
- Relevant to productivity assessment

- Sufficiently general as to allow use in multiple environments
- Adequately supported through self-instruction, reference documentation, and automated tools to facilitate its use.

REFERENCES AND SUGGESTED READINGS

1. Conrath, D. W., *et al.*: The Electronic Office and Organizational Behavior Measuring Office Activities. *Computer Networks (Netherlands)*, **5**, No. 6, 401–410, December 1981.
2. Tapscott, Don: How does the Office of the Future Measure Up? *Telephone Engineer and Management*, **86**, No. 1, 50–56, January 1, 1982.
3. Hammer, Michael, and Kunin, Jay S.: Productivity: The Means, Not the End. *Computerworld*, **16**, No. 13A (Office Automation Issue), 9–10, March 31, 1982.
4. Halatin, T. J.: Keeping Your Employees Turned On Professionally: *Supervisory Mgmt*, **26**, No. 10, 10–14, October 1981.
5. Goldfield, Randy J.: Is an OA Task Force for You? *Computer Decisions*, **14**, No. 3, 84, March 1982.

Advances in Office Automation, Vol 1
Edited by Karen Takle Quinn
© 1985 Wiley Heyden Ltd.

Chapter 11

PRINCIPAL PRODUCTIVITY . . . A FRUSTRATION INDEX

Noel J. Gilson

IBM Corporation

INTRODUCTION

The most difficult part of evaluating a concept such as an office system is trying to demonstrate its value to the people who will use it.

The justification for Office Systems is always explained to be an opportunity for increasing Principal Productivity. In their reading, in their meetings, and wherever they turn, today's executives in business and government are bombarded with news about productivity (Figure 11-1). The message is consistent: Office Systems will be one of the ways to obtain increased Principal Productivity.

The busy executives obviously want to increase principal productivity, but they are frustrated. They are not quite sure what anyone means by either office

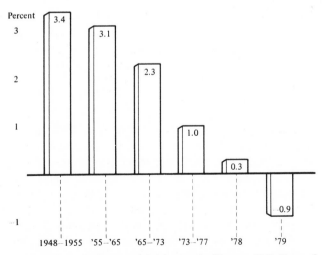

Figure 11-1.   U.S. productivity growth. (Source: U.S. Dept of Commerce. Reproduced from IBM Marketing Presentation 'PROFS . . . An IBM Product to Improve Productivity'.).

Figure 11-2. Office Systems are a productivity vehicle. Office Systems lead to greater productivity; the discipline of greater productivity leads to better business decisions.

systems or principal productivity. They sense that important decisions about office systems may soon be forced upon them, and they will be relying on recommendations from their staff people to help them make the right decisions. Staff people can be relied on to give quick answers; they can be depended on for accurate answers; but, sometimes, the executives seem to ignore their recommendations.

This chapter will reinforce the idea that the quick answers do exist. Several significant studies which were made recently can be used to verify the accuracy of the answers. More importantly, here is an attempt to define the answers so that they will influence the executive decision on Office Systems (Figure 11-2).

GLOBAL DEFINITION

Increasing productivity is a global concern; everyone's standard of living depends on it. If a nation's Gross National Product falls, it implies that fewer goods and services are being produced, fewer people are employed, and the nation's standard of living falls. It is easy to understand the concept of productivity in terms of anything that is tangible, visible, and in a form that can be counted and measured. Productivity implies that there is a product. Yet a principal is someone who makes nothing, and fixes nothing. By definition, he or she is a white-collar worker, someone who works in an office in either a management or professional capacity. What, then, is the product?

The modern world runs on information. The oil company analyzes a lot of data to provide information about the best places to prospect for oil before money is invested in a test drill. The farmer anxiously scans information from the weather reports to determine the best times to plant and harvest, to ensure the maximum crops, and to make enough money to go on farming. Each of us, as individuals, reads the monthly statements from our banks and credit card companies to see how much money we have (or have spent), so that we can decide whether we can afford that new car.

Those are three totally different examples. They were deliberately picked to appear totally dissimilar, but the information objectives were the same. Information was used to make a decision. All organizations conduct business in a similar fashion: when they make conscious and rational decisions, they do so based on the information that is available to the organization at that time.

It is important to recognize that the role of information may be perceived quite differently in your organization than in mine. Different because the *objectives* of the organization may be quite different: profit versus nonprofit, private versus public sector, manufacturing versus services, and so on. It is also true that the information *content* (i.e. what specific information is gathered and what will be used in the decision-making process) may be different. It is probable that the information *flow* (i.e. the formal or informal ways in which information reaches the decision-making process) will change from one organization to another. However, the information *form* and *function* are the same in every case (Figure 11-3).

The *form* in which information is transmitted or communicated is generally limited to the three ways that are similar in every organization and culture: it can be textual (i.e. the written word, sentences, and paragraphs, whether on paper or in electronic form), it can be pictorial (i.e. the diagrams and charts that convey an informational message), or it can be verbal (i.e. the spoken word, people talking to each other, whether face to face, or by telephone, or using some other medium). The *function* of information in every organization is always the same: to enable the organization to meet its expectations. Those expectations may be to increase revenue, or to lower cost, or to provide better service, but they will be reached via a series of decisions. The decisions will be based on information. Information is

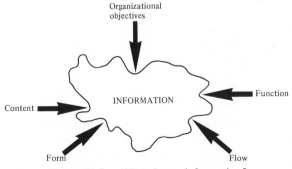

Figure 11-3.   What shapes information?

Information attribute	Productivity requirement
Justification	Information is used to support the decision-making process
Integrity	Is the right information available?
Accuracy	Is the available information right?
Completeness	Is all the information available?
Timeliness	Will the information be available in time?
Cost effectiveness	Is the cost of obtaining information less than the benefits of using it?
Control	Are there procedures to avoid, detect, or correct erroneous information?

Figure 11-4. Applying a productivity discipline to manage information. (Adapted from
IBM Programming Manuals.)

vital to the functioning of any organization, large or small. Information management is defined as the use of the information resource within an organization to
achieve the objectives of that organization.

Where has the information come from? Who has made it available?

An organization's information flow is generally through an office. The office is
where information is collected, manipulated, disseminated, and stored. Information is the product of an office. It is very real, even when it is not obviously
tangible, and it can always have a major impact on the success or failure of the
organization it was intended to support. Coffee machine gossip is an example of
intangible information. Everyone knows that it probably is not true, but it builds
attitudes that affect how we communicate with each other and, therefore, how we
work together (Figure 11-4).

Once you have accepted the idea that information is, of itself, a meaningful
product, then the concept of 'information worker' productivity becomes more
meaningful. A principal is an information worker. The principal's current work
assignment may be as an administrative assistant, as a staff professional, as a line
manager, or as a key executive, but the principal is working with information. The
input may be a weather report on the radio, the output may be a decision to invest
in a multimillion dollar (or deutschmark, or pound, or yen) expansion, but the
entire process revolves around information and how it is handled. How to make
this process work best, for the benefit of the entire organization, is what principal
productivity is all about.

EVOLUTIONARY PRODUCTIVITY

From the beginning of time, people have relied on information. At first it was
the knowledge needed for basic survival: where can we find food to eat, where
shall we shelter. Social anthropologists tell us that subsistence living was produc-

tive. People gathered only what they needed or could use, and no more. There was no waste.

Then came the 'agricultural revolution' with the cultivation of crops and the domestication of animals, and societies came into being. With society came government, and an organization that thrives on information. An early example of information gathering by a government was the Domesday Book (1084–85 A.D.).

Another example of information and organization is the Church. The Church represents a tremendous warehouse of information in all its variants: knowledge, data, fact, fable, legend, etc. At first, this information was communicated verbally, then much of it was written down. Mediaeval monasteries were centers of learning and contemporary knowledge during a period when the majority of people could neither read nor write. Certainly no information explosion or paper problem existed in those days.

Even the invention of the printing press did not immediately change the manner in which the ecclesiastical offices functioned. Written information was still hand-written. The scarcity of these documents enabled them to be treated as objects of beauty, as well as utility.

A third example of the office occurs historically in the military sphere. Until very recently, all the great military commanders worked in very much the same manner. Caesar, Napoleon, and Washington needed to communicate with their field officers. Yet if they wanted to do so to more than one person, in writing, and they wanted to tell each one the same thing, they had to copy each letter and every word by hand. There was no copier to reproduce them. Those letters were short and precise.

These old methods were, in some ways, more productive than the present ones, just as subsistence living was more productive. It ensured that the written word was essential and to the point. It avoided needless duplication and replication. Only the truly necessary was created in such an office. The system was immensely productive because there was no waste.

Then the Industrial Revolution (Britain, c. 1730–1850) transformed the pre-dominantly agricultural society (Figure 11-5). Machines could now duplicate and replicate, endlessly it seemed. From that era came the philosophy that machines are supposed to work (i.e. make something) and people are supposed to think (i.e. handle information). However, it is the Electrical Revolution, beginning in the 1870s and still going on, that has really changed the office. It was electricity that spawned the devices that are commonplace in today's office: the electric typewriter, the telephone, the copier, the calculator, and so on. Computers, and traditional data processing, are a natural outgrowth of the electrical revolution, but they have had little real effect on the operation of the office through the 1970s. Although changes occurred in numbers and speed, the office has not really changed for about a century. It is still essentially a manual operation. It has operated on the assumption that mechanized components have made us all more productive. Is that assumption valid today?

Agricultural revolution

Industrial revolution

Electrical revolution

Information revolution   Figure 11-5.   Revolutions that affect productivity.

CURRENT ISSUES

It is difficult to imagine an office in the 1970s that did not have a lot of equipment. Processing letters and text was done more quickly and in greater quantity. Yet this very equipment has helped to create a problem for the 1980s. Information is being produced, and reproduced, more quickly than people can handle it. However, a large part of the useful life of information is wasted; it is spent as paper in the distribution channels that we call the mailing system. The productivity gains that were made in the office, as a result of the equipment that was introduced, are quickly being dissipated by moving mountains of paper inefficiently from place to place. People are no longer managing information, they are pushing paper around.

The telephone is very much a part of business and social life. Yet it is not always a productive tool. A high percentage of the calls placed simply do not reach the person we wanted to talk to. Studies indicate that between two-thirds and three-quarters of all calls placed are in this category. The line is busy, or the person is out, and time is wasted, i.e. productivity is lost. The electric typewriter certainly made the secretary more productive if one measures how easy it is to churn out more letters and memos. A copier can now produce multiple copies of those letters and memos—duplexed, collated, and stapled—at a fantastic rate. It is too easy to make too many copies that are sent to too many people who put them in too many files. Then the real problem occurs when someone goes looking for information in the files. The particular document is hard to find.

That document was probably misfiled anyway. The secretary was trying to catch up on filing on a day the boss was out of town when the telephone rang and he/she had to stop to answer it. So, we call the originator, and ask for yet another copy....

Yesterday's technology made the office of today. It applied contemporary technology to automate a specific job, but it was a box approach. The boxes made each individual more productive at any one particular task. Now that technology is changing, and its cost is coming down, it would be quite simple to upgrade the technology of each box, and incrementally improve the productivity of any particular mechanical task. But what is the overall productivity gain from using the technology of the 20th century in typing a letter, just to drop it into a 19th century mailing system? Future productivity gains will be worthwhile when the principal has the tools to manage information effectively, from its origination to its final use.

Many people are looking at the overall question of productivity. Many theories and approaches exist, and they all agree on one point: this current decline in principal productivity must be reversed. Although many automated tasks in an office now were not possible over a hundred years ago, the investment in new office equipment is in no way comparable to the massive investment that has been made in manufacturing equipment. This is surprising since, statistically, over 50% of the U.S. workforce is employed in an office and accounts for approximately 65% of the total labor cost (Figure 11-6). Instead, office expense has increased, caused by growth in demand as well as inflation, but productivity has not increased when compared with the productivity gains in manufacturing.

One of the reasons may be that most organizations of the 1970s had no good way of measuring the productivity of their nonmanufacturing employees and, therefore, no good way of determining the return on capital investment on non-manufacturing equipment. Some obvious exceptions are seen in Figure 11-7. Information handling is not always a repetitive task with a known number of inputs and a clearly defined output. Some early studies were made which usually involved training observers who recorded, every two minutes or so, the activities of the people involved. It was technically sound from a task-measurement

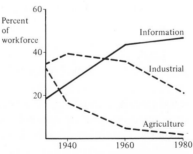

Figure 11-6. U.S. workforce distribution. (Reproduced from IBM Marketing Presentation 'PROFS . . . An IBM Product to Improve Productivity'.)

Profession	Quantifiable output
Insurance agent	$ value of policies issued
Lawyer	# of briefs handled
Loan officer	$ in loan revenue generated
Scientist	# of patents issued
Social worker	# of cases handled
Writer	# of words published

Figure 11-7.   Some ways of measuring principal productivity. (IBM Office Systems Study Guide.)

viewpoint, but not relevant to many principals. This method has been largely superseded by data gathering in a self-administered survey, as will be described later.

In general, though, most of the studies really only tell us what people are doing now, what they are actually spending their time on today. A few attempt to suggest what people should be doing, what equipment they should be using, and so on. Some excellent, fast becoming classic, studies have been published in the technical journals. Of these, the multiclient study performed by Booz, Allen, and Hamilton is a superb example. Yet the studies are going on, in organization after organization, often in different parts of the same company. Why? These studies tell us how we spend our time, and then attempt to measure productivity. A sensible attempt has been made to quantify these measurements but, in the quantification, some of the studies have completely missed the point. Only a very small number of them have attempted to *define* principal productivity. This is the missing link.

ACCEPTED DEFINITIONS AND MYTHS

The dictionary, it turns out, is not a very good place to uncover the meaning of 'principal productivity':

Principal, n., a chief or a head.
Productivity, n., the quality or state of being productive.

However, we have already defined a principal: it is someone who works with information. Our concept of using information fits very nicely with a productivity meaning developed by moving from productive through producing to:

Produce, v., to cause, to effect, to bring about.

In other words, a principal is someone who uses information to make things happen, or to make his organization more effective.

A 19th century concept of productivity was the use of machines to automate repetitive, mechanical tasks, rather than the use of people for production. The concept of reducing the workforce, and equating this with productivity, is firmly rooted in our perceptions of the work ethic. This would be true, for example, in an organization that employs 100 people to do exactly the same thing. If everyone is 10% more productive, then 90 people can do the same amount of work, and 10 of them can be laid off. This does not fit into the definition of a principal. Let us look at another example. You and I decide to write a new manual on hiring practices in our organization. You produce a 100-page manual in two months. I, on the other hand, produce a 200-page manual in one month. Who is the more productive: you because your manual is shorter, or I because I took less time? Is it possible to answer that question if the original goals are known: your goal was to write a shorter manual, mine to write a manual in a shorter time? It is still a matter of debate. The question can be answered only by a determination of which manual will cause greater effectiveness in the Personnel Department. Just as 'to produce' means 'to effect', so are 'productivity' and 'effectiveness' inseparable.

A number of atrributes or parameters have also come into usage to qualify the productivity question (Figure 11-8). They are:

Quantity, Quality, Time, Cost.

Then productivity becomes a linear equation involving some power of each attribute; or, productivity equals more quantity at less time and lower cost but higher quality. Those words convey very little meaning.

It is at this point that the thesaurus comes in useful for exploring the synonyms of each parameter in the above equation. You may wish to do this to select those words which will convey the meaning and structure that your organization

Attribute	Synonym
Productive	1. Prolific, resourceful, useful, beneficial
	2. Gratifying, rewarding
Quantity	1. Amount, measure, magnitude, size
	2. Total, aggregate
Quality	1. Excellence, distinction, worth, value
	2. Caliber, dignity, importance
Time	1. Interval, duration, span, speed
	2. Promptness
Cost	1. Price, expense, amount, outlay
	2. Detriment, pain, penalty

Figure 11-8.   Synonyms associated with productivity parameters.

considers important. I have done it:

1. to convey the generally accepted meanings of the word in today's business environment; and
2. to illustrate that these words also convey some different concepts, and that these may be the concepts that will ultimately decide the fate of principal productivity.

Let us look at quantity in terms of amount and magnitude. We generally accept the cliché that 'more is better'. So far, this idea is leading to decreased productivity. Automation of the mechanical task in the office gave us the paper explosion. It is not always an information explosion, but rather the same information repeated in many different forms. Organizations are inundated with data today and most principals are having difficulty digesting all that there is. A lot of information is wasted because selectivity is not possible and conciseness is limited. Less may be better. Similarly, a prolific principal may not necessarily be a resourceful one. A principal who can provide useful information is more likely to be beneficial to the organization. It is a question of the right information. The quantity of information handled is less important than the quality.

The quality of information is vital to principal productivity. In terms of the effectiveness of our manual on hiring practices, the real question is 'Which manual helped the Personnel Department do its job?' In other words, which manual is more useful and relevant to the jobs at hand. By expanding this idea to information in general, the words worth and value translate to relevance and usefulness. Productive information is relevant to the decision-making process and is used in the process. However, it also requires that the information is right. The wrong information may be counterproductive (by causing the wrong decisions to be made) or nonproductive (because work must be done over again and time wasted). Excellence, the concept of doing something right the first time, is a key concept. Distinction may be misleading. Sales organizations are notorious for providing distinctive-looking, glossy brochures that say very little, i.e. have no real usefulness. But, if your organization expects distinctive rather than substantive information, I may be misleading you.

Time is another key factor. The expression 'hindsight is 20–20' conveys an understood concept. If we had known yesterday what we know today, we would all have probably made different investment decisions as individuals. The same is true for organizational decisions. Therefore, it is important that relevant information be available to the decision-making process at the time it is needed. Not the day after! A better word to use is probably timely. Was the information timely? Was it available in time to influence the right decision? The time available to obtain information, before a decision will be made, can be a very short interval and so the speed with which information can be handled is important. It is also worth noting that information may be useful for only a short duration. In a rapidly changing economy, the life span of any single item of data can be very small indeed. Gaining access to the right information at the right time is the key to a successful business operation.

Cost reduction in the historical sense is really not an applicable concept at this stage. Principals do not sit by the hundred, all doing the same job, with a potential for staffing reductions. Cost in terms of outlay may be critical. As decisions are reached about investment in office systems, the expense will certainly be considered. What is the price of these systems? We may not know the answer yet. We can, however, address the cost of wrong decisions based on faulty, excessive, or late information. Rework and product recalls have been a major, measurable, expense for many organizations. The automobile and drug industries, for example, certainly know the amount of money that has been awarded in court after litigation against them. Could those lawsuits have been avoided if better product information had been available sooner?

Thus, we have many ways of looking at principal productivity. Viewed from the 1970s perspective, we clearly see a need to reduce the paperwork so that people can concentrate on information instead. Productivity will flow from the better management of information, not better ways of shuffling paper. However, it is an easier concept to grasp if the word 'effective' is substituted for productive. Principals support the decision-making process by providing information to it. An effective principal is one who can provide the needed information, when it is needed, with neither duplication nor oversight.

How do we appraise this individual?

MEASUREMENT AND METHODOLOGY

It is generally accepted that office systems will provide an opportunity to increase principal productivity. Historically, most product development and marketing activity seems to have been directed at relatively minor opportunities such as typewriter replacements. This will be contradictory if applied to the 1980s but, on the other hand, identifying the return on investment for office systems is a problem. It has been difficult to develop a benefit analysis because, historically, no system of measuring principal productivity has been widely accepted. If you cannot measure productivity satisfactorily, it is hard to realize the potential benefit from improving it. This has not stopped many people from trying to develop novel techniques to do so, however.

The conventional, or cookbook, method from Systems Analysis techniques is as follows:

- review current procedures
- review equipment status
- track document flow
- measure workload
- interview the people involved
- uncover the problem area.

Then a report is prepared which suggests ways of making improvements in the problem areas. Traditionally, this has included an economic assessment of the projected costs versus the anticipated savings. The approach has been tried many times before; it is logical and has been successful in the past. It is not enough for office systems. The problem still lies in trying to define and then quantify the costs and savings. It is very difficult to do this well when the office system, as it is defined by the experts in the field, is still a 'dream machine'. For many reasons, it still exists mainly on paper.

The next step came when studies were made on how principals spend their time (Figure 11-9). Several variations of the self-estimating, or 'opinion survey', questionnaire were used. In these, a principal was asked to estimate what percentage of time was spent each day, or during a week, on each of a predetermined list of activities. How principals spend their time has been averaged across so many studies that it should not be necessary to repeat this process. However, over and over again, people are being asked to repeat the study in their organizations to establish a base line, because it may be different. In fact, it is probably fairly consistent across types of organizations. Then the person who administers the survey is asked to make a presentation on the results. Anyone who has already done this has probably experienced the discomfort of defending the survey as an accurate, quantitative measure. The challenge is that the answers are not factual, they represent only feelings or impressions, they are perceptions. We tried to defend this, and missed the point completely. It is because these answers do

Activity	% of time	Information format
Meeting	22.6	Verbal:
Telephoning	11.7	34.3% of time
Writing	14.2	
Reading	12.4	Textual:
Filing/searching	8.1	38.7% of time
Handling mail	4.0	
Planning	9.9	
Traveling	7.8	
Other	9.3	
Total	100	
Time in office	52	
Time away from the office	48	

Figure 11-9. An average principal workday. (Source: IBM Corporate Office Systems. Averaged across studies in different organizations.)

represent perceptions of what people think they are doing that they are so important.

A technique that is more technically valid than self-estimating is to ask the principals to record, at stated intervals, what activity they are engaged in. The data is collected and statistically averaged across the organization. This may also be used in conjunction with a hypothetical, or paper, office system. In this case, the principal is also asked to check which feature would be used if the system were available.

Instead of conducting yet another study, it may cost no more to develop and install a pilot or prototype application. This would not be an integrated office system, but it could be used to test the concepts and the results would be based on actual experience. One additional benefit is that this approach would uncover any required changes or modifications in the assumptions and concepts.

In combination with what some have called 'guessing games' and 'sampling techniques', other people have used interviews. Once again, many tips are available for optimizing the results:

- arrange for no outside interruptions
- use two interviewers at each session
- avoid meetings right after lunch
- confirm time and place prior to meeting
- avoid tape recordings of the meeting

and so on. Unless the interviewer has some specific goal in mind, it is not clear what the interview offers. However, if there is an objective, and it can be described in ways that the interviewees understand, this technique can be useful.

More than one methodology has tried this with great success.

One organization became aware of frequent and wide-ranging complaints from principals. They generally cited a lack of specific solutions to their problems—all of which seemed related to information availability in one form or another. The company set about interviewing the principals involved. The objective of the interviews was to focus attention on the problems and determine if the existing procedures were correct. It is true that, once again, the study determined the perceptions of the problem: this is the main point. The complaints and the perceptions are often the clues to the real problems and, therefore, provide an opportunity to make improvements. Studies of this kind are more difficult to administer, but they uncover some very basic needs and requirements as well as the causes of daily irritations. What can they show?

First of all, the interview should reinforce any tentative assumptions that may already have been made about the office systems approach to productivity. It is a key opportunity to learn of major needs, values, priorities, and requirements. These may be at an individual level, or they may be at a corporate level, but they are important to the ultimate office systems solution. Many fascinating technological solutions have failed because the designer overlooked organizational, social, or psychological issues. The best system does not always give the best results. These issues do not always show up in predefined questionnaire formats. How will they show up in an interview?

Everyone, from the busiest chief executive officer to the newest hire, has a store of anecdotes and experiences that he likes to talk about. These tales can be interesting, and they can be useful. They can help to define the value system of the organization, the benefits that will be appreciated, and the problems that exist today. They provide insight into what motivates the organization and the individual, and perceptions of what should be changed. The office systems solution that ignores these perceptions will fail. Perceptions are important. Understanding them is absolutely vital to the ultimate success of office systems.

THE REDUNDANCY CONCEPT

The one thing that productive, or effective, people do not like to do is waste time unnecessarily. People are frustrated by waste of time. It may only be a case of perception: the individual may only think the time is wasted, but the frustration

Activity	How time is wasted
Telephone	● Waiting for someone to call with status information
	● Line is busy or not answered
	● Leaving a message to call back: playing telephone tag
Meetings	● Travel time to and from a meeting
	● The meeting has to be rescheduled
	● Every attendee and every arrangement has to be re-done
	● Waiting for a meeting to start (or finish!)
Mail handling	● Receiving multiple copies of the same memo
	● Re-addressing a memo to the person who should have received it in the first instance
	● Waiting for a letter to arrive in the mail
Searching for information	● Documents are misfiled
	● Files contain multiple copies of the same memo
	● Retrieved documents do not contain the required information
Rework	● Doing something over because it was not right the first time
	● Correcting typographical errors

Figure 11-10.   Some examples of how time is wasted in common activities.

is real. The great benefit of the Booz, Allen, and Hamilton study is not just that it measured where people spent their time, but that it showed where people *wasted* their time. Booz, Allen estimated, from its studies, that principals may waste as much as 25% of their working time.

We waste time in almost everything we do. It is the extensive search, for information, to determine the status of something, or correcting and revising, that keeps a principal from being productive, i.e. using information effectively. It is easier, perhaps, to understand the concept of nonproductivity, i.e. what is it that keeps people from doing the job efficiently and effectively?

In the past, we tried to place a value on some particular office activity or function or piece of information. It is difficult, if not impossible, to place an absolute value onto a particular telephone call that was placed, or a meeting that was held, or a memo that was written (Figure 11-10). We may not be able to decide the monetary worth of frustration, but we can all relate to the time we would save if we did not have to return a missed telephone call, or travel to a meeting in a remote location, or sift through too many memos to find the particular one we want. A true measurement of principal productivity can be obtained by looking at the opportunity inherent in redundant or ineffective time, i.e. measuring the value of time that is wasted.

Wasted time is caused by things that are often beyond our immediate control

---

The Frustration Index, F_I, is inversely proportional to Productivity, P_R such that:

$$F_I \times P_R = K, \text{ a constant}$$

where

$$F_I = \left[x \left(\frac{r \times c}{a \times t} \right) \right]^{-1}$$

or

$$P_R = K \left[x \left(\frac{r \times c}{a \times t} \right) \right] \frac{\int_i^o F_n \, (g + e + f + s)}{\sum_i^o [(w + n) - (p + l)]}$$

and

a = ambiguity in information
c = conciseness of information
e = ability to exchange information
f = ability to find information
g = ability to generate information
i = individual attributes
l = cost of lost information in the 1970s
n = cost of the organization's information network
o = organizational attributes
p = cost of paper system in the 1970s
r = relevance of information
s = additional information services provided
t = time to obtain information
w = cost of an office work station
x = organizational expectations

Figure 11-11.   The Frustration Theorem.

when we are trying to complete our work. It may not be realistic to reduce the total time we devote to information handling, to the thought process that we call 'making a decision', but the ideal office system will help to reduce or eliminate the redundant time spent. The potential for principal productivity lies in measuring the time that could be saved if there were no redundant or wasted effort.

Inevitably, you will hear that this is only an intangible benefit. Remember, what is intangible to one person may be real to someone else. But there are really no intangible benefits: these are only the ones that we do not know how to quantify. If you can obtain agreement that a principal's time has a value, and if you can identify areas where this time can be saved, then it is possible to quantify to a tangible benefit. Each organization's value system will determine how this productivity benefit will be used. It may result in better service, increased revenue from better decisions, or a number of other advantages.

It may simply mean that many principals, for the first time in their careers, may be able to go home on time and not take so much work with them.

This is also a measure of the frustration index (Figure 11-11).

THE FRUSTRATION INDEX

Early societal units survived by subsistence. It was a very productive, non-wasteful, way to live. Today we go to the supermarket where spoilage and waste are inevitable. We take it for granted that we need to work to earn money to survive, and the majority of us work in an organization of some kind or another. Once the basic needs for survival are satisfied, we have an opportunity to fulfill other, higher level, needs. One of them is job satisfaction. Is it possible that the office of the future can be a better place to work, with more choices, and with greater opportunity? Let us go back and look at the second list of synonyms associated with productivity parameters: quantity, quality, time, and cost.

People need to find their work gratifying and rewarding, in an emotional as well as a financial sense. They need to feel that their efforts are useful to the organization.

Would you agree that the people who are described in those terms are the ones who are productive, effective, and worthwhile? Someone who does not exhibit these characteristics is unproductive to his or her detriment and will suffer the penalty of loss of promotion or, worse yet, the pain of dismissal. Of course these words are qualitative and describe emotive perceptions.

Another example of perceptions is in the equating of equipment and a particular job or skill level, such as a typewriter which is considered a tool for typing, not for professional use. If people do not have a positive perception about something, they can easily prove that it will not work. This is true of equipment or procedures, and may well become a decisive factor with office systems. It is one thing to train people to do something a certain way; it is an entirely different matter to educate them on why it should be done that way. Education is a key to shaping future perceptions, but it does not affect present ones. Much of the technology that George Orwell described in *1984* has come true. It is our responsibility to ensure that the prophecy does not come true as well. Principals must manage the information technology, or they will be managed by it, just as they were ruled by paper in the 1970s. The question of productivity is one of discipline and attitude.

Well-conducted user interviews can reveal perceptions of what the problem areas are, and published studies can show where time is wasted. Frustrated people often feel so because they feel they are wasting time. If a principal can select when and where work will be done, less frustration may take place over travel that is perceived as unnecessary. When information can be located quickly and simply, frustration over current filing methods is less. People really want to do a good job and are happier when doing so. At a high level of job satisfaction, the performance level is high, and people are productive. Principals are people. If they are frustrated, they are unproductive. The relationship between productivity and frustration is inverse. How often have you gone home frustrated with the day's problems at work?

Management is not always a rational process. The final choices in office systems will probably be influenced by far more than just a cost/benefit analysis. It will still be difficult to translate qualitative benefits into quantitative ones. When the office of the future is finally installed and the information flow is fully integrated into organizational objectives, the question of principal productivity will probably still be a perception. Do you/your manager/the company president go home satisfied at having completed an effective day's work? Or are you frustrated?

Are you productive, or not. . . .

REFERENCES AND SUGGESTED READINGS

1. Curley, Kathleen Foley: 'Intellectual' Technologies: The Key to Improving White Collar Productivity. *Sloan Mgmt Review*, **24**, No. 1, 31–39, Fall 1982.
2. Tapscott, Don: How does the Office of the Future Measure Up? *Telephone Engineer and Management*, **86**, No. 1, 50–56, January 1, 1982.
3. Clear Case for Office Productivity. *Data Processor*, **23**, No. 5, 17–20, December 1980.
4. Conrath, D. W., *et al.*: The Electronic Office and Organizational Behavior Measuring Office Activities. *Computer Networks (Netherlands)*, **5**, No. 6, 401–410, December 1981.
5. Mellor, James R.: Office of the Future? It's Here Right Now. *Office*, **93**, No. 1, 137, January 1981.
6. Panko, Raymond: Facing Basic Issues in Office Automation. *Computer Networks (Netherlands)*, **5**, No. 6, 391–399, December 1981.
7. Executives Change with Office Automation Tide. *Data Management*, **20**, No. 2, 38–40, December 1980.
8. Buntz, C. Gregory: Problems and Issues in Human Service Productivity Improvement. *Public Productivity Review*, **5**, No. 4, 299–320, December 1981.

INDEX

The index is arranged on a word-by-word basis. When authors have used different words or different forms of the same words to express the same concept or overlapping concepts, the terminology has been standardized. Cross references have been used freely to provide broad access to the concepts. Acronyms are usually listed under the acronyms unless the fully spelled out form is more common. Names of individuals, corporate bodies, subjects, and the references and suggested readings have been included. The page numbers in parentheses represent those from the reference sections to allow the user to readily distinguish between index pointers to the bibliographic materials and index pointers to the text.

Comments and suggestions are welcomed and should be directed to the Editor.